DECEIVING THE EAGLE

**What you need to know about
the influences that evolution,
religion, business, the press &
government have on America**

Table Of Contents

Introduction

Let me begin by pointing out that virtually all attitudes that we think of as being "ours" are derived from sources outside of one's self. While this may or may not be obvious, it sets the stage for what you will later read about making choices and exercising what we mistakenly call "free will".

The intention of this book is to help raise people's consciousness regarding the copious deceptive and deceitful practices that occur in society by discussing their root causes, and then presenting some of the negative manifestations of those behaviors. We can not expect to advance society by allowing these antisocial actions to go unacknowledged and not dealt with.

Also described are some of the ways in which we voluntarily become victims, whether they are derived from social interaction, religious indoctrination, the press, our government, or the ever present manipulation of consumers by big business. These are all areas in which we can benefit from having reasonable insights.

Before approaching those subjects it would be helpful to spend time getting to know the brain, decipher how and why it functions the way it does, and then examine the implications.

Pogo: *"I have met the enemy and it is me."*

While there are many adverse behaviors discussed herein, the most flagrant of them may come from politicians… virtually all of whom are indebted to the corrupting purse-strings of corporate America for their political livelihood (*reelection funding*). It is the officers and directors of the major institutions who manipulate this country with their legalized bribes and surreptitious illegal perks. And this corporate achievement is accomplished without a great deal of detection, fanfare, or concern for who may be in office at any given time. Have you noticed how often big business give money to both parties? This tolerated graft is why nothing much changes from one Administration or one Congress to the next. Big business owns both.

People may imagine that they are voting for change if they cast their ballot against an incumbent. The reality is that any perceived difference between candidates is only a function of the false and exaggerated rhetoric that is issued for the purpose of vote-capturing. This carefully-constructed posturing can be quite different from a politician's actual beliefs, which may only be expressed in the back rooms of power. This is where political platforms are created, with an unwavering eye in the direction of the candidate's next campaign and toward those who will finance it.

Business owns government, and it will until we accept that reality and act to prevent it.

Many of the points that are made in this book may fall into the category of *I already knew that*. However, there should be more than a few ideas that will elicit an *aha!*

As you will discover, I take frequent issue with many counterfeit statements that emanate from our institutions, a feature that has been a function of their business-as-usual plans and the political landscape for uncounted decades. It is these persistent fountains of misinformation and disinformation that we should be aware of and deal with if we are to counteract the negative side of people's pursuit of power. Just don't imagine that you can label me un-American if you should happen to disagree with my contentions.

Being a good citizen is <u>not</u> being inclined to accept all that the government may want of us. On balance, it is an entity that is made up of regular people who have their own prejudices and personal agendas, and we should not expect otherwise. Resistance to the evils that are inherent in bad government (*the quest for power*) is everyone's duty in order to promote a stronger, more just America.

I am aware that in some cases I may be preaching to the choir. Those who are most interested in this book's subjects might already be well versed in them. In contrast, those who have the greatest need to understand these issues are precisely those who may make the least effort in that direction. This is not an indictment of our country with its great beauty and fine citizens. Rather it is meant to shed light on understanding the malevolent motivations of some and the pervasive lack of attention by others.

While many of the presented ideas represent logic and analysis on my part, others deal with an accretion of knowledge through the practice of skepticism. These are two essential mental processes that are underrated and underutilized by society. People who are not steeped in logic may not grasp the importance and elegance of using this technique in their daily lives. There are also those who may consider skeptics to be little more than malcontents, and choose to ignore their "rantings". Yet others may be so thoroughly indoctrinated in their belief systems that questioning of what they "know" to be true is unthinkable, and is therefore virtually impossible.

I have also devoted some content to the misadventures of our past President, George W. Bush and his band of advisors as examples of power driven failures. GWB was clearly a President of limited intellect… severely limited when you take into consideration his position of power. Too often he used the authority of his office to promote welfare for the rich and the expansion of religious dogma into government, which are two qualities that should be unacceptable to all Americans.

Additionally, his actions were not accomplished through the exchange and acceptance of dialog among a broad-based audience, but they were achieved through the muscle of the Presidency and the efforts of his narrow-minded clique of advisors. Fortunately for the rest of the citizens they were relatively incompetent at advancing their causes.

My rebukes of GWB do not, however, color me a Democrat or imply that he was the only sinner to come down the presidential pike. I would prefer to be labeled an Independent. Beyond that, I weigh ideas as they apply to the welfare of people rather than to the promotion of questionable codes of belief. Being an Independent should be an attractive concept, but one might not draw that conclusion from the political arena where people are encouraged to commit to the party of their choice.

I recognize that there is much to say about how and why many of us do not gain an effective knowledge about this country or the world in spite of, or perhaps because of the vast amounts of information that surrounds us. Among the reasons that may be pertinent are…
-- society is not terribly adept at transferring new knowledge from parent to child and from peer to peer
-- there is such a blizzard of data circulating around us that real effort is required to analyze and process it… with many of us being too disinterested to do so
-- we have developed relatively low expectations of people, and we may also philosophically feel that it is neither our place nor our right to challenge their beliefs or behaviors
-- we frequently find it easier to suffer the consequences of people's slings and arrows rather than to transgress into the social taboo of criticism of others

As a result of learning disabilities or personal inabilities, which are respectively genetic and social in nature, we tend to experience problems repeatedly because we can not seem get the learning thing down right. Being deficient in social development can readily be seen in those groups where criminal behavior or abject poverty has been perpetuated from one generation to the next. It is not extraordinary to have a parent and child or perhaps two siblings incarcerated at the same time. Nor is it unusual to have consecutive generations mired in the disincentives of the welfare state.

I recall a report in which an inner-city youth said that he expected to be killed or jailed before reaching adulthood. Not only did this reflect a great despair regarding his personal circumstances, but it also expressed the belief that there is a lack of opportunity which might lead to better life. And it is people's perceptions, whether they are real or imagined, that are difficult to overcome.

This state of affairs is especially true if children do not have the insight and benefit of a helpful mentor, parent, or friend who can provide them with countervailing information. An opinion about a lack of opportunity is surely one of the more destructive influences that confront America. A close runner-up to this is that jails are the solution to crime.

In the next chapters I discuss how the brain developed through time, forms conclusions, and can be flawed due to genetic and external influences. This will include a few thoughts relating to the genesis of indoctrination, how it corrupts society, and result in inappropriate beliefs and behaviors. Because of these varied subjects, this is essentially several books in one... evolution study, brain study and people study.

Meet The Brain

How We Learn

Apparently the brain is not formed with logic as an imperative. Rather, its programming is more about situations and pattern recognition. This means that we are inclined to learn by the absorption and correlation of events that are experienced than any other way. The mind's processes determine what it already knows, learns what the nature of logic is, and begins to understand how using this tool can be beneficial. Unfortunately a few of us don't become accomplished at taking advantage of that ability.

In the early stage of life children do not know the rules of the world, but they come with minimal logic and background to help them in forming sensible conclusions. They consciously and subconsciously take in ideas and compare them to other thoughts they have accrued in an effort to make reasonable deductions. This learning process is heavily prejudiced by the coaching of parents and their interactions with others. Like a computer, if there is garbage in, there will be garbage out. So part of accruing effective learning is being able distinguish the good from the bad, or "data filtering".

For the most part when we are provided with legitimate information, valid conclusions may be formed. This improves over time as we think about what we know, learn which behaviors have better outcomes than others, and why. Since we do not effectively teach logic in most school environments, it must be gleaned from our peers and experiences. Some of us will develop this helpful insight more effectively than others do, while some may defy the benefits of being immersed logic their entire life.

Nature of Learning

Let me emphasize that education comes essentially from without, not from within. The best that we can hope to accomplish by ourselves is to contemplate and correlate the various bits of information which have been accumulated from external sources. While some of us may start out being more capable of applying this process than others, we are all offered copious opportunities to enhance our understanding of the world by analyzing our own experiences and those of others. Some will take full advantage of this prospect. Some will not, and will undoubtedly suffer the consequences.

In my case I attribute becoming a Computer Systems Engineer (essentially and analyst) and science junky to the influence of a bright neighborhood youth. He was several years older then I and had been more exposed to the wonders of the universe. We would occasionally sit on the curb in the evening, look up at the heavens and speculate on what it was all about.

As children we tend to look for simple, uncomplicated answers to the events we encounter while growing up. Life is preferably cast in black and white. Grey is difficult and annoying. When my uncle invented a garbage disposal many years ago, I recall his relating to my father that the cutting tool had to be heat treated in a specific way so that the edges of the blades would remain strong and sharp (*and consequently brittle*) while the rest of the blade would have to remain flexible enough to avoid snapping. This was too complicated for a child to get his head around. Couldn't life be simpler, I wondered? In getting older however, grey (*and not just in my hair*) has become much more interesting and richer. As I have aged I have become able to see past the need for simplicity, and have consequently embraced a keen interest in discovery, analysis and problem solving. Not only did those fascinations eventually allow me to become a first class programmer, but it eventually nudged me in the direction of evaluating the nature of human nature itself. However, this latter interest took many years to come to fruition.

Since the incentive for learning can be greatly enhanced by a mentor, parents should make every effort to guide their children in a direction that is appropriate to the child's disposition in order to maximize their potential for success. Because my mother loved the piano, which she could not play, she pushed lessons on her children. My eldest brother took to Chopin and Rachmaninoff like a duck to water. But because I was not the least bit interested in piano playing (*and was also dyslexic as I later learned*), I resisted mightily… wasting everyone's time and energy. Eventually I discovered that my passion was computers and went for that.

It wasn't until much later that I decided to express what I had gleaned about America and its institutions in the form of a book. While I have confidence in my conclusions about the array of subjects that are presented here, there is little doubt that some readers will take exception to the ways in which I view the world. A few controversial conclusions certainly go against the prevailing wisdom, and they may they even provoke people's anger. Let me point out a few ideas that can be useful when reading this book…
-- a response of anger usually indicates a closed mind
-- no one has a lock on right and wrong – not you, not me and most assuredly not those who would deceive us into believing that they have that gift
-- skepticism is a useful tool that is underutilized by society
-- repetitive assertions of "the truth" are mind control, pure and simple, whether they come from politicians or preachers

All Wired Up

An analogy about the human mind might portray it as being like a living sponge because it soaks up information somewhat akin to the way the sponge soaks up nourishment. The sponge has passages which can be thought of as representing our brain's original wiring. Our learning is like the nourishing ebb and flow of the tide which promotes the creation of new and delicate channels during a sponge's lifetime. Sometimes the nutrients have a strong effect and can create more permanent passages. At other times they are weak and less effective. The result is an ever changing structure that evolves, to a greater or lesser degree, as a result of those ocean influences.

In a similar way our brain comes with pre-wiring (*original passages*) thanks to our heredity. At this stage it is like a computer that is manufactured with "POST" (*Power On Self Test - in computerspeak*) software so that it knows it is a computer and not a toaster.

Subsequent learning is the process by which the brain evolves and creates new synapses and clears or enhances old ones. In addition to the original wiring and re-wiring, we have an "operating system" which knows part of what it is to be a human and something of what its capabilities are. With this knowledge the brain has an almost incomprehensible capability for processing new information, given its small size.

None of us begin with identical brains, not even identical twins. We each come out from a different starting gate. As a consequence of this we develop different abilities and propensities that correspond, in some degree, to the environment we live in. A few of us may even have extra-ordinary wiring. I think we can agree the Mozart had a serious musical advantage over his peers. There are also a lucky subset who are nurtured by a mentor and consequently manage to attain achievements that go beyond what would have been normal or expected with their native abilities. Others have such unfortunate original wiring that they may never be capable of interacting with the outside world in realistic ways. Still others may encounter corrupting influences and become harmful to themselves and to society. This last group produces a real challenge for the rest of us to cope with when they inflict their life remedies on others.

John C. Crosby, writer: *"Mentoring is a brain to pick, an ear to listen, and a push in the right direction."*

Brain Divisions

According to those who purport to know these things, there are multiple areas of the brain that are somewhat specific in nature and are used for discrete functions such as language, analysis, artistic ability, hearing, seeing, imagination and the like. When we learn a new word, we remember its meaning so that is can be reused in the future. This brain re-wiring provides us with a method to advance our communications through written and verbal cues, as well as through facial expressions and body language. In addition to this we store rudimentary pictures in the brain which are more like schematics (*which use less brain power*) than they are like detailed photographs.

These images are then used to make broad associations and connections to our visual world, and they may also serve a function in dreaming and daydreaming. I suspect that our having occasional feeling of deja vu comes from the viewing of an image which promotes a flashback to one of these pictures that were almost forgotten. As a result, the connection that we conjure up may be strong, or only a weak remembrance. These images are, for the most part, what allow us to recognize objects that are similar to what we have seen before, whether they are mountains, trees or people. This could also be the case with deja moo... when we have heard that bull before.

As an aside to dreams, as a child I was told that if one has a recurring nightmare there may be two possible resolutions... wake yourself up (*which can be done with practice*) or simply let the monster get you. Waking up is the short term solution. Letting yourself be eaten, fall from a height, or in some way be assaulted will usually stop the nightmare from returning. It worked for me. I no longer fall down elevator shafts.

Brain Programming

Unlike a computer's operating system which functions with a rigid set of rules, the mind's programming is capable of both subtle and dramatic changes depending on the strength of its inputs. It is this ability to learn a broad range of reactions to stimuli that is built into our initial makeup. It can be seen in our going from babies to adults and, to some degree, back to infants as we age. This learning process contributes to and constitutes our value system, beliefs, attitudes, agenda, goals and self-perception. Without this facility we would be a single purpose program regardless of the circumstances that surround us. Compare us favorably, for example, to the shark that is said (*incorrectly*) to be little more than an eating machine.

As for our initial wiring, it appears that certain processes must occur within a specific timeframe in the brain's development for them to succeed effectively. It has been reported that if a language is not learned in the early years, the brain can not learn one because its accommodating programming has evaporated. Similarly, if chimps do not learn to use tools from their troop-mates by the age of eight, they can never pick up that skill. So as it turns out, some brain subprograms come and go, never to return. However, once a language is learned, picking up a second or third is only a matter of effort because the requisite wiring has been established. Learning a language is also easier while that particular program is functioning to it maximum in our youth.

If this language theory is correct, it sets the stage for understanding why some recidivist criminals can not learn a new trick no matter how much inducement or incarceration is used. At the point in time when they should have learned reasonable socialization they were deprived of this education by incompetent or missing parents. Or they may have been unduly influenced by their peer group with a lower social conscience. This may be one of the factors in why the poor tend to remain poor.

George Bernard Shaw, author: *"A fool's brain digests philosophy into folly, science into superstition, and art into pedantry. Hence university education."*

Brain Integration

There are two ways in which the brain and body function on an automated level. One is the autonomic nervous system that responds to body needs without the time consuming requirement of passing through central brain processing first. If we touch something that is hot, our hand reacts quickly by pulling away even before the brain has had a chance to evaluate the stimulus. This also explains why it takes a brief moment to feel the pain. The other facility is what I will call a quick response system. It is as fast as the autonomic system and does not use the awareness portion of the brain to initiate or validate reactions. This ability comes into play when we make movements without conscious thought in order to be efficient at a task. It can be exemplified by petting a cat or driving a car. We may not consciously process the steering wheel movements, but we can easily become aware of them and then modify them as necessary. If we were to take time to think about each hand and eye movement we would not be able to function because of brain overload. Our brain is fast, but not that fast. In a study designed to show "non-thinking" implications, people were asked to simulate their lane changing motion at a steering wheel while seated in a chair. Invariably the movements were exaggerated, and they would have led to greatly overshooting the lane.

The quick response system may also help to explain some of the so-called "thoughtless" behaviors in our daily lives. Because the brain does not have sufficient power to deeply process our every situation, we learn many predeterminations and soft-wire those decisions in our lower-level brains in order to reduce higher-level brain workload. This allows us to enact run-of-the-mill responses to situations more easily. Getting effortlessly from one well-known destination to another in an automobile would be an example of this capacity. This ability to go on automatic control, however, can be both good and bad. On one hand we are able to get more done with less mental effort, and this leaves the brain's power available for more critical tasks. On the other hand we experience less control of our behaviors because we are not exercising as much management.

Brain Training

Another characteristic of learning is what I will call pattern driven thoughts. That is, we subconsciously store some experiences as vague or nebulous events that can be referred back to when appropriate. The next time a similar incident occurs we may recount a previously stored event, or perhaps a composite of several similar events, and will hopefully react appropriately. This type of connection can give us a feeling of comfort or anxiety depending on the nature of and reasons for the stored pattern. People generally experience some anxiety when visiting a doctor's office because one or more experiences that were uncomfortable, or because of negative stories that were told to them by others. When one's blood pressure is taken in a doctor's office it is usually higher than when taken at home… an indication of a discomfort level.

On the positive side, remembered patterns are conveniently used to prepare us for an upcoming occurrence that can be helpful. In a way this is similar to our "fight or flight" wiring, just not as extreme. It is the method by which our brain gets ready for potential events. You may know of someone who regularly experiences the negative aspects of their thoughts. They will obsess on what may be about to happen to a degree that is out of proportion to an impending incident. Their sense of anxiety may even outweigh their ability to make a rational assessment of an event. As a result, problems can be invented when none exist or when none were probable. A person might dread flying in an airliner and insist on driving to destinations, or not going at all. The relative safety of planes verses that of cars and buses is not part of their thought process. Their exaggerated sense of anxiety overwhelms rationality. This type of fear may be the result of unfamiliarity (*not knowing the dynamics and risk-level of flight*) or of a feeling that they lack of control (*they are not flying the plane and may not trust the plane or the pilot*). A well known sports commentator would average thousands of miles per week in his RV going from one game venue to another just to avoid flying.

There are also people who simply like to attract attention with their behaviors which are related to certain types of avoidances. Food mind-games fall into this category. Science has not conclusively demonstrated that people who have diets devoid in particular foods, like red meat, are healthier than those with diets consisting of moderate meat consumption. I think it is fair to assume one or more of the following may be occurring...
-- they do not care to thoroughly understand nutrition
-- they do not want to eat anything that they could pet – so to speak
-- they enjoy the attention they receive (*even if negative*) resulting from their behavior
-- they are doing what they think is best

One theory about the evolution of brain development is that our switching from exclusively eating plant food to focusing on eating red meats was instrumental in the growth of the brain. It apparently provided us with the requisite nutrients for its enlargement that were absent from other foods. A straight vegetarian diet required too much of an time/effort hit to be efficient because of its low energy value. Since early man hunted during the day when most other predators were resting, they needed to ingest fat and protein to be able to run down their prey (*the grass eaters*), a task which might take hours before the query was too exhausted to go on.

According to a scientific article, in early humans there was a trade-off between the sizes of our guts and our brain. As we moved towards a diet of meat, we reduced our digestive needs by cooking meat before eating it. Our guts became smaller for a mammal of our size, and the energy freed up by smaller bowels would then power our brains.

Brain Intuition

Intuition occurs when we experience feelings (*a form of knowledge*) which have been translated into our genes over the generations. When these attitudes repeatedly keep someone out of harms way, the wiring becomes reinforced (*by living and not dieing*) and is subsequently passed along to their offspring. The longer that the reinforcement persists, the more likely it is that it will become a part of our intuition's repertory. Or more succinctly, learning will perpetuate itself when it contributes to one's survival and facilitates the passing on of one's genes. For example, it is thought that our innate fear of snakes and other dangers relate to events in our past that eventually became hard-wired into our brains. Our ancestors confronted these situations often enough that the fear we now experience is a result of their reactions being transferred onto the future. These fears can be thought of as the magic of seeing the world through the eyes of those who came before us. It can also be thought of as education without learning.

Feral cats that have become tame pets and are then released into the wild will revert back to their wild intuition. Those that then escape danger by being wary will have that behavior reinforced And with each successive generation they will become more wary. This reversion behavior has also been shown to occur with house cats.

With what I will call "situational intuition" we can experience thoughts about people who are perceived as not being in our clan or who are not like us. This may prompt us to feel uneasy about persons we do not know. "I knew I didn't like that person from the moment we met" might be the reaction. This intuition can also reveal itself when we are watching a movie or television program and an unknown actor is instinctively liked or disliked. A majority of viewers may even have this common reaction to an actor's appearance. In fact Hollywood is adept at typecasting actors because of a semi-common response. In other cases the movie makers will create this feeling for us over time, such as with dressing villains in black. We may then associate the bad guys or good guys with the color of their clothes or even the look of their horses.

Other associations may refer back to our previous encounters with certain colors, smells and shapes. Some years ago Nissan came out with a bold-yellow colored Z-car, a 280ZX, I think. Having learned somewhere in my past that this color was predominately used for run-down taxis, I had a strong dislike for the color. However after observing it in its new context for some time, I was able to give up my previous bias and accept that this particular shade of yellow was ok, or perhaps even appropriate for a sports car. As a result I was able to unlearn an earlier attitude, being none the worse for it.

Past experiences can be a predictor of the future attitudes – or to put it another way, current attitudes can be rooted in the past

Brain Filtering

Our life is not much different, at least in a figurative way, from the computer software programs that I used to write for a living. Input flows through the program and produces output. Input flows through our brains and produces immediate or delayed responses. In some cases the outflow can be invalid with computers because of faulty coding. Why should the human mind be any different, except that we use many learned filters to assess the input and determine what may actually be garbage-in? Because of our adoption of these filters we can reject information as being irrelevant, inappropriate or flawed. Even some sophisticated computer programs have a limited filtering capability in order to solve potential conflicts. However, these filters are unable to provide favorable results if they too happen to be faulty, such as when they motivate us to see events and people in unacceptable ways, such as with...

-- white supremacist groups which may see it as their duty to purge undesirables from their country

-- government-hating groups who have a revolutionary bent that views politicos as having the power and interest to abridge their rights and freedom

-- others who believe the propaganda of elected leaders, even though they may say whatever it takes to get elected

For the most part we process information accurately and make sense of it because of the filters we have accumulated. As we may know, children have very few filters, and adults can have too many, or they may have inappropriate (*read faulty*) filters such as when they do little to resist the deceit of persons in authority. It is the development of these various data sifters which makes up much of the differences between each of us. Some will have a perspective on society that another does not. Occasionally their filters can be altered by events that are not easily control…

-- a pacifist may choose to kill a person responsible for harming a loved one

-- a severe illness may reduce a person's will to live

-- politicians may give up their integrity to be reelected

-- when drinking, alcoholics may react with unwarranted anger, or perhaps drive a vehicle without regard for its deadliness

Get the filters right and the output has a chance of being be right

Brain Subconscious

This is another aspect of the brain's ability to process the huge amounts of the data that we are subjected to. Even though we are busy with our conscious thoughts, known as explicit memory, a part of the brain is processing information in order to keep us in touch with our environment. Because of this facility the subconscious brain can absorb information that we are not fully conscious of… hence the prefix: sub. The implication of this ability is that we can learn without being fully aware of it taking place. This kind of data acquisition contributes to our implicit memory which is the subconscious knowledge we acquire (*things we know without knowing why we know them*). You may recall that sleep-learning tapes attempted to exploit this facility ability years ago.

We must be careful of unfettered reliance upon memory, because though helpful, it will occasionally be based on faulty information or be passed through to us by the faulty filters that we have developed. If we start out with a skewed or flawed perspective, it is likely that our memory will carry those same flaws and social difficulties.

Another way we get into trouble with subconscious thought is through our natural confidence in concepts that we were taught as children. Those ideas are not really learned ideas as much as they are our adopted ideas through indoctrination... a process which some choose to deny. These thoughts may then become a relatively inflexible part of what we have come to accept as the truth. Childhood is the stage at which we have not yet learned how to develop sufficient, workable filters, and we tend to believe much of information that is passed on to us. Early indoctrinations can include this faulty information which may then be carried for a lifetime if we do not stop to examine our beliefs as we get older. We should learn to question the ideas that others impose on us in the formative years in order to insure that we form more valid perspectives

Brain Imprinting

As we know, ducks and other creatures have a scheme for staying near the safety of their parents, called imprinting. This is a temporary brain program that serves a critical social function and then mostly disappears. When I lived at a waterfront apartment my neighbors took in a baby duck that had lost its parents to predation. The chick followed them inside and out for weeks until its imprinting wore off. Then it was a permanent good-by. In a similar way we humans are also subject to imprinting at an early age as we...
-- become aware of our environment and we don't want to leave it
-- insist on being close to mom
-- smile when someone smiles at us

-- learn who is similar to us and who is not, and tend to stay within that comfort zone

But unlike with those chicks, the effect on us does not completely disappear. Even with age we manage to maintain some of these same behavior patterns because of reinforcement. While we tend to develop biases against others, the widening of our experiences can allow us to have a greater appreciation of others and develop healthier, worldlier attitudes. Strangely there are a number of cultures that disparage this kind of openness. Some Arab tribes practice such closed societies that they are in a constant state of "war" with their neighbors. There is no rationale for this type of behavior except that it is the way it has always been done. No wonder it is so easy for them to hate the Westerners when it is also so easy for them to hate their own neighbors. Our mores about community have evolved differently from theirs. Their mores about who is and is not in their clan may continue to receive negative reinforcement throughout their lives. A twist on this culture is that some of these clans will freely give food and the comfort of their home to a needy "enemy" if asked. Presumably all bets are off after the guest leaves.

Brain Dispositions

Because of our initial wiring (*heredity*), some of us may be more susceptible to inappropriate behavior than others. I had a good friend in high school and another in college who followed in the footsteps of an alcoholic parent. Since alcoholic propensity is not uncommon within families, it is likely that there was something in their initial wiring which contributed to problem drinking. Smoking addiction is another example of how a predisposition can have a greater effect on behavior for some more than for others. Both my wife and I used to smoke and quit many years ago. This was not an unusually difficult process for me because my chemistry did not make me addicted to nicotine… just to the socialization of smoking. My wife, on the other hand, had more difficulty with quitting. A number of people are not able to make the smoking cessation transition due to their own personal chemistry or learned attitudes. One lady I knew ran out of cigarettes at night while she was in the middle of recovering from a facial peal. Her face was bright red, but she was so desperate for a smoke that she went to a convenience store one evening wearing a ski mask. I can only imagine the clerk's reaction. I can't put myself in the position of others with such a compulsion, but it must be major problem for them. I do suspect, however, that having knowledge of the reason(s) behind an unwanted behavior works toward mitigating it.

Our wiring is the commander of our ship's journey through life – but mutiny is always a possibility

Brain Copying

When we are born, our minds are something of a blank slate as far as an understanding how the world works. Most of how we first function is the result of our initial wiring which manages breathing, hunger, discomfort, etc. Included among these abilities is the propensity to copy what we see our parents and others do. This is how animals come by their early training, and this is why we know that children are so easily indoctrinated. Concepts that become ingrained before the age of adult reasoning are the strongest and most difficult to counteract with logic and effort. On the plus side, the benefits of copy-ability might be obvious. We do not have to go through a protracted trial and error processes to learn an old trick. Those who came before us have accomplished that tasks for us. The down side to this rapid learning is in the copy function itself. Because it is semi-automatic, it does not come to us with a censoring mechanism built in. We tend to accept what we see, as being legitimate, worthwhile to be emulated, promoted, or defended.

Initially we use this copy adaptation to fit in with others in our society. Our personalities are developed in direct correlation to the input we receive via the feedback of social interactions. On the other side of the coin, this is not terribly productive when it involves the blind adherence to the negative ideas of others. Being a member of an antisocial group or gaining association with criminal organizations are prime illustrations.

Beliefs that we unreservedly accept as legitimate can have other adverse effects as well. You don't imagine that the idea that America is the greatest country in the world was your idea, do you? Right or wrong, this belief has been ingrained into our thoughts since we were first able to understand the word's meaning. As a result of this notion about our superiority (*which is incumbent in the conviction*), we have repeatedly succeeded in getting ourselves into troubles with the rest of the world. In spite of this, most Americans would take strong exception to any suggestion that we are not the greatest country, even though they might not be able to statistically defend the idea.

Since the copy function comes so naturally to us, we don't always question the premise, validity or appropriateness of what we have learned. As often as not this true-believer inclination tends to work against us when it causes us to put reliance on the self-serving statements of others, and pay little attention to the evidence that contradicts them. For example, we may foolishly believe that the platitudes of politicians actually express their sincere feelings and represent honest beliefs.

Shakespeare's Cassius: *"The fault, dear Brutus, is not in our stars, but in our selves."*

Image Creation

Admiring movie stars, music celebrities, or other public figures is a practice we may indulge in but is actually an exercise in self-deception. We really know next to nothing about them and their off-camera lives regardless of what the tabloids and broadcast media reports. The news about stars is mostly fashioned by public relations managers and publicists who are in the business of creating positive illusions about the stars. And they presumably work very hard at it. The images that they fashion can be enticing to believe, but usually have little substance to them. I recall hearing about Tom Cruise jumping up onto Oprah's couch (*on the live set*) and giddily professing his love for so-and-so. Do you really believe this wasn't a carefully staged event by those who were involved in the skit, including Oprah? And do we really need to know anything at all about Tom's love life, even if it were true? It's not as if this was the first time that we have been subjected to this side show either. His previous marriage had been heavily promoted in the media for years. If it worked once, why not try it again appears to be the logic.

Mark Twain*: "Good breeding consists in concealing how much we think of ourselves and how little we think of the other person."*

To be clear, the star-directed media outlets that pretend to present news are in the business of portraying people in the most enticing fashion they can for the benefit of themselves and the industry they purport to report on. They are as much a part of promoting a movie and its stars as are the producer and their marketing department. Truth and honesty take a back seat to publicity and income. Would you watch a program that portrayed these personalities as bland? So is this a bad thing? I guess not if you enjoy living in someone else's constructed fantasy.

Generally it isn't until years after a person's fame has faded or their life has come to an end that we are may get an inside story about their marginal personalities, frequent tantrums, excessive drinking, inappropriate behavior or whatever. You don't think the revelations about Mel Gibson's hostile-to-Jews personality weren't glossed over by the media for years, do you?

Prior to having a star with a mal-behavior personality that can no longer be obscured, there are the persons who are involved in the business of false portrayal. This is because they also benefit financially from those personalities that they have so diligently manufactured. Later on there may also be money to be made by exposing the "real" person in an article, biography or movie. These personality architects have an occupation that is similar to the aids to politicians who are employed to parrot the political line in spite of the fact that they know how bogus it is. They have much to gain from their deception, and will likely continue to indulge in that practice until any benefit arising from it disappears. The lack of reality that is incumbent in this type of theatre is why some politicians are apparently able to discover a social conscience after they leave

29

office. Even then many continue to indulge in their contrived posturing. Perhaps the silliest example of this phenomenon was when Clinton set up his post-Presidential office in the ghetto. Hmmm, were you impressed? For me it was just another proof of President Lincoln's observation that: "**You can fool some of the people**..."

Star image is a constructed fiction that we must learn to see through

Right vs. Wrong

Due to their local environment, other people's views of good and bad may be dramatically different from yours or mine. The result can be their engaging in antisocial or criminal activity. Any punishment that we might dole out for those acts could very well be ineffective at modifying a recidivist's behavior. They just can't get the message. Continued incarceration may be the only suitable protection for the rest of us.

Right is right no matter how <u>few</u> agree with something
Wrong is wrong no matter how <u>many</u> agree with something

Obviously having a different view of life from others is not dire, but in many cases it can materially contribute to not fitting in. We had a neighbor, for the most part a decent chap, who had decided to cut down a tree on our land before our home was completed, and presumably because no one was watching. This was done, we later learned, so that he could more easily view the cities' ten minutes of fireworks display across our property. Some time after moving in, the tree subject came up, and amazingly this person did not feel remorse over his actions. The explanation was...
-- he did not know the tree was on our land – as if that mattered
-- the tree was dead anyway (*we happen to like dead trees as an attraction in themselves and a haven for birds*)
-- it blocked his view

All of these excuses, and especially his associated anger when the subject was broached, were designed to relieve himself from the reality of his guilt. So this person's perception was probably that he was not a bad person and we were to blame for making an issue (*however small*) of the downed tree. In his own mind he had already denied the seriousness of the offence to protect his ego. This ability at denying an uncomfortable reality undoubtedly influenced his other behaviors and relationships as well.

Anger can be a common byproduct of denial and the associated guilt that is part of getting caught

All of us go through life with various misconceptions about what is right or wrong, and invariably suffer the consequences of that mindset. A significant group will fail to learn from their mistakes because they did not get their wiring straight at an early age. They may not be capable of judging their own behavior accurately and acting wisely. This is one reason why child nurturing and setting good examples for youths is so important. As an aside to this theme, there is some evidence that the violence that children are subjected to on TV and in video games has a correlation to their own violence. This exposure apparently dulls an internal sensor.

Let me offer a mild example of example of inappropriate behavior. We should understand that walking down the left side of an isle in a store will eventually result in a conflict (*however small*) with another shopper. But many people will do this over and over again anyway. This self-centered behavior demonstrates people's tendencies toward an it's-all-about-me attitude, and how they show little awareness or regard for the interests of others. This conduct occurs even though they may be occasionally inconvenienced by their own actions. This is because their I-want-to-do-what-I-want-to-do attitude is too strong for them to control. Any annoyance that they experience is just part of doing business in the manner that is preferred. The probability of negative consequences may not enter into the equation.

A more serious example would be drivers who intentionally run red lights to cut a few minutes off of their travel. They are aware that it is a dangerous practice which might lead to a citation or worse, but they have their selfish imperative to fulfill. The welfare or convenience of those around them is secondary to their own wants.

A somewhat more common anti-social behavior revolves around being stingy to excess. We have all known people who look for ways to offload their financial obligation onto others such as…
-- the singles guy who manages to be in the men's room when it is his turn to buy
-- the couple that never seems to do the math quite right on their portion of a dinner tab
-- the woman who borrows money from another to pay for a drink and than fails to repay that companion
-- the adults who come to a party or dinner empty handed

Those who live in residential environments may know about or have personally experienced the inconsiderate fence builder. No, I am not referring to the typical yard enclosure type. I mean the neighbor who asks you to share in the expense of building a common fence between the homes and then makes sure any unattractive design features are facing your property. In one particular case the neighbor on the unattractive side refused to pay for half of the fence.

Rarely does one escape an eventual penalty for misbehavior. Life has an interesting tendency toward balancing the score over time. I had a friend who was a college graduate and stock broker at a large company. He was a generally likable fellow with a good job, but he had a deceitful side that was, from time to time, manifested against friends and family alike. One of his more odious episodes occurred when he pocketed his father's half of their house payment for several months and then filed for bankruptcy… all because of a drug habit. The last time I heard about him he was employed at a fast food restaurant in another state. I would guess that he sees his situation as being caused by others rather than by his senseless behavior. It's interesting what an impairment one's mal-wiring can create.

What goes around generally comes around, so learn to behave accordingly

It's Us vs. Them

Some of our less social behaviors can be traced back to being taught certain lessons (*both explicitly and implicitly*) about connections, from the simple act of cheering on one's team, to seeing others as like ones' self. This conduct may have been part of a rudimentary script for the development of cohesive, constructive interactions among the earliest roaming humans. It was required to cement the relationships that were used to facilitate procreation, food gathering and group security. In the eons since this development we have retained this imperative to connect ourselves with familiar groups. Some people, for example, are so fixated on one of those associations that their team's loss can be a depressing event. It may not matter whether the game was technically good or not because of innate wiring which tells us that winning is more important than content.

Today we use this behavior in cooperative and competitive ways in order to produce better widgets or to improve a service. This instinct is still serving us well. The downside, however, can be seen in how we may treat other people. Feelings about their not being part of our local group can lead to disharmony. This is especially true for those who have chosen criminality (*street or business*) as their vocation. They have little or no empathy for their victims because they don't know them, and don't think of them in any caring way.

What Comes Naturally

Christian Nestell Bovee, author: *"No man is happy without a delusion of some kind. Delusions are as necessary to our happiness as realities."*

In a previous paragraph I used the word senseless as if the person's behavior was irrational, and that he was unable to make more reasonable decisions. The reality is more subtle. Antisocial actions actually reflect one's delusions and desires at any given moment. The future implications of our behaviors may not be well considered, and we may deceive ourselves about the consequences of our actions due to inappropriate wiring and filters. So my point is this... people do exactly what they want to do. And they will do what they want to do regardless of any conflicted thoughts that they may have on the subject. In point of fact, it is not possible to do what we don't want to do, despite our prevailing attitudes to the contrary. If the outcome of our behavior is negative, it may well be because we do not have remedies at our disposal that can act as a deterrent to this behavior. That is why some of us require serious retraining, when possible.

Choice is an illusion, not an option – you are who you are, and you will always do what you are inclined to do at any given moment

Imagine what it would be like if we were truly capable of doing what we didn't want to do. This situation would be analogous to a computer program that was occasionally capable of giving an alternate response even though the input was the same. Not only is this virtually impossible, but the computer would be hopelessly unreliable. If we were somehow able to be wired in this strange manner we would be living in a schizophrenic cloud that could be devoid of adequate reason and rules. Red could be blue on one day and not the next. Since this clearly is not the case, believing that we do only what we want to do is the most rational conclusion to be drawn about human behavior.

Having mixed emotions about a situation does not imply that we will occasionally do something we don't want to do. Certainly we all will do things we shouldn't have done, but that is not the same animal. As time passes we may be able to clearly see the implications of our actions and have regrets about them. However this does not contradict the reality that at the moment in question we did what we wanted to do. It just means that the regretted behavior was not particularly well considered, and that the ramifications of the action may come back to bite us in the butt.

Making decisions about which action to take or not take is not much different from bidding and playing bridge. Before offering up a bid one should consider the possibilities that may be derived from their call. If enough education and consideration is at hand, bids will be logical and reasonable. If not, the results could be disappointing. But even an undesirable outcome in no way implies that the person did not do exactly what they wanted to do at the time. Again, their decision may just have been poorly considered.

If I were to purchase an automobile because I imagined that I would be able to cover the payments, I may later come to regret that decision. But at the time it would have been what I wanted to do. Such an ill-advised action would suggest a lack of maturity more than it does of having a choice. Or let's say that I acted unkindly toward someone which then resulted in alienating or embarrassing them, to my dismay. The reality is the same. I did what I wanted to do at the time, without adequate regard for the implications. Accepting this premise is critical to understanding and dealing with human behavior.

Brain Programs

It's a Busy Place

You have no doubt heard of the unsubstantiated statement that the brain only uses 10% of its available power, and that this can be dramatically increased using various techniques. Not likely! That is just propaganda from those who want to sell some bogus remedy. The brain uses 25% of the body's energy and is already quite busy running its native functions, with only a modest amount of energy to spare on additional tasks. The evidence that I offer to support a not likely contention is that the brain uses ten times the energy for its size compared to the rest of the body. Most of our brainpower is used for non-thinking tasks. It has not been shown that persons of brilliant intelligence use more energy then those with lesser abilities. Brain power may be more a function of providential genetic wiring than of personal effort. Savants have an extreme version of this wiring.

Scientists have speculated that a portion of our brainpower is also dedicated to subconsciously preparing the brain to receive new input by using predictive routines (*if this might happen, then that should happen*). It occurs when we crunch the data that has come to us from past experiences and was transferred to, or available to our built-in, problem-solving routines. Who has not gone to sleep with a vexing dilemma only to awaken with a fruitful solution? These routines and other brain programs will suggest support for my thesis that there is no such thing as free, which is explored later.

Nature of Nature

Tendency is a term that we can use to describe the probability of a particular action taking place given a particular stimulus. This suggests the reasonable rule that actions lead to reactions. The probability that some behavior will occur after a stimulus is how we make sense of the world using the brain's initial wiring and its ongoing rewiring. It is our brain programming which determines…

-- how we conduct ourselves
-- what we are able to learn
-- what we might believe about our surroundings
-- to some degree what we are capable of achieving
-- how we will journey through our life experiences

Tendencies are the expression of our brain programming and its subsequent output. The implication is that we, by ourselves, can no more change our programming or tendencies than can a Dalmatian change its spots. If this hypothesis is valid, it negates what people believe about the curious and nearly indefinable term free will. By indefinable I mean that doing what you don't want to do is not a possible explanation for anything.

Subprogram Startup

At any point in time we are precisely who we are, even though that condition is in a constant state of flux because of our changing environment, the inputs we receive, and how they interact with our personalities. Our brains are continuously being subtly or dramatically altered as we process new data and form conclusions about what we have encountered, even if those inputs and changes may be imperceptible. Sometimes our behavior may be the direct result of one or more brain subprograms that kick in or out on some sort of genetic schedule. Among these subprograms is...
-- the willingness to become loyal followers like the animals that instinctively track behind their mothers
-- the ability to learn a language, which develops in our youth, but strangely can not be implemented if it is never used during youth
-- similarly, chimps must learn the use of tools from their troop mates before the age of eight or they can never learn to use them
-- the propensity of males in their teens, 20s and 30s to be more capable of violence then are other groups
-- the different forms of affection that we can experience toward prospective and potential mates as we age and our attitudes may change from...
-- puppy-love
-- to lust

-- to love
-- to the best of all – warm love and affection, and having fun together every day

Helen Keller, educator: *"The best and most beautiful things in life can not be seen or touched; they must be felt with the heart."*

While I am on the subject of love, people can have a difficulty describing it, and they may revert to the non-explanation of "I know it when I feel it". Let me help out. Love is, among other things, a combination of need, pleasure and giving. The vast majority of us have a genetically motivated need to cultivate companionship because we can not procreate alone or easily fend for ourselves. Part of love is the pleasure of another person because of what they can add to our lives. An occasionally underrated aspect of love is giving, so that the recipient of the affection is inclined to reciprocate. This last area is where many relationships fail because one or both of the parties is too self-centered (*really stupid*) to give. Yes this makes love inherently selfish on the one hand and potentially generous on the other. In the final analysis it must be a win-win situation to flower.

Mark Twain: *"Love seems the swiftest, but it is the slowest of all growths. No man or woman really knows what perfect love is until they have been married a quarter of a century."*

Shared history is an important factor in how well relationships survive the differences between couples. These are the big and little events that contribute to a knowledge and appreciation of each other, or to disrespect and dislike. Because this is so important, substantial effort must be made to have as many positive memories as possible. These memories will bounce around in our heads for a long time and will consequently color future attitudes for better or worse.

Getting back to brain subprograms, another curiosity may be curiosity itself, although my evidence for this conjecture is purely anecdotal. Females appear to have less interest in things mechanical and in discovering how the world and universe works. Perhaps this occurs because they were not raised around mechanical toys or scientific discussions. Girls may be given dolls and stoves that they barely interact with. Boys may be given toys that move and require action, like bows, toy guns, action figures, trucks and trains. These toy associations may occur during a time when one's curiosity can be either enhanced or retarded. When we do find the occasional woman that works with automobiles or computers, it may be that she had male playmates or siblings with whom she interacted as a tomboy. Given identical environment stimuli, boys will be girls and girls will be boys. Or to put it another way, they will be more alike than different

Herd Synchronization

People are intimately connected in ways that they may not realize. When someone yawns or laughs, we are inclined to follow suit. This innate behavior explains why comedy shows add artificial laugh tracks to their programs. They are designed to put an audience in the mood to follow suit with their own laughter.

Correspondingly, flocks of birds and herds of animals are well known for taking flight or stampeding when a single member of their group does so, all without having direct knowledge of an imminent danger. They intuitively know that their group's quick movement represents a threat. And like them, we may not always be aware of the reasons why we play follow-the-leader. This propensity is also an explanation for the formation of clicks, gangs and true believers.

Common forms of herd synchronization occur at sporting event and with television audience-participation shows. There is no true need for shouting or applause, but we do it any way. For some reason sports are more attractive to men and daytime TV talk shows are more appealing to women. While an athletic game might prove to be interesting even with the sound turned off, having talk shows without a cheering audience would diminish audience interest. This is why all entertainment shows have them. It is the producer's way of involving people in the event, especially when the content is just so-so.

Having gone to a number of entertainment events over the years, one thing has become very clear. People will feel an obligation to cheer at the "appropriate" time even though the content may not be all that motivating. While a few will laugh at nearly anything that smacks of humor, others will simply go along with the program so that they do not look out of place. As an aside, on one occasion a person seated behind us laughed so hard and so often that we had to change seats during the intermission. She apparently had a need to be noticed and (*as science of the brain shows*) got a mild high from the experience. This also explains why there are politicians who are willing to go through the rigors of a bitter campaign in the hopes of getting into the limelight. Their need for and fulfillment from public acclaim is a brain high that they can't resist. And of course they will end up selling their souls to the corporate bribers in order to get there.

Not Just Our Wiring

Even though we have a genetic push towards aggression, especially with the "hunter oriented" males, the expressions of this behavior are more likely to occur due to the incentives derived from one's social environment rather than from their own wiring. And to exacerbate this situation, society tends to incentivize (*a coined word*) this group with their rewards of appreciation and encouragement. Just look to our attitudes towards contact sports for confirmation of that thesis.

Children may be encouraged by passive-aggressive praise they receive when adults pronounce that "boys will be boys". Teenagers may have moderate aggression because they have their hormones to contend with, which favor excitement over caution. This lack of control occurs primarily because the frontal, calculating lobe of the brain tends to develop in the later teen and early twenty's years. Gang members have their negative and destructive behaviors reinforced by...
-- the influences that are promoted in their peer group
-- a learned addiction to power and cruelty
-- a cultivated hate against outside individuals and groups as a way of asserting imagined superiority
Felons may feel the need to perpetuate their violent or illegal behaviors because they...
-- were treated harshly in their youth and it is the world they know best
-- feel detached from or cheated by society
-- are robbed of their dignity in prison – ignoring the behaviors that brought them there in the first place

-- have aligned themselves with a prison group which can provide protection and other perks
-- are incarcerated for life and see no viable alternative

While we may be born with aggressive tendencies, it is unlikely that we are delivered from our mother's womb with antisocial dispositions. Most negative behaviors are learned from close associations. To some degree these acts are perpetuated by the tolerance found in society, such as with...
-- school bullies
-- social network (Internet) harassment
-- unnecessarily aggressive athletes
-- road-rage drivers
-- cultures that are based on aggression
-- businessmen who illegally work the system
-- leaders that use repression as a tool to maintain power

All of these genetically inspired behaviors are symptomatic of a permissive society that has insufficient incentive to police itself. And the perpetrators of aggression believe that they have or will achieve something positive from their behaviors. So our social conflicts will continue until we offer or impose positive rewiring opportunities and effective sanctions on those who are in need of them.

Dan Olweus, social scientist: *[Bullying is] "a pattern of repeated aggressive behavior with negative intent directed from one child to another where there is a power difference."*

A word about the nature of bullies is that they may...
-- learn to thrive on the fear that they instill in others
-- use intimidation to prevent being bullied themselves
-- feel superior in some way
-- learn the practice in their homes where they were bullied, and then continue to exhibit the behavior in public

Society needs to be aware of the substantial damage that is caused by bullies and have these offenders publicly and frequently exposed. Imposing this lesson on them could be productive in suppressing their need to be tormentors.

41

Another way to look at bullies would be to draw a parallel with a study of the bird Nazca Boobies. Researchers at Wake Forest University have learned that these birds are capable of perpetuating a cycle of violence that was initiated against them as chicks. These bullied chicks tend to become bullies and pass that pain onto others. When the parent birds leave their nests to eat, baby Boobies are often visited by sexually and physically abusive, non-breeding adults. Then these chicks, when they are grown, are more likely to abuse other unrelated chicks. The link indicates that their nesting experience, and not genetics, influences their adult behavior. It is supposed that this may have to do with hormone levels in the brain. Researchers have found that concentrations of the hormone corticosterone in Nazca Booby chicks increased five-fold during bullying events. The team believes that these spikes in hormonal levels could have a long-term effect on the boobies' brains, causing their aggressive behavior later in life. Perhaps something similar occurs with human bullies when they are molested or abused as children.

As for social bullying, there seems to be a certain degree of implicit tolerance in our school systems toward this behavior. An occasional excuse for this attitude is that the administrators and teachers were not aware of when this was taking place, who is the offender was, and who the victims are. To which I would ask why not? It's not as if this is an unusual or isolated phenomenon. Bullies have been a fact of life forever. Anyone who is not aware of this trait is being intentionally blind to that reality.

So the answer to this problem is clearly that school personnel must take a proactive approach to root out and discipline those who are guilty so that the other students can live without fear or harm. And when this dread of abuse occurs, it can last for years. Just as anyone to recall when they were first bullied. It is likely that they still have memories of the event(s).

Antisocial Influences

From time to time we run up against those who just can't seem to get in sync with the logic and benefits of society's rulebook. They may profess to have good intentions, and say that they will try to do better, but they just can't change their deviant behaviors. On a television program about an apparently intelligent, but negatively disposed homeless person, she demonstrated that selfishness is not always a learned reaction. To put this more clearly, her self-centered behavior may not have been derived from others who exhibited it. This person clearly understood the rules of those who were trying to help her, but no matter. She needed to do what she wanted to do regardless of being made aware of its destructive implications for her. Making the intelligent choice was not an option since having a desire to conform to the rules was not a mental imperative.

Having known two friends that fell loosely into this antisocial category, I gather that they probably possessed a genetic disorder guiding them down the more difficult path, like the propensity for some to become alcoholics or drug addicts if a parent is. Additionally these people failed to appreciate their situation or to acquire the skill set required to deal with their problems. One would think that those who are able to recognize their frequent missteps would eventually be able to take measures to correct them, unless there is something more powerful at work. And that something is their emotional-genetic brain in action. Logic is cast aside when a person's imagined needs supersede their common sense. For those people, defective brain programming may be too strong to overcome… and the divorce courts and jails are filled with this personality type.

On the extreme end of the scale are the serial killers that range in modern times from Manson to Osama, as well as others who have permeated history with dreadful deeds. No doubt each of them felt that their behavior was part of their destiny. They had delusions of supreme importance, and a seductive inner voice moved this urge along without self-control. The possibility of their being captured or punished may not have been on their radar. They were driven by the misconception of a providence that had been created for them alone. As they transitioned from being nobody to somebody, their destiny was reinforced by their misguided followers.

Another aspect of these individual's personalities and some of ours as well is the empathy factor, or more to the point, the lack of it. When people can not make a sympathetic connection with others they will be inclined to treat them with minimal respect, or in extreme cases with great harm. Again, the logic that would tell them that they may eventually receive what they have meted out does not calculate. And jail time can be ineffective at encouraging these individuals to see the light.   Their wants and needs are too strong to overcome, and they can be unrepentant for life.

What becomes clear in a study of extreme deviant behavior is that some people have an overwhelming need to attain and hold onto power. Take away their audience or followers and they are nothing, which can barely be tolerated. On the milder side of this behavior are those who seek the highest positions of social, business or political status. Why else would some of them spend millions of their own dollars to be elected to office? The answer is a deep-seated need to acquire and hold power, feelings which may border on pathological.

Educational Influences

A few people with favorable genetic wiring may have the ability to become great educators or scientists. Others can never attain that level of skill regardless of any efforts that they might expend in that direction. Still others may be able to be guided into fulfilling higher achievement by the encouraging efforts of a mentor. Our ability to be encouraged in a particular direction is an important part of our brain's adaptability which permits us to adjust, within limits, to the influences and pressures around us. This essentially amounts to riding the horse in the direction it is going, and therefore becoming beneficially conforming. It also precludes our having to learn everything from scratch.

Jews may constitute a disproportionate number of doctors and lawyers in this country based on their percentage of population. This happy phenomenon probably occurs…
-- not because they have a doctor or lawyer gene helping them
-- not because they exercise control of those professions
-- not because they were in the right place at the right time
-- but because they may have been subjected to an encouraging ethnic push to succeed in those directions

Failure vs. success is often related to how we view ourselves and our capabilities in comparison to others. As children we embark on our lives with palpable insecurity. Those who are fortunate enough to receive the insight that they can do almost anything they set their mind to, will undoubtedly succeed to a far greater degree than others. Those who doubt their abilities and are not subject to encouragement will be less successful. The importance of having positive mentoring can not be overstated.

Living as Yourself

One of the most difficult dilemmas to solve, especially for children, is learning to be comfortable within their own bodies. By this I mean, accepting that you are ok, and then not try to be someone you are not. As a child I did not have a home environment that promoted self confidence to any great degree. This resulted in my being distant from most children, even though I wanted to fit in. While it didn't permanently stunt my social growth, it did put up roadblocks that I had to learn to overcome. Fortunately too, I married a loving woman who helped me deal with an undercurrent of disappointment that I carried from childhood as silently as I could. Because of her I got that I could be the person I wanted to be, just by being myself.

Incarceration Q&A

Question:

Why does America have a higher percentage of its population in jail than most other countries? Among what are surely many reasons, I offer the following.

Answers & Options:

<u>**Ineffective Drug laws**</u>: We have an entrenched bureaucracy that <u>benefits</u> from today's prohibitions. There are large numbers of people

employed in this ineffective army, and they do not seem to care that more damage than good is being done by their actions. A reasonable person should be able to recognize that this out-of-control, drug-repressive experiment is not working... not even a tad. But that does not stop bureaucrats and politicians from their illogical blather and pumping increasingly more money and resources into a failed drug-abatement program.

Option: Decriminalization and government control of prohibited substances (*like we do with alcohol and tobacco*) would go a long way toward eliminating the illicit drug trade and the crimes that are associated with its cultivation, turf wars, transportation, and sales. And a sales tax on these drugs would create substantial revenue bonus for the states.

Lack of Opportunity: Crime can be perceived to be a viable alternative to poverty or to taking menial jobs. This, in part, is because the perpetrators of criminal acts lack the education that can lead to success in the business world. Even if they go to prison without an education, they come out with one (*if you take my meaning*).

Option: Institute a policy of not permitting early parole for felons unless the inmate has obtained their GED and an employable trade through prison training. This would give these miscreants practical options to utilize when they get back on the outside. As it is now, criminals learn mostly criminal activities in prison, which they fall back on when they can not find, hold, or appreciate a job.

Lack of Education: This is what prevents most people from attaining the expertise that is required by employers. Unwillingness to make an educational commitment at an early age is a life long sentence of mediocrity or crime. While it can occasionally be overcome, those who have rejected learning at an early age are unlikely to change their stripes as they get older.

Option: Among other bits and pieces that could be used to correct this situation, we need to...

-- make education interesting, not just dry textbook lessons - stop emphasizing what-happened-when in history and teach why-it-happened and why-it's-important
-- teach practical classes on obtaining and holding jobs
-- incorporate both manual and cerebral education into the mix

Please note: *In the following subchapters when I use terms like options, choice and select, I am not being literal. I'm using them figuratively.*

Choice & Free Will

Definition of Choice

So what can we glean from the previous analysis into the manner of how the brain functions...
-- at any given point in time we will be slightly different from the preceding moment due to those influences of both our initial programming and our encountered experiences
-- if we are exposed to positive behaviors it is likely that we will improve our coping skills
-- conversely, if the pressures on us are negative we can be expected to suffer adversely from that experience

Sounds reasonable, right? What you may not conclude from the analysis is that people have only a limited ability to alter themselves independently of the outside world. They also possess the illusion of having more than that minimal capacity. The vast majority our behaviors result from our brain programming acting in concert with external stimuli, not from independent thoughts.

The Illusion of Choice

Intriguingly, we are so accustomed to our stimulus-reaction scenario that we may not have deciphered what it is or just how it makes us who we are. Yes we can live our lives, and yes we can have our lives altered, but being in control of them is an entirely different matter. Having this power over our behaviors would involve the ability to make independent choices... independent of ourselves. And that does not even sound reasonable. While we can influence others by our own conduct, and we can be swayed by theirs, we can not change ourselves because (*and this is the essence of it all*) we are always ourselves. In other words we simply respond to the outside world's events in the one and only way in which we are destined to, due to our birth starting point and our life experiences, and that is by reaction. Each event that we detect produces a response that is unique to us, generally repeatable, and which could potentially be predictable to someone with brilliant insights and the appropriate training. Short if that impossible skill, people can generally know each other and have reasonable expectations.

The ability to process what we have previously taken in may be the mechanism that allows us to believe in free will in the first place. But we will always do whatever (re)processing we are inclined to do. On the surface, accepting this concept can seem reasonable because we may form new conclusions while reflecting on past events and from mulling over of current ideas. However this does not technically support choice or free will. Only previously established instincts and tendencies, along with our adaptations to the everyday stimuli is what continuously updates our brain program.

The illusion that we have about choice probably comes from our ability to detect what appears to be a range options that we may see as being available to us, but are actually not. In the end we will always select door number one because it is the "option" that our makeup dictates. This selection will not necessarily result in our exercising the most effective action. It may just happen to be the behavior that we have become predisposed to "choose" because our initial wiring and subsequent rewiring. While the illusion of choice appears to be real, we simply follow our constantly evolving nature.

Doors number two, three, and beyond may fall within our awareness, but they will never be accessed, except with what only appears to be an exception. That circumstance occurs when we contemplate an existing idea, draw on its implications that did not readily occur to us, and then that process changes our mind. At this point the new idea becomes door number one, and the original number one is no longer available to us.

Free Will Fantasy

One definition of free will could be:the ability to do what we might not want to do. For example, I want to "date" my wife's sister, but on reflection I choose not to. In reality we do exactly what we want to do at the time unless encumbered by something or someone that prevents us. No exceptions! We may imagine that we want to carry out an illicit act, but electing not to do so, if that is the outcome, is what was actually and only wanted. Since we are always who we are, how could we possibly express an alternate behavior that is not us? All of our "choices" are predetermined by our current (*evolving*) makeup, and we can not deviate even slightly from that program, except in the two quasi-ways that were mentioned earlier.

When we deliberate about the wisdom of eating an ice cream cone or buying an automobile, our tendencies will invariably dictate what we actually do, regardless of any feelings that we might appear to harbor to the contrary. Even the interesting emotion of ambivalence about having multiple perceived options is part of that programming.

We are only passengers on our train, while we mistakenly believe ourselves to be the engineer in charge

Since our potential reactions to every scenario are essentially fixed in place (*and subject to change based on influences or contemplation*), how could choice ever come in to play? Part of people's difficulty in accepting this thesis may be that life's events are approaching us at a rapid rate and generally involve significant complexity. This makes the process of pinning down what is happening to us very difficult. Presumably we were not born with this insight because it did not serve an evolutionary purpose.

Having a choice would imply that we possess the ability to pick from a variety of different behaviors (*like from a menu*) that may or may not be appropriate or advantageous in a given situation. But the reality is that we will act in the exact fashion which is appropriate (*even if not beneficial*) for us at any point in time. This of course does not mean that we might not come to regret an ill-advised behavior, or that others won't take exception to the ones that we exhibit.

In order to be able to modify one's tendencies we would need to have a supervisory program that is both knowledgeable of us, yet separate from us. It would have to come with the ability to make autonomous (*non-reactive, capricious*) decisions that could then be used to alter

our programming on the fly. Does that even sound plausible? If one's tendency is to...
-- cry at emotional movies, then that is what will happen
-- over eat, then that is what will happen
-- spend beyond one's means, then that is what will happen
...until new programming changes the tendency.

We have no internal supervisor that will change the behaviors that are us. However, pre-destined behaviors are not absolute and will vary with time and circumstances. So a different reaction from one similar event to the next does not disprove the thesis. An assumption that can be derived from this analysis is that all of those things that could contribute to the alteration of our behaviors must come from without... again, short of a subprogram kicking in, or reformulating what we already know. So if this logic is true, it means that there is no such thing as free will, no matter how attached one is to the idea.

The concept of free will is something like the concept of having a soul. If we all began as simple organisms which had neither of these qualities, then just when did they appear on our evolutionary path, and for what reason? The answer to this is that neither of those qualities ever came to into existence, no matter how much we are inclined to insist that they did. There is no genetic imperative and no physical mechanism which could have made this happen. You may wonder... is it possible to believe that there is no free will even though we can see it in action? Yes, we just think we see it.

A Deterministic View

Again, a way of thinking about the concept free will is that it is the reformulation of thoughts on the fly. By that I mean we may pause to analyze a situation before reacting to it. If this is what you think of as free will, the argument has something approaching a validity. It is just not my definition because a behavior is not really alterable by what people call choice. Pausing to recalculate our options, if that is what happens, is just another preset brain mechanism that makes us who we are. The outcome from a deliberation will always be what it will be.

Isn't There Choice?

Ok then, how is it that we appear to make decisions if we really don't? The answer to this intriguing conundrum is that we have little consciousness as to how this brain process takes place. We simply view our options as if we had the ability to make a choice between them and then "allow" the brain programming to take the only course that is valid for us at any instant. We will always make the exact same decision given the exact same circumstances, just like the computer programs that I used to write. There is no real choice or free will at work, only built-in tendencies or propensities that are the result of genetics, education, and other influences. To put it more succinctly, our reactions are based on original wiring (*from our inherited traits*), rewiring (*from external stimuli*) and precious little else.

Another factor that leads us to believe in choice is that we can apparently make something out of nothing, so to speak. We can take two or more ideas, examine them, and perhaps create something new. Einstein was proficient at this type of thought process when he contemplated the universe's space/time continuum. But note that he did not start with nothing and then make a leap into something. He began with his own wiring, which gave him a very genetic-rational brain, and then added external data from other scientists into the mix. The result was that he developed spectacular insights into the nature of universe. But this was not the result of independent choices. It was just his brain doing what it had evolved to do... process input and correlate it with existing knowledge. This is why cave dwellers did not postulate the speed of light. They did not have a data stream of information to work with.

Intelligence is evolutionary. It is built up from fact after discovered fact. While most of us do not have the ability to reason on the same level as Einstein or other great thinkers, this is none-the-less the same method by which we all resolve our own problems and challenges, just in a more limited way. We take what we already know and extrapolate new conclusions from existing information. It may seem to us that choice is at work, but it is only our programming that is functioning in this manner. Does that make us lesser beings or somehow out or control? Not at all! It just makes us what we are.

All About Illusion

As I type this book I appear to make a myriad of choices about what to write and then what needs to be rewritten. In actuality I am only a spectator of my actions, not an originator, even though that does not appear to be the case by me or anyone else. If people could truly make choices, wouldn't we all have become far better for it, by not making so many of the harmful decisions that affect ourselves and society? Or do you believe that some of us just prefer to be antisocial, unfair, ruthless or vicious. The fact that there are educational disciplines which are focused on improving the mind should stand out as an argument against our having the ability to make independent choices and construct improvements from within.

Choice is like a magician's illusions... interesting but not real

One last thought regarding the illusion of choice. Since I wrote and rewrote this book many times in order to make the logic more lucid to the reader, it demonstrates how the mind accomplishes learning as it reorganizes what it already knows, but doesn't know it all that clearly. Perhaps this is what some people think of as free will. An example of how this learning takes place is in the reading of my own text. I am able to discover mistaken word choices and difficult phrase constructions through rereading. It is a matter of examining what I already had written in order to improve upon it. Rereading the text became my external supervisor, just like reading any other book might be used to enhance learning.

This manner of revisiting an issue is similar to the technique that programmers use to resolve coding problems. At times the process of verbalizing an issue to an associate can help to clarify various aspects of a program. This type of intercourse may then lead to a workable solution, and occasionally without any feedback from the person who has become relegated to the position of listener. This is one of the ways in which we consolidate, reorganize and reconstruct what we already know, but do not know all that clearly.

Robotic Similarities

In many ways people are like computers… perhaps far slower at some tasks and more complex in our programming, but similar. Can you imagine anyone believing that even the most advanced computer robot of tomorrow would ever be thought of as having a soul, free will, or having the special ability to make non-programmed choices, even if it eventually mimicked humans? We would always be aware that it was someone's programming at work. Curiously we do not make that same judgment of ourselves.

When contemplating robotic programming, the analyst has to imagine every conceivable circumstance that the machine might reasonably encounter in its intended environment. Then they would have to program appropriate responses for each of them. These decisions are then eventually scripted into the robot's software and hardware. With the advanced form of programming called Artificial Intelligence (*AI*), robots must additionally possess a supervisory type program that can, through the detection of new events or things, reprogram its basic system. This is very tricky stuff. In fact it is so difficult a concept to enact that a Masters AI student I met was unable to describe how this process worked. However it is still programming that allows the robot's adaptation to unexpected circumstances.

For a robot with AI to become human-like in the distant future it would have to possess…
-- self awareness
-- sufficient memory
-- learning ability
-- problem solving skills
-- empathy with its surroundings
-- creativity
-- prejudices – hopefully of the good kind

Basically AI is a complex form of dual layer programming as opposed to the single layer programming that is required for spreadsheets, word processing, or humans. While there might be something in AI that is akin to learning going on, there are still no independent choices involved. It boils down to exhibiting behaviors that were defined by its programmer. If a robot is able to detect where a curb is and how high it is, it may be capable of taking avoidance measures given the right anatomy and directions. What it can not do is determine what a curb is if it does not have any rules which would lead it to that discovery. A robot's existing set of rules can not be changed, however, unless there is intervention by the programmer. We are still in charge.

As humans we can not act as both the program and supervisor because we have no such ability, or split personality. All of our potential decisions are predetermined until new education (*which might be thought of as our supervisor*) intercedes to alter our current programming. In a way, we are stuck being who we are.

An interesting idea for a sci-fi story might involve a clever programmer that was able to have a robot miraculously reprogram its own supervisor. Then there is no telling what that might lead to. More likely than not, it would result in chaos, rather than taking over the world.

Are We Responsible?

Evolution has created the human brain with input/output capability. When the brain's output is faulty it can usually be traced (*however convoluted*) to the input and not to a problem with the brain. Similarly, good behavior flows from good influences. This is why we must create positive role models for our youth so that they will learn how to cope with their lives in the most reasonable and productive ways. Though one can not technically be blamed for their negative actions because they had no real choice, this doesn't mean that they can not or should not learn new tricks from their environment. For the wrongdoer, the execution of punishment and incarceration may or may not go a long way in that direction. When this type of social re-engineering occurs, we act as the offender's supervisors in an attempt to reprogram them into becoming more acceptable.

Here is a simple set of questions that is designed to suggest how the appearance of choice functions...
-- If I were to propose that you should make an effort toward making an advantageous choice, and you seemed to comply with that advice, did you choose that course yourself or did I do that for you in the form of urging?
-- Would you have made that particular choice without me?
...the answers to these questions are: **yes** and **perhaps not**

In an experiment in Southern Arizona, some DUI offenders received the dubious honor of having their faces displayed on DUI billboards for all to see. While this test did not have universal support (*the ACLU was against it - no surprise*), it did reflect an earlier punishment theory that was used by the British and early settlers in America... the stocks. The logic was that if people can not maintain a reasonable behavior on their own volition, they should be shamed into it using public humiliation. I have been a mild advocate of public shame (*not necessarily the stocks*) for quite some time. I adopted this attitude because it is clear that if people are allowed to act with anonymity, they will be less responsible to others, such as with road rage, bullies, and graffiti. We might not be subjected to these people's offences so often if they knew that others would be made aware of their misbehaviors.

Brain Confusions

How It All Began

When humans first began to recognize that they were in a relationship with their surroundings, they were fearful of those areas which were discovered to be dangerous or that represented unknowns. And with their limited life experiences there were many unknowns and much to be feared. Due to minimal knowledge about the nature of life and death, explanations were invented for their comfort value. As the concept of guilt became attached to horrific events, people began to blame themselves for adversity (*drought, war pestilence and epidemics*) - hence the creation of, and the looking up to gods for salvation.

Another "solution" was to blame the cosmos for what occurred on earth. This led them to harbor many false conclusions about the mystifying effects that were witnessed. Eventually they contrived the creation of multiple gods that were believed to control the various forces of the world in order to have a better connection to nature. The gods that had been invented were eventually replaced with a single god, although there were different gods for different peoples. These singular gods were believed to be all-powerful and maintain dominion over living creatures. The one-god concept was perhaps easier to rationalize then relying on the conflicting tales about what the function of each of the many gods was. For different groups, different folklores evolved that were used to teach a variety of life lessons. These various stories were eventually employed to consolidate the power of the god-promoters who set themselves up as authorities.

The Universe & Us

Some of us might choose to imagine that the universe was created in seven days exclusively for our personal gratification, and that Heaven was devised as a place of reward for those who lived a particularly devout life. Those who do not accept this folklore might still believe that mankind is unique and holds a special relationship with God. Others might label themselves as spiritual, but it is hard for me to determine what that it is or why it is important. I guess it just feels good.

These imagined possibilities could be reassuring if they were true, but are they even realistic? Can we somehow manage to rationalize that an unimaginable volume of space and an uncountable number of stars, molecules, atoms, photons, quanta, etc. were all devised for our existence? The more we know about the evolution of man's thoughts, the less inclined we should be to believe in a God as the creator of the universe.

Several years ago a scientist took a number of commonly available ingredients including water and put them into a sealed vessel. He then subjected the concoction to electric sparks in order to simulate the effect that lightning might have had on our early atmosphere. The result was an accumulation of sludge that contained amino acids, the building blocks of life. What this may demonstrate is that the earth, and certainly all of outer space, is ripe with those components that are necessary for the evolution of life. And since there may be zillions of planets that have a similar climate to earth, how likely is it that not a single one of them would harbor life or even intelligent life? And if there is life elsewhere, our singular place in the universe is not so singular. Recent studies that were based on satellite discoveries have revealed that inter-stellar space is indeed a breeding ground for molecules and proto-life compounds.

When I look at the science of the universe, two facts that stand out are its…
-- incredible complexity
-- unerring faithfulness to a grand design…
-- the stars in our galaxy behave in the same manner as do the stars in far flung galaxies
-- the speed of light and other constants appear to be the same here and elsewhere
-- super massive black holes have been deduced to be at the center of all galaxies
…and so much more

Part of the universe's complexity is that there is more going on inside a single atom than we can hope to imagine or perhaps ever discover. One of the stranger mysteries of the universe is called quantum entanglement. Simply put, each of a pair of "related" particles can be affected by an effect on the other, even if they become a distance apart. That makes me think that our perception of space is way off the mark.

A second mystery revolves around dark matter and dark energy which can not be observed directly. They can only be deduced by the effect that they have on normal matter. Based on its influence (*acceleration*) on the disbursal of galaxies, dark matter is believed to make up the major portion of the universe, which leaves very little remaining for us, the earth, the solar system, and all of the galaxies. We on earth are getting smaller all the time.

If these dark forces and other cosmic complexities exist, how do we square that with the chauvinist attitude that the universe was created for a group of human beings who appear to have been created as aggressive, ignorant, superstitious and self-centered? Is that how you would have shaped life if you had been in control?

Earth and its inhabitants represent virtually nothing when compared to the entirety of space. We are infinitely smaller than the proverbial needle in a haystack. What then is the point of all the other stuff that surrounds us? It can't be a matter of attractive cosmetics having been created just for us, can it? Are we worth that kind of effort? Is there no more reasonable explanation?

Denying Intelligence

On one hand we may learn about how complex the brain is, and be told how our intelligence sets us apart from all else in God's eyes. Then on the other hand we are advised that we can not know the mind of God when some event goes against our wishes or our expectations, such as with deformities, catastrophic illness, major casualties or the untimely death of a loved one. Any reasonable person should not have a problem finding this belief totally arbitrary and contradictory in the extreme. In addition, we are induced to follow the teachings of those who may not be more insightful, or superior, nor have demonstrable insights into the universe's grand design. To the contrary, many of them have chosen to deny science when it poses a conflict with their indoctrinations. But it is because of these very leaders that we are strangely comfortable justifying adherence to a set of unproven and improbable stories from a distant past.

Curiously not all of our religious teachings tell stories that resist change. In 2000 the Vatican came to the conclusion that alien life was a possibility. This turn-about flies in face of what was taught about how mankind came to be. I don't imagine that Adam and Eve made trips to other planets, so how could this be possible? The obvious answer is that science was making it more difficult to believe in the tales about creation, and the church was grudgingly listening.

Where would religion be without the false guarantee of an eternal life after death and the potential of entry into Heaven to persuade us? These teachings about the afterlife may be appealing stories because the alternative of eternal death is a less desirable or perhaps a less understandable alternative. But that does not make these promises so, or even make them plausible. It does however, make them unlikely beyond measure.

Faith has long been the empty answer to explain the unsubstantiated and improbable statements that are promoted by its leaders. But isn't faith just another way of saying "I don't know" while relying on the hand me down words of others who also did not know? Even as a child I was aware that faith had a hollow ring to it. Nothing had to be proven or demonstrated. We were all supposed to take the word of someone who was taking the word of someone, who was taking….

Religion is about the power that comes from the making of enticing but un-provable promises to the faithful… and far less about man's humanity to man or his true place in the universe

To insist that one buy into these unsupportable beliefs is to ask that we accept an ancient dogma that was invented by those who were more likely as interested in exercising power and influence over others, as they were in salvation. As a demonstration of this contention about power, just look at any religious institution. You will find a hierarchy of positions that are similar to those in the military, which is clearly all about power. It is those at the top of religion's ladder who dictate policies and a litany of mandatory beliefs and behaviors to the people below them, and so on down the chain of command. There are, so to speak, generals, majors, sergeants and privates (*the flock*).

Two qualities that perpetuate religion are the attraction of power that comes with attaining leadership, and the herd instinct that is responsible for creating devoted followers

Cause and Effect

Cause and effect appears to rule everything in the universe, without exception. Something always leads to something. As far as we know, matter and energy can never be destroyed or created. They can only be converted from one form to another. And how could it be any other way? Where would they go to or come from? We should understand and respect this notion about the natural order of things, and discard those false ideas to the contrary. It is having this insight into the nature of things which will allow us to understand, appreciate, and respond more properly to the events and details of our world. Nothing in the universe ever happens without a reason, regardless of whether or not we understand its rationale or have an explanation for it. Everything we see was set in motion at some point in time. Or perhaps it has always been in motion based on the theories about space/time itself, which we have yet to unravel.

As far as we know the universe has progressed along its current path since the Big Bang some 13.7 billion years ago, in the only direction that it was destined to take. That path is absolutely, unequivocally, and unerringly straight ahead. However there are forces that might turn straight ahead into a circle, with gravity being the most well known of them. It reins in what energy pushes out. And while dark energy is apparently working against gravity, we may find that its power is not forever, and that gravity will force the universe to come full circle. Dark energy might turn out to be like a stretchable fabric that gradually resists expansion the farther along in time it is stretched. Or perhaps it is a manifestation that itself will turn into gravity at some point in time. After all, the age of our current universe is nothing close to the length of eternity, and it must have "begun" in the middle of infinite time. What would be the point of a universe that goes out with a cold whimper as all matter eventually decays? What are the chances that there was nothing before the Big Bang?

Going back to cause and effect, the possibility of there being randomness (*which is an absolute impossibility*) anywhere in the universe would ultimately have led to chaos long ago. A little shift here, a little deviation there, and over a great period of time the eventual accumulation of these inconsistencies would overwhelm the perfect order that we see today It would not be unlike what we may think of as the fanciful butterfly effect where…
-- the flap of a tiny wing effects…
-- a tiny air current, which affects…
-- the tip of a tiny wave, which affects…
-- a grain of sand on the beach, which affects…

Imagine what nature would be like if the speed of light or the force of gravity could somehow be subjected to the vagueness of randomness. The laws of perfection must also apply at the quantum level, which we have yet to fully understand. Without unalterable laws in the universe there would be anarchy. There would be no certainty. No order. Therefore nothing of what we observe around us and none of our actions can be accurately be described as random, even though they may occasionally exhibit the deceptive appearance of randomness. Theories that would embrace unpredictability as a function of reality deny the pure and elegant logic of cause and effect, making the notion patently impossible. There is and can be no randomness anywhere… period.

Casino slot machines are about as close to random as we can construct a device, and that only appears to be close. In getting to that point they must start-up with a built-in random number generator, which is initialized with a seed number. This is done by the machine taking the time of day or some other number and feeding it into the generator to simulate randomness. And when you start with something, there can be no randomness. The events that follow start-up will always be identical given the same seed and a lack of machine failure.

Going back to the concept of perfect order, it contradicts the virtually-indefinable and logically-indefensible idea that most of us cherish about free will. There is simply no reality to this widely held belief because it challenges the law of cause and effect. Like the slot machine's wheels, everything that happens in the universe is based on something that preceded it, and therefore everything that exists does so as a result of something else. If we were to extrapolate backwards, the universe must have always existed because of the need for a prior action to have created a reaction (*the current universe*). And if this law of nature is true, then any contention that a person could exercise free will independent of their personal history is illogical. Since all of our behaviors are dependent on something that has occurred in the near or distant past, they can not technically be free. Hence, no free will... at least by my definition. I suppose some define free will as the ability to choose between alternatives freely. We certainly appear to have this facility but how free is it?

History determines everything that will occur in the future – but that in no way means that we can make accurate predictions about it

Choice or No Choice

Our lives are little different from the universe, in a way. We react to events because there is perfect order, even though we may not always like what is playing at any moment in time. We are part of nature's ebb and flow. The best we can aspire to is being directed onto the preeminent path, like the comfort of first class over the more cramped seating in coach, and having the genetic make-up to facilitate that "selection". If this sounds contradictory and appears to support free will, it does not. Various options will be presented to us instant by instant, and we must hope our existing makeup permits us to generate the better outcome. It is our native instincts (*wiring*) and ongoing education (*re-wiring*) that make those good or bad choices for us. The grand illusion is that we make choices at all.

Because of our hereditary and continuous reprogramming, our behaviors are potentially predictable and essentially fixed at each instance in time, while awaiting the next action-provoking stimuli to occur. If you love blue cars, you will likely buy a blue car. If you prefer sweetened coffee, you may add sugar or substitute to the cup. If you are in awe of jewelry, you will want to obtain more of it. Our current disposition dictates what our future propensities will be (*which may or may not be exercised based on the prevailing circumstances*), and therefore dictate our potential behavior. Could it logically be any other way? If our life could be different than this, with an occasional or random twist, how could we be expected to have any confidence in our own thoughts and actions? We might act in one manner at one moment, and then not in the next under identical circumstances. We might select one course of action to engage in, or we might not, regardless of the circumstances. Our behaviors could potentially become so unreliable that having stability in our life would be highly unlikely.

Instinct, re-education, stimuli and the brain's processing of what it has learned and believes is what compels our reactions

Logic is Universal

Logic rules everything in the universe because logic is the nature of everything in the universe. This does not mean that people will always act in ways that may be interpreted to be logical. They will dance to the tune of their own thoughts. Their behaviors may not conform closely to the ideas of others, but this does not deny that they have their own logic. What it does mean is that there is a personal logic (*based on one's particular tendencies*) and a communal logic (*based on the standards of the group*). Sometimes our personal actions, which appear to be unreasonable by others, may actually boil down to being a flawed interpretation by those viewers. After all, each of us brings our own biases to the table when making judgments about others.

No one can truly be illogical within themselves because people are exactly and only what they are. Just don't expect others to allow them to break society's rules with impunity. There are many who have and will travel down a path of unacceptable behaviors because it conforms to their flawed personal logic. Even the mentally impaired persons are dancing to their own logical beat. Their wiring is just a bit haywire.

The difficulty with not having a clear understanding of communal logic for some is that they may not always aware of its great truths and importance. They may go through life ignoring rules and reason only to be straddled with those hardships that did not have to happen. There are easy paths and difficult paths, and understanding this is requisite to a experiencing a trouble-reduced transition through life. A few are never able to make this connection due to being subjected to negative, heartless, or cruel "training" that impacts them for a lifetime.

We tend to suffer our personal problems by doing exactly what it takes to create them

Another aspect of logic is that is not subject to human labels, such as right and wrong or good and evil. It simply is what it is. In a manner of speaking, it has no fundamental meaning. We may assign descriptors to details, events and actions in order to suit our own attitudes or to promote particular behaviors, but the logic of the universe is completely neutral. Right and wrong are designations that are the convenient tags that we use in an effort to guide society in particular directions. Accepting these labels may sometimes create adverse effects for us as people in positions of power promote their own definitions. We should certainly not assume that the conclusions and dictates of these label-makers are infallible. We should instead, become aware of how often it is that they indulge in deliberate misstatements in order to gain an advantage when they stage the world according to their own viewpoint. In point of fact, we are all guilty at times of engaging in this counter-productive behavior.

Truth, on the other hand, does not suffer from the above caveat. It is an absolute form of <u>what is</u>. While "truth" is often twisted to serve the purposed of the giver, fundamental truth is not subject to the interpretations of individuals. It is, however, sometimes difficult to ascertain due to the agenda of the giver. People will always color the truth to suit their own motivations.

Deceit is Common

We are unanimously devious in great and minor ways. We do things to satisfy our own needs, sometimes without a regard-for or having an awareness-of the potential outcome. There is also a contingent among us whose preference is to hang out on the "great" side of this continuum much of their lives. This likely happens because they have developed less workable solutions and attitudes due to their personal history.

Children are fond of saying: "I don't know" or "I didn't do it" when they are questioned about a negative behavior that they exhibited, in spite of there being evidence to the contrary. On some level they may not actually know the reasons for their behavior because they have yet to develop those adult insights about their motivations, which could lead to actual knowing. Or they may think that being in denial changes everything because they have come to view this technique as workable… a quality some adults still employ in an attempt to gain an advantage. Children are born selfish (*normal*) for valid evolutionary reasons and must learn what the implications of their behaviors are in modern society. They may discover that there are real benefits in denying their guilt, depending on the circumstances. At other times, a perceived benefit is internal, as with the fostering of feelings that they are not a bad person.

Occasionally the misdiagnosis of our actual role in problems or our repetitive denial of guilt can persist for a lifetime and serve no legitimate purpose. Pathological liars manage to deceive themselves into thinking that there is something to be gained from their ongoing use of prevarication. They are not in touch with their own actions, or in sync with the reactions of others. Some may even adopt the posture of believing that they are innocent, and that this posture will mitigate the retribution of others. As a result they may not experience the internal contentment that others do. Telling lies is hard work when you consider the difficulties incumbent in keeping track of them. Or they may adopt unfortunate justifications for their actions because of childhood traumas. If one is damaged in their youth, they may go on to express that damage in antisocial ways in the future.

An everyday example of social deceit is the institution of religion. Its exaggerations and false promises follow from culture to culture and country to country. Virtually no individual goes untouched by these fantasies that can sometimes have positive influences. If a business were to indulge in this level of prevarication, the principles would be wise to consider how to avoid jail time. Yet we give religion a pass for its many false contentions. And their substantial tax breaks go against the separation of church and state, regardless of justifications that are put forward.

Mother of Invention

For as long as we have had civilization (*communication, rules and community*), we have demonstrated a need to believe in the most unbelievable ideas, such as...
-- fire and water were gifts of the gods
-- Mars has creatures living on it
-- crop circles were made by aliens
-- mystical vortexes are near Sedona and other places
-- a sea serpent is living in the Lock Ness
-- the Bermuda Triangle causes plane crashes and ship sinkings
-- our government is hiding aliens and their technology

The more ancient of these beliefs were so arbitrary that they could not be proved or disproved by the masses. The origins of fire fall into this category. It only took a blind trust in the information giver to become a believer. Their assertions could neither be proved or disproved.

The lack of repudiation of an idea is not the same as it having been proven

Some of our recent beliefs have repeatedly been debunked by scientific evidence, such as there being intelligent life on Mars. Our modern telescopes have made vast improvements in long distant viewing, and our soft landings on the planet have gone on to dispel this idea. Until subsequent pictures of the "face" on the surface of Mars revealed as nothing more than shadows from ridges on a mountain, there was a cry from the I'll believe anything crowd that the Martians were trying to communicate with us. It was a ludicrous belief even before it was dispelled. They had the expertise to carve out mountains, but not the skill to employ radio waves. Right.

The intriguing crop circles that were found in England were assumed to be extraterrestrial in nature to the point where a quasi-profession evolved to investigate the phenomenon, Cerealogists, no kidding. A few deep thinkers actually promoted themselves to this profession. That is until a number of night-vision cameras were set up at the edges of crop fields and subsequently photographed the two highly creative, practical jokers who started it all. But even after that disclosure there are still those who favored an "aliens" answer.

In another case, a small town was treated to a cluster of lights in the night sky which bounced around too fast to be a natural event. Did the viewers consider that the bouncing was so unnatural that it required an explanation other than the alien classification? Did they consider that there might be a mirage effect in the atmosphere occurring with the light coming from the exhaust of several airplanes at a distance, and that the light was being manipulated by different densities of the atmosphere? Yes, there is an Air Force base nearby.

Over the years we have uncovered countless frauds ranging from forged pictures of Nessie the Lock Ness Monster to those of flying saucers. One might think that these exposures might deter or limit our gullibility, but that appears not to be the case. There are still those who believe that Area 51 in Nevada houses an alien spaceship, and spend their vacations there scanning the nearby skies for evidence. But alas, no validated sightings are forthcoming after years of observations.

Since we evolved in a superstitious, unscientific climate, it is not surprising that some of us would easily believe in the fantastic.

Presumably those attitudes evolved a long time ago, became part of our instincts, and have subsequently affected our current attitudes. Remember too that is was the churches that first promoted the ideas of werewolves and zombies... not the Steven King types. Until the movie "The Exorcist" was released, few of us knew that the Catholic Church had this bazaar ritual... one that is still being practiced in quiet places.

While these and other beliefs may be entertaining or harmless, there is a major contingent that has failed to get past the idea that society's truths require substantive evidence to be considered true. It seems that we have a great need for drama in our lives, and these invented stories serve to satisfy that craving. That would of course be for others since I have been a life long skeptic, requiring proof that there is a sufficient level of water before diving into a pool. If this is also how you function, welcome to the choir.

In another facet of our drama craving we may know people who will go out of their way to create incidents even though there is no reasonable logic beyond there own wants to justify the behavior. They need stress in their lives and will go about doing what it takes to get it. Then they lament their lot as if they have had no part in their created problems.

Resistance to Invention

In addition to being willing to believe in the unbelievable, we paradoxically exhibit a remarkable reticence toward adopting new ideas, or being able to comprehend their value. When an inventor named Goddard developed the first reliable rocket, fellow scientists rejected it as being fundamentally useless... nothing more than a toy. In Germany at the beginning of WWII however, a few German scientists were no so myopic, such as Werner von Braun and his colleges. This enterprising group successfully utilized Goddard's notes to successfully kick-start their counties' rocket aspirations.

Throughout the history of inventions there have been many initial detractors. This is because humans are inherently reticent to adopt change. Visions for modifying the future were not high on our genetic hit parade because they did not evolve as survival techniques. Early man benefited from determining a solution to a recurring problem and then sticking with it until it became instinctive. Sometimes that involved rejecting alternatives that may have been more suitable. Because of this background we may regard newness with such negativity that we denigrate an inventor and postpone progress. History is filled with those who were not given a fair shake by their peers, especially in the scientific societies. Even very good ideas can have a difficulty making the grade.

When the Japanese started exporting small cars to the US, the CEO of General Motors promised the public that his company would never make a compact car. Eventually GM relented and did build the Cadillac Cimarron. It was so much smaller than a standard model (*it was a baby Chevrolet in Caddy dress*) that its market failure was guaranteed… kind of a: see, I told you so endeavor. Presumably this was done to discourage the pundits from criticizing the high priced, gas guzzlers that GM wanted to build for their greater profits.

The shortage of American-made, commuter-sized cars vs. the proliferation of SUVs and large trucks (*that routinely carry a single person*) continues to define our glutinous mindset. How high does the price of fuel have to go, and how many terrorists do we have to subsidize before the light goes on for the auto industry and its myopic supporters? Did Detroit really have to go broke in 2010 before those running (*ruining*) the Big Three got the message? Maybe you can remember back when GM held over fifty percent of the auto market. Well that was then and this is now… or about twenty percent.

Invention resistance can also be targeted toward highly effective ideas. A professor of psychiatry at Harvard demonstrated that a natural brain chemical has the undesirable effect of reinforcing traumatic memories. A person's strong, negative memories can produce even more of this chemical, and an adverse cycle is created. He showed that another drug will interrupt this cycle and suppress negative memories, thus preventing people from being disturbed by them. Resistance to his studies came from the President's Council on Bioethics, populated with witless Bush appointees. Because of their view of the world, they condemned the work as unethical since it risked undermining a person's identity, whatever that means.

The Harvard professor who made the discovery rejected the council's criticism as being a bias against psychiatry. Don't think so. A more reasonable take on this subject would be that this government group was primarily interested in interjecting their view of God into the equation. In effect they are saying that we should not have too much power over life because that is His work. This is not much different from the attitudes surrounding stem cell research and the use of a morning-after pill. For some it is better to let people suffer or die then to interfere with what they imagine to be God's plan, if I get their message right. Would this a case of man being potentially stronger than God, or is it just another example of man's inhumanity to man through religion?

Short of using a drug, there may be a viable technique to counteract the difficult memories that we are all saddles with. This is, however, pure speculation on my part since I have not conducted anything approaching scientific method. Having experienced a number of events in my childhood that were either traumatic or potentially embarrassing, I have had to work on being ok with them. What I mean by this is reviewing those situation in a new light that excuses my behaviors or those of others who had adversely effected me. We are all raised in imperfect environments and will do things or be subjected to traumas that we come to regret. But regret is not the answer. The solution may be to justify those happenings to yourself and forget about the associated guilt or frustration that is incumbent in the memories. Those episodes are in the past and it might be healthy to deal with them as a learning curve, in spite of the scars that were left.

Going back to our apprehension of newness, being wary can also be found in the way we view each other's cultures. Each of us is a similar human being, but prejudices often prevent us from making that self-evident judgment. Some feel that those people who are not like us should be avoided, denigrated, persecuted or worse. An early encounter I had with this mentality came in childhood when I learned that the local drug store owner would not hire anyone who was outside of his Catholic faith. I can still recall how angry that made me feel even though my mother was also Catholic. I suspect that my reaction to this prejudice coincided with my observations of how badly children can treat each other… a disturbing similarity.

Religion vs. Logic

Deceiving Ourselves

One of our least productive traits involves the capacity to deny reality. This allows us to be repetitively duped by circumstances or by the unscrupulous who prey on us for their own benefit. Prayer fits well into this phenomenon because so many people believe in it without being able to demonstrate the slightest effectiveness. Has anyone ever done or even considered a statistical analysis of its success or failure rate, or heard of such a study? Of course not. This would be an affront to the faithful. In the event that providence has been favorable, they claim their prayers have worked. Or perhaps they identify it as a miracle, which would be God changing his mind about his grand plan. When an event remains negative, they remain mute, but none-the-less continue to believe in the fantasy.

A miracle is a positive event for which we may not be able to derive a reason, but that does not mean that the event does not have a simple explanation if we were able to identify and understand all of the circumstances

In an experiment showing how easily people are able to fit dubious explanations into their beliefs, test subjects were shown two pictures of different faces and asked to identify the more attractive image. After choosing one, the experimenter turned the photos face down. Then through slight of hand he switched the images and presented each subject with the picture that was not chosen and asked them to explain the reasons for their preferences. Many went on to construct justifications for what they believed was their choice. The urge for people to accept what they falsely believed was their choice had supplanted the memory of their actual selections. This reality flexibility is also what makes eye witness testimony so unreliable.

Hook Line & Sinker

Some time back a good friend professed his belief in how gifted a Native American woman fortune teller was. She could, so he said, tell him intimate things about himself that should not have been knowable to a stranger. This event reminded me of a show put on at the Magic Castle in LA. An entertainer told me personal things about myself after I had a brief conversation with his aide, but before the two had any obvious chance to speak to each other. While the information that was related about me was relatively accurate, it had nothing to do with any supernatural talent and perhaps everything to do with…

-- there are many truths about all of us (*most likely*)
-- maybe I heard what I wanted to hear (*possible*)
-- a code was passed between the aide and the performer (*maybe*)

I was amused, but not surprised. However there are people with a genetic disposition toward the easy acceptance of supernatural explanations because it satisfies their temperament. It is a part of human nature to look for answers when we are confronted with the unknown, and more than a few of us possess <u>really superior</u> skills in that direction. But common sense does not always go hand and hand with this innate behavior. Our society doesn't seem to learn a lesson from being repetitively duped by those who are anxious to engage in that sort of fun-for-profit. An example of this would be the "ghost stories" programs in TV. They manufacture "evidence" that fits into their agenda, and there seems to be a willing audience for this contrived "proof". That fantasy creation goes hand and hand with the various hotels around the world that claim to be haunted by someone who died there.

I am a little non-plused when I hear someone express their belief in the mystical vortices that are claimed to be located around the Sedona AZ airport and elsewhere. They are comfortable with these stories even though there is no evidence to support them. The anecdotal testimonies that abound are the result of people's easy beliefs, or perhaps they are deliberate deceit on the part of those who would make a buck off of the idea.

Common sense can be in such short supply that people will occasionally take classes to gain a bit of this skill. Classes like "est" in the 70's may have been in vogue for the moment, or they may have been deemed to be interesting by those who attended, or they may have actually served a learning purpose. While I did not attend, I had friends who did. I recall thinking that some of this education could be beneficial, such as *be here now* and *ride the horse in the direction it is going*. Others may have gotten the questionable message that *making mistakes was beneficial because it leads to a positive learning process*. Well maybe it does at times... just don't count on a high frequency of this.

Attention to Dress

One of our evolutionary traits is to deceive, and curiously, another is to be deceived. While this may seem slightly illogical, there must have been sufficient justification for both of those traits to evolve into instincts. One of these dispositions, to be deceived, can revolve around the dress and demeanor of the person being listened to. Politicians may wear conservative dark suits and "power" ties to elicit respect from their audiences. Women, more than men, have taken up the role as card readers and other fortune telling activities. They fit well into the expected stereotype which we have learned is appropriate for that profession... not unlike having the clergy generally be predominately men. As for dress, this is critical to our taking the bait of the illusion. Can you imagine a fortune teller not wearing some sort of gypsy garb, or a preacher not being dressed in a distinguishing robe or suit? What credibility would the latter have if they were wearing jeans and a T-shirt that said *power to the people*?

Wearing the appropriate dress is so persuasive that we are able to assign capabilities to the "properly" dressed people who claim to have special qualities. The downside to having this propensity to have beliefs based on a persons dress is in how easily we can be mislead and manipulated by it. Revival meetings are a fine example of this potential, where excitement is generated by, and people are swept up by the dress and captivating behavior of the presenter. The media is the message, and it works like gangbusters.

Some years back the entering freshmen members of Congress tried to gain admission to the Capitol building without wearing ties. They were quickly threatened with sanctions if they failed to fall into line with the illusion creators. As we should be aware, Congresspersons benefit from our willingness to believe that they are professionals because they are wearing the garb we associate with professionals. It is this clever veneer that they have successfully hidden behind forever, while simultaneously engaging in activities that are seldom in our best interests.

Judgment from Others

We tend to believe that it is <u>we</u> who have determined what is right or wrong, good or bad, beneficial or detrimental. This is because of our being presented with options to evaluate, and then making "choices" that come from that education. But the reality is not so clear. Our choosing between alternatives is never made from a clean slate or from perfectly logical wiring. The truth is that we express those attitudes and inclinations that are based on our instincts (*history brought to us from our forefathers*) and those experiences that we encounter throughout life.

Some of us may have been fortunate to have a mentor who provided us with a clearer, more beneficial picture of life's options and truths. Others may become so mired in negative social environments that they acquire destructive beliefs and behaviors. What we all end up with is the adoption of beliefs that are derived from <u>other</u> people's indoctrinations, insights and behaviors. Then these ideas become thoughts that we mistakenly assume were of our own creation.

Adopted beliefs can be either beneficial or detrimental depending on their value and implications for us. Sometimes we become an integral part of the social consensus of ideas, and manage to fare relatively well with what we have learned. At other times we may travel along destructive pathways due to the *garbage in, garbage out* principle. As you may guess at this point, I am offering these thoughts as an initial argument against the concept of *free will*.

If we spend only a limited time on productive personal behaviors, there must be something at work that prevents us from being there more often. The answer is that negative lifestyles come from the inappropriate ideas which we have adopted from others. Society has not gotten its communal act together all that well, and we collectively suffer from some of its behaviors and teachings. To make this point, do you believe that the evangelist, construction worker, or fireman down the street had elected to pursue their positions purely by independent choice? They were certainly influenced by the ideas of others… perhaps without being able to recognize or evaluate that education.

What we actually believe in will be the myriad of ideas that we have adopted through the processes of instruction and osmosis, but not always because of in-depth, critical examinations of those thoughts. In effect we do not develop reasonable or antisocial attitudes out of the blue. They require contact with others to acquire theses positive and negative viewpoints. So knowing something is not the same thing as having come to it by independent conclusion, because nothing in life is independent. In point of fact, the word *independent* is not unlike the term *random*. It is an absolute impossibility. The only way that anything can be truly independent is if nothing came before it… a concept we should all grasp and accept. Even if the universe was created in the big bang, it is not possible that this was the first cosmic event to occur. Something must have preceded it. It did not come from nothing. It would be a mistake to think that time and the universe began with that event.

Without Resistance

Your next thought might be *why do we know what is "right" if it is occasionally wrong*? The short answer is childhood. This is the time when our minds are a like a sponge, and we have not yet learned to assign the appropriate true and false labels (*filtering*) to the thoughts and arguments that come our way. At this age we are susceptible to even the wildest, most improbable ideas if there are no countervailing arguments at our disposal, or if detrimental ideas are presented with sufficient impact and authority by the giver. Why else would some societies condone or relish the massacre of others? Why would some parents reject traditional medicines for their dying children?

Logic is a valuable skill which can come to us in degrees as we progress along the pathway of life. However it will not always arrive in a timely fashion to dispel some of the notions that have been incorporated into what we already believe about the world. Because many of those thoughts arrive before the age of full reason, we are at the mercy of the idea-givers that we have encountered, who were in their turn at the mercy of the idea-givers that they encountered, and so on. This is in fact the exact method by which folklore and false stories becomes a part of our communal belief systems. Such counterfeit ideas can be perpetuated nearly indefinitely, and they may gain in stature over time.

The books that have been written about history are good examples of the phenomenon of adopting someone else's truth. They are written by those persons with an agenda (*honorable or not*) that may include both unavoidable and deliberate, factual flaws or perspectives of events. Occasionally these false thoughts may become accepted by us as evidence to the contrary is either lost in time or is infrequently contradicted. The Bible is a collection of books *(initially verbal Jewish stories)* which made the popularity grade at some point. But they are clearly not the only set of ideas that were around during the era of their early history. There were other disparate beliefs moving in then out of public favor as they did or did not attain a sufficient level of orthodoxy (*legitimacy*) with the common man. This occasional lack of acceptance reflected a lack of popularity, not necessarily a lack of truth.

If an idea is not interesting or popular, it is more easily discarded, perhaps without regard to its legitimacy... as in contrast to popular beliefs

Did the orthodoxy that many people attribute to the Bible occur because God (*who seems curiously unwilling to speak to us directly*) guided its drafting? Or was it because some of its ideas proved to be more interesting than others that were promoted at the time? Isn't it likely that the people who crafted the stories in the Bible did so by including those ideas that they preferred and rejecting those that they didn't favor or found undesirable for whatever reasons? Isn't the acceptance of ideas frequently a matter of natural selection in what amounts to a popularity contest?

We read interesting stories and articles, but avoid those that do not appeal to us. Similarly we will gravitate toward ideas and persons that we have come to like because of what they say to us, and avoid those that we might not agree with. This concept is most certainly true about the accretion of ideas that contributed to the making of the Bible. Some thoughts were voted in while others were voted out. So if this is the case, what does that have to say about its truth?

To demonstrate the Judeo-Christian diversity of ideas, there are Jesus-based religions that do not even agree on His status as the Son of God, such as Jews and Universalists. And conflicting attitudes were even truer during the formation of the Christianities. Back then people viewed Jesus as a mentor rather than the Messiah that was sent to earth by God. Apparently that lesser status was not appealing enough to garner wide-spread acceptance, and the more well-liked Son of God viewpoint won out.

In the Bible we have the ancient record of misinterpreted or improbable events that have been depicted by generations of the faithful as the truth. It is likely that these stories were originally a set of useful social lessons (*do this, don't do that*) which over time became transformed into fundamentalist stories and commandments. There is a high probability that they evolved in order to make Bible stories more interesting, understandable, and transferable down through the ages. This is similar to the way in which lessons had been passed down through songs in Great Briton and other countries before people became literate.

As an aside, one might ask why are there 10 Commandments and not fifteen or seven? Surely there are other admonitions that are worthy of being elevated to that status. Perhaps it was nothing more than being a function having ten digits on our hands, much like our Arabic numbering system that is a function of base-ten counting. FYI - computer systems use a base-two system which is represented by a multitude of on and off switches (*gates*).

As for people centric stories, we should be aware of our tendency to unduly (*unrealistically*) elevate the status of well-known persons after their death. The stories that we tell about Jesus may well fall into this category. Our ability to indulge in a progressively greater series of exaggerations can create fictions around people which continue to grow as one fantasy is heaped and reinforced onto another. Few of today's believers have the will to subject the origin and evolution of Biblical stories to any sort of critical scrutiny. This reluctance is likely do to the result of our early indoctrination as children. The Bible is said to be the truth, and any arguments to the contrary are deemed to be blasphemous. They are not something to trifle with, as the legions of crucified can attest to.

A few years back, a biblical scholar determined that the world began some 6000 years ago based on his family-treeing the persons who are depicted in the Bible. While these calculations have not generally been accepted, his effort demonstrates how easy it is to "prove" whatever you like about the notions found in religion. Yet if those writings should turn out to be reasonably accurate, blind acceptance of them is still not healthy practice.

Just because a great number of people insists that a writing is true (or false) does not make so

Is it Fact or Fiction?

Occasionally the concepts that are presented to us as being factual can be historically false. Most of us assume that the institution of marriage had been sacred within the Christian church since its founding. The reality of this matter is much different. In the Dark Ages, when Kings and Warlords were running amuck, marriage was viewed more flexibly. Multiple wives and concubines were not frowned upon, and in some cases they were encouraged. This was because there was a high mortality rate during delivery, and additional male children were required to balance out the losses from an endless succession of religious wars. We can imagine that because of this male attrition there was an abundance of women who were eager to have mates, no matter how tenuous the relationship.

Charlemagne, the Christian warrior King in the region of France, single-handedly (*so to speak*) saved Europe from the marauding Islamists. He had five wives, at least as many lovers, and twenty or more children. There was no conflict with the church over this matter. In fact the Pope went on to crown him Emperor for his many military successes. And this high reward came even after he had purged the countryside of infidels by beheading thousands of his own people who did not fall quickly into line with the current thinking. There were also the Popes who had mistresses and children outside of the (*now*) sacrament of marriage. It was more expected then condemned. I can imagine that the nuns were pretty much fair game. Does this sound like an early justification for having men run the church's affairs (*double entendre intended*)?

With our current dogma we may be taught that marriage and only one marriage is forever, and that committing murder is a sin. The lesson to be learned from these turnabouts in belief is that today's truths have not always been histories' truths. Since moral flip-flopping has been a long standing convenience with religion, it might be revealing to question why these concepts have changed in order to ferret out the nature of that evolution. In this way we may learn who had pulled the strings and why. This may even lead us to a healthy cynicism.

As for the murder side of the coin, today we entreat our military to kill thousands of people without having the traditional justification of self defense. We have conveniently substitute the expedient of self interest, and the people go along with this new line of thought.

Questions to Answer

If one is to have a rational belief in religion there are several simple questions that should be answered with logical replies...
-- Why is there a God?
-- Why is prayer beneficial?
-- Can we prove that it works?
-- Why is there a Devil?
-- Why aren't we born in Heaven?

-- Why do all of those people who were not exposed to religion allegedly end up in heaven anyway?
-- Why is it that your ideas about God are correct even though there are many religions with conflicting beliefs?

Is it in the Genes?

A modern study of our human genome has lead researchers to the unexpected conclusion that our ready acceptance of teachings about God and related religious issues may be linked to a specific gene. The head of the National Cancer Institute sited a study in which pairs of similarly religiously-minded twins who had been separated at birth suggested that there may be a genetic component involved in their intrinsic religiousness. In the general population, this characteristic may include the tendency of people to pray often and to feel the presence of God. Other researchers have found similar links to our genes as well.

Genetic makeup might well be a motivation behind those Evangelists who feel a great need to convert others to their way of thinking about God, and to promote fundamentalism wherever they can. These advocates will readily proclaim its imagined virtues to the world while simultaneously ignoring its shortcomings and many contradictions. So this blind acceptance may not be based solely on indoctrination during their childhood, but also on brain genetics.

While perhaps little about genetics goes very far beyond the working theory stage at this point, it does raise the question of how religion became so embedded in some people's psyche and not in others. I for one was raised in my mother's environment of regular church and Sunday school, but became a skeptic like my father at *the age of reason*, as George Carlin put it, as I began to wonder…
-- Was the wine and host really changed in to the blood and body of Christ when the little door was closed?
-- Why did the little door have to be closed anyway?
-- Why doesn't everyone go to Heaven?
-- How fair is Heaven's admission testing if we are not all subjected to the same challenges in life?

-- Why did I have to go to church anyway?

Perhaps I did not have the appropriate genetic-emotional makeup or the specific genes sequences that are requisite to becoming a believer. Or was there something else at work here, like having a genetic-rational perspective which required some shred of evidence that the genesis of religion was more than the result of a people who were easily indoctrinated, uneducated and superstitious?

It makes sense that genetics could be a factor in evolving belief systems. It is also likely that for many thousands of years people were killed for not following the witch doctors teachings, or for professing belief in the wrong religion, in the wrong place, at the wrong time. The believers had a better chance at survival and therefore passing on that instinct. History is filled with religious purges that may have been a factor in skewing the gene pool.

What is Reality?

Turning away from history for a moment, there seems to be occasional confusion as to just what reality is. A few people claim that it is only something within our brains rather than something concrete. I wonder if these people are merely having a problem with language. If reality were only located in our heads, we would all have a notably different view of reality because our wiring is so different from person to person. What they may mean is that perception is within our brains, and that individual's understandings are not always accurate. I would buy that explanation.

The closer our perceptions approach reality, the more accurate they are, and the better we are able to function.

The gist of the above is to suggest that people first need to find ways to get in touch with their perceptions, and then make an effort to have them become more relevant to reality.

Rejecting Reality

When Galileo Galilei (*based on Copernicus' teachings and his own observations*) wrote that the sun, not the earth, was at the center of the solar system, and that the earth revolved around the sun (*heliocentric*) not vise versa, he was condemned by the Catholic Church for his un-Godly writings. Whether he was correct or incorrect with his observational evidence was hardly the issue. Substantiation was not particularly important to the church, and was not permitted to be presented to the Court of Inquisition. Their job was to rubber stamp the determinations of the Popes and Cardinals and hand down appropriate sentences. They were not the judge and jury. They only worked for the decision makers.

The Catholic Church, along with other religions, has had a long standing interest in maintaining its infallibility, and their earth-centric mindset was a part of that dogma. It did not matter to the Pope that Galileo had been a close friend, or that he was able to support his contention with telescopic observations. It was simply heresy to disagree with fundamental elements of the church's teachings. Have things changed all that much since then? Galileo's punishment for transgressing on church doctrine required that...
-- he sign a false confession in front of the Inquisition
-- his confession would be posted in various towns
-- it would be read to the population
-- he would spend the rest of his life under house arrest

During his house arrest Galileo continued to write his findings and smuggle them out to receptive scientists, to the great benefit of all. One of his supreme (*and virtually unheralded*) contributions to man's knowledge was to elucidated that it was not appropriate to validate information simply from oral discussion, as had previously been the Roman practice. This contention brought about a debate as to how ideas should therefore be justified. Eventually the process of making valid observations was deemed to be a requirement for formulating accurate determinations. While this sounds eminently reasonable today, it was a radical departure from the style of the time when the elders ruled by consensus and what they took to be common sense.

Many other dissenters, because they were not so famous or so well connected to the Pope as was Galileo, were not treated nearly this well. In 1600 Giordano Bruno, a mathematician and Dominican friar, was stripped naked and driven through the streets of Rome, tied to a stake, and burned to death. The records of his prosecution by the Inquisition have been lost in time, but one of his major heresies was cosmological. He advocated that other points of light in the night sky were stars were like our sun, and that they might each support planets teeming with life. Orthodox thought of the time (*and with some of us today*) dictated that Earth and humanity were unique.

Ayn Rand, author: *"Reason is not automatic. Those who deny it can not be convinced by it."*

Since proclamation was considered a valid form of teaching in the past, is it any wonder that people became believers so easily? And because this ritual took place over a long period of time, it is likely that the acceptance of this format became instinctive as the non-believers (*with the "bad" genes*) were purged, and the believers (*with the "good" genes*) survived. Today there is still an ongoing issue over dogma's legitimacy when religion is the topic, with proclamation retaining the top billing for many. We continue to have a contingent who believe that the scientific theory of evolution is little more than pointless speculation because that is what they had been taught to believe. Perhaps they also trust that the physical indicators that construe a 4.5 billion year evolution of this planet were put here by God to confuse us.

Louisiana Learnin'

A Louisiana's voucher program, starting in the 2012 school year, gives some students the funds to attend certain highly rated public schools and private institutions. A number of these schools will be offering ignorance to their students by having curriculum that clashes with science. One of their textbooks makes the creationist claim that no transitional fossils that show evolutionary changes have been found… which is an out and out lie.

According to their unsupportable text book: "This gradual change from fish to reptiles has no scientific basis. For the change to have taken place many transitional forms would have been developed. However, no transitional fossils have been or will ever be discovered because God created each type of fish, amphibian, and reptile as separate, unique animals. Any similarities that exist among them are due to the fact that one Master Craftsman fashioned them all."

This excerpt comes from a high-school science book used in the Accelerated Christian Education (ACE) curriculum, an educational tool in many Louisiana schools. Religion trumps logic once again.

Theory Confusions

Controversy Ahead

While I have alluded to this elsewhere, this is where I expect a greatest number of people will disagree with me. Perhaps they will even look with hostility on what I have written. Religious beliefs, as we know, are a sensitive subject because people have a deeply vested interest in retaining their point of view, and they may resent having those beliefs challenged. Some of us just don't like being told that we might be wrong.

The religiously inclined spend years or a lifetime holding onto their illogical view of the universe, and they are generally not interested in subjecting their entrenched beliefs to any arguments to the contrary. When I say entrenched, I essentially mean that they also exhibit the same faith-based, god-worship that our earliest ancestors engaged in when they looked up at the sun, moon and stars with wonderment. Our modern religious beliefs may have become more sophisticated, but the concept of worshiping the unknown as if it were a known goes on virtually unchanged and mostly unchallenged. In spite of what may be some protestations to the contrary, religion does deal with the unknowable, un-provable, and the tales that surround those beliefs.

Evolution Theory

Evolution is called a theory because much of what we presume about it can not be proven beyond a doubt (*notice that I did not use the term reasonable doubt*). Rather, theory is based on what we have learned from observations, experiments, and the execution of logic in forming deductions (*extrapolation*). From these efforts we are convincingly able to demonstrate how life evolves (*mutates*) and even why it does so. But for the most part we are not able to indisputably establish the origin of life, whether we might say it was by God's hand or by some convenient circumstance.

Evolutionary theory is interpreted by some doubters to mean that since there is no absolute proof, its foundations are based on little more than speculation. Sorry doubters. The fact is that most scientific theory has a great deal of evidence attached to it, just not enough to permit changing it from its theory classification. In other words, it is not the speculative hypothesis that its detractors would like us to believe. We should actually applaud the scientists for exercising definition-credibility rather than dismiss their findings because they are not absolutely verified.

Stuart Chase, writer: *"For those who believe, no proof is necessary. For those who don't believe, no proof is possible."*

As we examine the fossil record we run across gaps in what is described as the evolutionary chain. "Ah-hah" say the creationists, as if anything that is less than 100% of the record proves that it is 100% false. As a consequence for them, Creationism (*or its stalking horse - Intelligent Design*) is the answer to life. So using their explanations of nature we should accept a conjecture that has no proof whatsoever rather than a theory that has considerable evidence attached to it. And then to be fair we should teach that belief in our schools as an alternative theory to the normal classroom curriculum. That would be fair to whom? To the close-minded parents and their children who have been indoctrinated? To those preachers who make a good living espousing questionable beliefs?

Perhaps some of the most compelling arguments in favor of evolution are...
-- without evolutionary mutation there would be no new strains of viruses or bacteria – which we know there are
-- drugs that were effective at one time would remain potent forever – which they aren't
-- we would not have grown taller in response to an increased food supply in the relatively recent past – which we have
-- the average IQ of today would be the same as it was years ago when humans couldn't build a fire

While some may find it repugnant that our ancestors could have been related to chimps or apes, they certainly wouldn't want to consider that our earliest ancestors may have been single cell organisms called Stromatolites. This earliest of life forms evolved in the oceans about 3.5 billion years ago, and are believed to be the precursors to all existence on this planet.

Another facet in our evolution lies in the human genome. This is the complex set of genetic information that resides in the nuclei of each of our cells and controls all manner of functions in our bodies. Not only does it contain active, working genes, but it is also comprised of *pseudogenes* that are long-since-unused genes that had a purpose at some time in the past, but no longer do. It was the mutations of the human genome that caused these transient genes to become "turned off" as they become irrelevant, counter-productive, or perhaps even dangerous to the continuation of life.

Through genetic tagging we have been able to determine that mankind roamed out of Africa some 200.000 years ago, and that we are all related to every other human being, however distant, on this planet. We can show that more than 99.9 percent of our genes are identical to those of every other person alive. In spite of the notable differences in our appearances, we are essentially one. Yet some remain inclined to believe in the Old Testament's story of Adam and Eve to explain our origins, while continuing to make too much out of our dissimilar looks and birth countries.

Evolution has served the difficult, beneficial, and necessary function of *in with the good and out with the bad*. That is, those human features, inclinations, and behaviors that produced positive traits (*which may be referred to colloquially as jungle law*) were more likely to be perpetuated by natural selection. Those genes that fostered negative traits may not have survive into the future for the same reason. So based on this scenario, one might pose the question "If we have been evolving for so long, why do we still have criminals?" The answer is that nature, while not static, is exceedingly slow to incorporate positive alterations into our innate behavior. Genes that promoted life in the past may work against our having constructive interactions in the present. Circumstances change far faster than human do. If we make the reasonable and popular assumption that our behaviors are essentially designed to pass along one's genes into the next generation, we must further assume that our current set of behaviors had played an important roll in our past, no matter how antisocial they may appear to us today.

Creation Theory

Since God is not something we can query for answers (*unless you believe that imagination is reality*) we have several ways to explain our existence. We can...
-- believe the stories of those who claim to have the special circumstance of being close to God and understanding some of His intensions
-- believe that because Adam sinned, we innocents are being subjected to a life of struggles rather than a life in paradise (*as if God had no clue that this alleged sin would occur, nor have no hand in it, nor was able to prevent it*)
-- accept the writings of a poorly educated, aggressive, and superstitious people from hundreds of years ago
-- believe that if one is a Christian, it doesn't matter how evilly you lived your life, because as long as you confess and repent your sins in time, you will go to heaven (*such a deal*)

Or we can rely on what we have learned of life, and then extrapolate additional theory regarding those areas which are still a mystery, regardless of any conflict that they may pose with religion.

In relying on the Creationist theory we might be inclined to believe that...
-- the universe, our world, and all of its inhabitants were created in six days, and then God rested on the seventh day (*rested?- are you kidding?*)
-- the unimaginable vastness of the universe was designed just for us on this insignificant planet
-- everything from deadly viruses to extinct dinosaurs were placed here at the same time
-- evolution is not something we should use to define the nature of our existence because it often contradicts religion

How much more illogical, irrelevant and unsubstantiated does a belief about the past have to be before it is summarily rejected?

In spite of the absence of any demonstrable proof, there are religious leaders who claim to have a special insight into the mind of God, while at the same time saying that He acts in ways that we can not always understand or appreciate. And they do not find this belief to be prima fascia contradictory. Yet the insightfulness of these leaders comes to us with absolutely no means of verification.

Often their guidance takes on the form of well-intentioned but gratuitous statements that are conveniently invented as needs arise. An example of this type of counsel might be the guidance that is dispensed during personal hardships. They tell us that God is good and loving on one hand, and then explain that it is His grand plan which has a child die in an accident or lets a loved one suffer a debilitating disease, on the other hand. We are advised that we are not privy to His reasons for these events, nor are we expected to comprehend His behavior. Curiously these are the same preachers who allege to know what is going on. Rather, we are exhorted to believe in those things we can not see, hear or touch by believing that He...
-- knows everything there is to know, everything that ever was, and everything that ever will be
-- has intentionally made us imperfect for some reason - we are imperfect, aren't we?
-- expects us to pay homage to Him through prayer as if we were worshiping an Easter Island statue - and because why, exactly?
-- allegedly watches over his flock, but then inexplicitly lets us solve our own problems
-- can be induced into action through prayer, as if we might have the power to have Him change His mind - how illogical is that?
-- alters His plan to permit the offering of capricious miracles

Going back to Creationism, if there can be an argument made for this concept it might go something like this...
-- God created everything that there ever was and ever will be
-- He gave matter the unchanging properties that included the existence of the tiniest sub-atomic particles, the largest black holes, and everything in between

-- He can perhaps be induced to modify His perfect design (*intervene in our lives*) when we implore Him through prayer

The problem with that belief system is that it is totally arbitrary and illogical. We have nothing but the word of a few preachers, who bought into the word of other preachers, who bought into… They attest to its veracity as if someone somewhere actually knew God. But if God is perfect, why would He ever need to change His plan for us, anyway?

Christian Theory

What do most of us actually know about the varied beginnings of Christian beliefs? Not much as it turns out. This is perhaps because some aspects of its origins did not constitute a marketable story at the time. Many of the original beliefs were rejected and left to evaporate in the past. In other cases, certain stories made up more engaging tales, told more enticing "truths", and therefore survived through the ages. What we profess to know what about Christianity is what we have been taught in church schools, and not through a record of historical accuracy. It is the consolidation of a series of stories and teachings that eventually made the grade into the present (*its own kind of evolution*).

Many of us may hold the prevailing assumption that today's truth was also yesterday's truth. We might believe that the church began with Jesus and has been carried on without significant or conceptual change for more than 2000 years. Oh sure, there may have been a share of bad apples in the church leadership from time to time that caused it to wander, but we might none-the-less hold that the church's truth has managed to transcend those behaviors. The reality of the church's beginnings are, however, quite different from those that are presented to us. There were actually a wide number of competing Christianities, with each of them struggling for their own orthodoxy. What survived that tug of war became what is now presented in our churches, and it bares little resemblance to the early and varied teachings that failed garner wide spread acceptance.

Some of us may be aware that Jesus initially had a limited number of followers, but few of us know that they were mostly the uneducated poor that had been disenfranchised by the Roman religion of the day. In other words, a backlash. It was the establishment's religion which served the wealthy, and subsequently catered to their spiritual needs. Christianity began by accommodating those who had been left out.

Other religions have also been created as a rebellion against an entrenched establishment. Martin Luther broke away with his version of a Protestant (*protest*) religion as a backlash against the Church of England. Our Pilgrim forefathers were persecuted by their church for their contrary beliefs. In their quest for freedom to worship as they saw fit, America was actually the second country that these rebels tried to relocate to in order to find the self-determination that was missing in England. In spite of fleeing from their religious oppression to this country, they continued to suffer the stigma of being outside of the main stream. And their repression did not lead them into freedom *of* religion.

Even today we do not completely agree on what Christianity is, hence the many denominations that exist. The precepts that we may take for granted today, such as the resurrection of Christ, or a single God were not universally accepted by the early Christians. Undoubtedly it was the most palatable of the stories that survive through to today… not necessarily those that accurately reflected Jesus' life, or his teachings, or the reality of the times. So what conclusions might be drawn from the early churches? Here are a few…
-- God must have had a good reason for letting religion evolve, and that this evolution is presumably not over
-- some of the Christianities' early teachings died out because they failed to gain legitimacy
-- the teachings of today's church are a significant reflection of the past's attitudes rather its accuracy

Indoctrinated followers will always believe that their current church is true to God, and any statements to the contrary are an unforgivable heresy

My Own Theory

Early humanoids were without a sophisticated language, and they had few daily motivations other than finding food, mating and avoiding dangers. They may have clicked or grunted for attention in order to make others aware of danger or to announce the presence prey. Perhaps little attention was given to thoughts that their clan was much different from other, less sophisticated creatures. When a companion died, they were left behind to revert back to nature. No ceremony, no burial, perhaps only a minimal grieving and limited memory of a passing. This was the way of the world and they had no reason to question or change it.

As their brains and abilities grew, humans made their way up the food chain and came to dominate their surroundings. They learned how to make tools, and utilized animal parts for weapons, shelter, and clothing. Eventually it came about that they imagined themselves as something special because of being more advanced than their fellow creatures. This observation eventually told them that they were supreme among the these creatures, and that they warranted special consideration from the difficulties of the day. They eventually learned that their bounty was related to the sun because they observed its movements and the changes that the seasons would bring. This wonderment became a thing to worship in the hopes that it would continue to bring prosperity.

In time, when one died there was grieving for the loss, the initiation of grief ceremonies, and most importantly, the creation of reasons for the tragedy. It was this early capacity for sorrow and beliefs about the unknown that was the impetus for the formation of rudimentary religions. This process resulted in the creation of many gods who were looked upon as their benefactors as the age when personal comfort, cooking and irrigation took hold. The purely nomadic life of the past became less necessary with the advent of civilization (*communication, rules and community*) when people became more stationary, specialized, and organized. Whoever was in charge may have gotten to say who the gods would be. On occasion the masses were instrumental in initiating new religions with new gods, such as with the advent of Christianity in Rome.

Along with a relative measure of prosperity, the dominance of many early provider gods lessened and the emergence of social leaders took their place. Religion then evolved to cater more to ethereal needs (*hope and salvation*) and less to the physical needs, which were no longer in a daily crisis mode.

It wasn't until spiritual qualities had been attributed to "endowed" individuals did religion moved away from being little more than a localized set of beliefs for each specific clan. At that point the early religions could have been compared to the newer versions, and cream rises to the top. Not that this led to a universal faith, but it defined which type of beliefs could succeed and which of them would fall by the wayside. It was a protracted trial and error period with the winners telling the most enticing stories.

As it was necessary for most of the people to be followers, they submitted easily to the leaders of their clans. Occasionally they were required to promote them with their lives. This harsh method for the accumulation of followers worked well until the expanding influence and power of religion made that effort less productive and rewarding. Religions then settled into flock accretion by more by persuasion than by force. As a result, the group with the most enticing "truth" to tell had the better chance of adding to their flock.

Today there are still many religious stories that are vying for acceptance, with each of them declaring their singular connection to legitimacy. A common thread among these groups is their need to control the hearts and minds of those who believe their story and to recruit those who don't. Religion is not quite a personal thing, but rather a group experience. Its leaders disseminate their version of the truth, and then they benefit from the accumulation of power that comes with having worshippers. Another commonality to these groups is the use of the carrot and stick approach for recruitment and retention of new followers. The reward may be...
-- their God's love
-- a graced after-life in heaven
-- a flock of virgins for those who are willing to martyr themselves

The punishment side of religion's coin is the rather vague concept of hell and damnation. This condition is said to go hand and hand with a so-called loving God, with no second chance for salvation… as the story goes.

Man created God – Not the other way around

Belief Confusions

Origins of Belief

Imagine for a moment of being whisked off to a far away place where the rules of nature that we take for granted were off kilter and difficult to fathom. The brains reaction to this scenario would be to try to put things into "proper" perspective... to make sense of it. After all, if perception does not lead to understanding, life will not advance very far. We need to use the information that surrounds us correctly to feed our brains or we could be among the extinct.

Now consider that over the millennia our life evolved from creatures who did not understand much of their world... just enough to avoid making too many life-threatening mistakes. As time passed these creatures began to notice important characteristics of nature, and they learned that dealing with them in productive ways brought an advantage. These reactions did not suggest that they had an in depth understanding of the events. Rather it meant that on occasion, trial and error brought about workable conclusions. Eventually it was recognized that expending this effort to comprehend could lead to rudimentary understandings.

Along with that elementary knowledge and the passage of time, the creatures developed instincts (*brain programming*) that enabled their descendants to "know" and utilize practical information pertaining to their environment without the need to re-learn these skills generation after generation. Again, practicing these tasks did not imply that they had correctly deciphered or analyzed the problems in each case. What it meant was that they were better off doing something about the challenges that faced them rather than doing nothing. And this conviction about making an effort insured (*with repetitiveness*) that the resultant instincts would become imbedded in their genes. As they came across new phenomena, these instincts may have guided them in the direction of useful insinuations and survival techniques. If there was no countervailing wisdom to argue against a conclusion, a belief could be formed based on pragmatism, but without a strict proof. As this acceptance of unsubstantiated ideas began to flourish, it became easier for the creatures to accept interpretation and dogma as valid roads to the "truth".

Friedrich Nietzsche, philosopher: *All things are subject to interpretation - whichever interpretation prevails at a given time is a function of power and not truth.*

Eventually there were those who began to manufacture reasons for new phenomena (*some valid, some not*) which helped to promote themselves as authorities… and the medicine man was born. From those initial steps it was a short path to the generalized acceptance of authoritarian rulers. With this new era also came the reluctance to question that authority, which is a posture that many of us still ascribe to today because of our misguided beliefs about people of stature and charisma.

Since death was no doubt seen as mysterious, rituals evolved concerning its meaning and purpose in an effort to make sense of the senseless. Religions were formed around the belief that death could somehow be controlled, since not on earth, than in some hereafter. Because society had evolved into leaders and followers, the rulers were believed to disseminate legitimate answers to their flock. Their proclamations may have been accepted out of fear of the unknown, or they may have been accepted because of a desire to avoid the sometimes harsh retribution for being a non-believer. So arbitrary beliefs prevailed over proof, and were given the name *faith*.

Voltaire, philosopher: *"Faith consists of believing when it is beyond the power of reason to believe."*

Nature of Belief

Until a few thousand years ago the Romans believed that the truth of a matter could be determined through the arbitrary discussions of senators in the forum. Because of this attitude they did not rely on the more arduous presentation of factual evidence. Conclusions, in stead, were derived from the deliberations of respected leaders. That simple "logic" was then utilized to shape conclusions and make determinations. Use of a group dialogue did not necessarily imply that a problem had the correct solution. It simply meant that their answers led to the Senator's into agreements based on their current understandings.

Benedict Spinoza, philosopher: *"Comprehension of a statement carries with it the tacit belief that it is true."*

In the 17th century the Dutchman Spinoza expressed the belief that people are inclined to believe what they understand regardless of its actual truth. For example, if one grasps the concept that God is the benevolent creator, then belief in this idea is likely to follow.

The acceptance of people's assertions is more likely to become established in our youth when our attitudes and filters are not yet fully developed. Common sense resides in the frontal lobe and develops slowly until 20 something. The unquestioning faith that is derived during our formative years can be so strong that being confronted with obvious contradictions may do little to change one's mind. In for a penny, in for a pound.

Robert Harris, neuroscientist: *"Understanding a proposition may be analogous to our perceiving an object in physical space… we seem to accept appearances as reality until proved otherwise."*

In sharp contrast to belief, disbelief requires an explicit rejection. For this to occur one must question ideas, and that predominantly flows from being exposed to new experiences in ways that lead to non-traditional insights. Belief is initially more natural than disbelief, at least until one develops a serious level of skepticism. Becoming a skeptic is a process which can be hastened by the recognition that a significant percentage of what is purported to be true turns out to be false, and it is being provided by those with their own agenda.

On the plus side, the evolution of human nature has dictated that having an acceptance of dogma is a powerful means for moving society forward. Imagine the turmoil that might exist if wide-spread and unyielding skepticism were the prevailing attitude. Maintaining order would be nearly impossible because so few would be willing to view leaders as credible. This does not mean that skepticism has little value in society. But because this questioning perspective is rarely taught in social or educational environments, we tend to remain victims of those who choose to deceive and control us.

Statements about how much of our learning is actually false would not prove to be excessive if we were to look at the vast amount of deceit that dominates corporate advertising and business practices. This reality is also undeniable when we examine the self-serving statements of politicians. No matter how ardently we might choose to imagine that they took office to do the public's bidding, we are constantly being deceived and manipulated by them for their own advantage (*reelection*). And we do not easily learn this lesson in spite of the many examples of their egregious behaviors that abound. Our willingness to forgive and forget far exceeds our rational thought process because we have been propagandized to the contrary.

The trouble with being a skeptic is that it is something of a lonely gift. True believers often find this quality anathema to their idea-accepting personalities. Many have yet to discover the benefits of regularly questioning statements that are presented to them, and thereby avoiding situations where political posturing, or religious training, or corporate ads turn out to be patently false or misleading.

Lest we suppose that nearly everyone is a religious believer on some level, a survey indicated that sixteen percent of the adult population are actually non-believers, whether atheists, agnostics, or just have no use for organized religion. And that is based on what people are willing to admit to an interviewer. It would not be unreasonable to assume many of those respondents wish to keep their contrary attitudes private, and that the percent of non-believers is significantly higher. Even so, this reported percent of non-believers is greater than many groups in America including Blacks, Jews, Hispanics, veterans, gays/lesbians and more. The problem for this largely-silent faction is that they are a minority, and there is a strong bias against disbelievers specifically and minorities in general. So while we may not often run into admitted atheists or agnostics, it is likely that they exist in numbers that are greater than one might assume.

Perception and Belief

In a study conducted in the Netherlands, scientists attempted to deduce whether there was a detectable difference between the thinking of neo-Calvinists (*a religion*) and those of atheists. They reasoned that because neo-Calvinists believe in the concept of sphere sovereignty (*each sector of society has its own distinct responsibilities and authorities*) there might be other perceptions that are crafted by this manner of thinking. In a test, the participants were shown images of large rectangles and squares that consisted of a smaller rectangle or square. They were asked to quickly identify the shapes of either the larger or the smaller images. It turned out that Calvinists scored measurably lower than atheists in a statistically significant number of cases. The perceptions of atheists also trumped the narrower-minded viewpoints of those neo-Calvinists in other areas as well. What the study hinted at is that the religion choices that are based on a non-religious ideology may be one of the dynamics in the rejection of contrary viewpoints. To put this more clearly, a person's history of choosing illogical ideas can create perception difficulties elsewhere, thus inhibiting the use of logic to view the world.

Conviction is what you believe something to be – reality is what it actually is – knowing the difference is what we need to learn

In a study of genetic disposition, researchers found that people tend to stick with the advice they have been given, even when their own experience contradicts it. That propensity is linked to one's genes according to a study published online in the Journal of Neuroscience. The findings suggest a possible genetic component of confirmation bias, or the tendency to focus on new information that agrees with what you already know, and to ignore information that contradicts your views. It is hard to imagine that even the staunchest believers in religion are not aware of, and maybe a little bit concerned about the many contradictions that exist. Yet the fact that these discrepancies are of minor distress to the faithful is indicative of their perception bias and logic difficulties.

A simple example of this lack of concern for facts can be seen with the seven deadly sins that are a part of many religions. These sins were actually invented by Dante Alighieri in his book Dante's Inferno, written in the early 1300s. They were later adopted by the ruler Constantine as a method to blunt the growing Christian power in his part of the world. This shows how the beliefs that we may hold can have very different origins than one might suppose. This may also demonstrate how difficult it is to purge religion of false ideas.

Power of Belief

There are Bible fundamentalists who tend to believe that every word therein is the truth. A part of this unquestioning acceptance comes from being grossly unaware of, or intentionally close-minded to the contradictory ideas that revolve around the onset of religion. Among the numerous orthodoxies that had vied for acceptance in the early years, Christians are known to have debated as to whether or not Jesus actually existed. Now if they couldn't agree on that fact, what are the odds that they got much else right?

On one talk show, a religiously oriented panelist expressed the conclusion that mankind did not exist before Christianity began some 2000 years ago. In her mind we apparently all just popped up one day and got around to writing the Bible some two hundred years later. For this believer, the facts about history that are taken for granted by virtually all of us somehow managed to escape her education and interest.

Bertrand Russell, author: *"It is undesirable to believe a proposition when there are no grounds whatsoever for supposing it true."*

In our early history, a group's social indoctrinations may have meant taking an overtly aggressive posture toward their neighbor tribes. Occasionally it also ordained the driving off members of one's own group because of a rules infraction. The result of these punitive actions was to implant important, negative instincts about others who were not quite alike. Today we continue to believe that those who are not part of a local group are different or may even be a threat. We still retain our inclination toward these social biases. Just check out the White Supremacists and Hell's Angles if you need the most extreme conformation of this.

In the past, in order to protect and not deplete our early food sources we adopted the practical disposition of restraining tribe size and avoiding over-utilization of a territory. This meant becoming semi-nomadic before a habitat was denuded or polluted. Curiously, not over utilizing critical resources is an accomplishment that we have rarely achieved in the modern world. This is a remarkable omission from our genetic wiring since our ancestors must have seen fit to engage in that practice for eons. This lapse is part of our genetic-emotional brain that allows us to ignore what we know is right, as well as what may be the inevitable result of our actions. We will...
-- over-fish our river, lake, and ocean stocks
-- over-hunt our wild life
-- decimate our oxygen generating forests
-- squander our finite supply of fuels
-- pollute our streams, rivers and oceans with industrial runoff
-- poison our foods with heavy metals and pesticides

There is an interesting story about Easter Island that makes this very point. The island is now without a single tree because its previous inhabitants (*who are also extinct*) used up all of the wood for their fires. After the last tree was cut down and the last fire was made, the people died off. Whether or not this tale is true of false, it makes a good point about overusing resources.

Problems with Belief

This may be an appropriate time to bring up our past President, George W. Bush. His religious indoctrination undoubtedly allowed him to believe that a dedication to God was sufficient to imbue him with the solutions to problems he could not begin to understand. George was after all, guided by his strong faith. He knew what was right, what was wrong, and would willingly apply that "knowledge" to his decisions. This behavior occurred in spite of evidence that some of his actions brought on cultural, economic and military failures. He was not even able to grasp the simple proposition that our presence in the Middle East has created the very terrorism that he then chose to fruitlessly engage with the military-industrial-complex.

Going hand and hand with the flawed mindset of GWB was one of his more intellectually challenged, seriously corrupted, war-mentality advisers, Vice President Dick Cheney. When he was questioned about the war by a reporter who offered up the statistic that "two thirds of the public was against the war", his response was "So?". Wow! Apparently he was under the impression that gross arrogance is an acceptable quality in public office. Cheney went on to say something to the effect that the polls go up and the polls go down, and that reality doesn't affect government policy. So his take on being a political leader was that listening to the public and then conforming to their reasonable interests is not a relevant trait for being in government service. Perhaps he also imagined that the war would eventually bounce to the top of the hit parade, and that those who opposed it didn't possess his brilliant insights into the workings of the Middle-East.

The Need to Believe

An amusing example of people's easy gullibility was brought to light in a national news story. Someone had discovered a ghostly figure (*attributed to be Mother Mary, wouldn't you know*) that appeared on a garage door in an alley at the same time each day. This vision eventually drew a crowd of true believers who assumed that they were witnessing the hand of God. In reality it was the sun's reflection off of some distant object because it shown on the backs of people's hands as they touched the garage door and disappeared after the sun moved on in the sky. Did this countervailing evidence alter the belief of the faithful? Probably not! Did the press expose the explanation for the image? Not that I noticed. We just don't like to tamper with people's beliefs no matter how ill conceived they might be. But reflection or not, the image itself carried no information about its actual purpose. Everything of a religious nature attributed to the vision came from the viewer's imaginations. There were…

-- no subtitles on the garage to offer an insight
-- no voice out of the blue that conveyed a message
-- just people's need to believe in the unbelievable because it gave them comfort and a small confirmation of their religion

Friedrich Nietzsche, philosopher: *"The irrationality of a thing is no argument against its existence, rather a condition of it."*

The Right to Believe

Having criticized what some people believe, I should say that I defend their right to believe what they choose. However my caveat on this matter is *as long as they don't impose those beliefs on others.* Our society has a plethora of thought police who would transform us into rigid lock-step with their views of an In God We Trust world. Because this need-to-impose is so pervasive in virtually all societies, one conclusion about the conduct could be that it came about through a protracted period of evolution, and that it satisfied early social needs. Perhaps it brought about a cohesiveness that had allowed humans to prosper. But that was then and this is now.

Today there is little justification for having these religious attitudes encouraged, and none for having it imposed on people. There is a dearth of evidence that religion has produced more pluses than minuses in the long run of history. Nor is there proof that the Bible's stories have anything more than a hint of veracity. And if true, what is the point of a continued emphasis on religion? Well the easy answer is *the perpetuation of power by those who hold power...* with religion being their vehicle.

Atheism vs. Religion

Lest we ignore the sad fact that religion has a long and bloody history of being imposed on people, consider the following behaviors which are in sharp contrast by those of atheists and agnostics. These groups are not known for...

-- sending missionaries out to convert the unconverted
-- teaching innate guilt or everlasting salvation
-- ignoring those aspects of history that fail to support their ideas or contradict their beliefs
-- forming group affiliations in order to influence the political process
-- rejecting candidates because of their belief in God
-- killing massive numbers of people for not believing in and not following dogma (*were there atheist crusades that I missed?*)
-- repetition in places of worship

Franklin Delano Roosevelt, President: *"Repetition does not transform a lie into a truth."*

Yet the above arguments largely fall on deaf ears for great numbers of the faithful because of the effective indoctrination by the religious institutions that promote their God based ideas against minimal opposition, and along with government assistance.

Science vs. Religion

There are occasional arguments as to whether or not science supports religion or can religion coexist with science. These debates are generally irrelevant because they take prevailing biases and attempt to construct accommodating logic for them, which invariably fail. To make this point, science is the study of the real world and consists of proofs and theories about the nature of nature. While the theories are not held at the same high level as proofs, they do rely on substantial objective and empirical evidence for their support. In other words, theories are serious business. And they are not the hypotheses that they are sometimes portrayed to be by those who wish to put down science when it contradicts their beliefs. Religion on the other hand consists of a web of folktales that are presented as being factual portrayals of a long-ago time. While these teachings do not diminish the educational value of their lessons, they do not lend credibility to stories of an invisible, benevolent entity being behind nature. Nor do they convince that there is a deity that is interested in caring for us after death.

One of religions recurring arguments against evolution and Darwin is that this process can not be observed, and that it requires taking the word of its proponents. Darwin's ideas are alleged to be little more than the result of speculation, not of a substantiating proof. Couldn't this same argument be directed more accurately at religion?

An interesting corollary to the argument about evidence regards the story of a man who was arrested for biting off the ear of another person. A witness to the event was asked if he had actually seen the defendant bite off the man's ear. When he replied in the negative to the question, the prosecutor demanded to know how he knew the act had been done. At that point the witness replied "I saw him spit it out". Using this same logic we can readily see what evolution has spit out. We have...
-- fossils and intermediate forms of life
-- similar genomes
-- development of new breeds
-- genetic engineering

Doesn't this constitute substantial evidence to anyone who is paying attention and who doesn't apply specious arguments against it?

Science is a little about a lot - religion is a lot about a little

Sanctity of Life

This is a subject that is hard to get your head around when trying to determine just what it means. If *sanctity* means that life is sacred, exactly who says so? Well of course it is the religiously inclined with a drum to beat. Maybe an explanation for their belief that life is sacred...
-- is a natural result of our winning the survival battle against other animals and elements
-- was invented so that we could imagine ourselves as worthy of God's care
-- like faith, sin, hell and heaven, it is a convenient invention that is used to further the goals of religion

…and we fall into this transparent trap without judging the situation for what it is… the control of one indoctrinated human being by another

Pro-Life/Pro-Choice

Well here is a subject to avoid at your next social event. Most people are firmly on the side of one "pro" issue or the other… some to the point of being hostile towards an opponent's perspective or life. Their minds have been firmly made up because their viewpoint consists of ideas that they were induced to believe in from an early age, and not necessarily because there is any underlying logic or common sense on their side of the argument.

Indoctrination is <u>not</u> a form of education, logic, or common sense

The definition of life appears to be whatever suits people's agenda, no matter how arbitrary their conclusions might be. Without taking sides, but to further the discussion, it might be helpful to ask…
-- Is a sperm or an egg life all by themselves?
-- If they can die, weren't they alive?
-- Or is it that sperm and eggs are simply a quasi half-life until they are joined together to form a whole life? Well, did you ever try to dig half of a hole? No matter how small the hole, it is still a whole hole, if you take my point.

For those who like to quote the Bible, Leviticus concludes that "life is in the blood". This is generally taken to mean that life begins when the embryo is first infused with blood at about eighteen days. For those who prefer the Catholic offering of a 16th century Pope, life begins at forty days, which was promoted without any evidence to support the contention. In the end it is likely that the pro-lifers will continue to point to selected passages of the Scriptures to render support for their unsympathetic arguments toward others, while the pro-choicers will continue to consider the real-world struggle for mental health, physical health and justice. Which side of the argument do you fall on? Maybe there should be a third option available to us… life-choicers. This is when everyone minds their own business and lets others do the same.

Another consideration in this debate might be that all arguments about when life begins are irrelevant, and that we should consider what is good for people rather than what is good for religion. If we were to concede that abortion is indeed killing, but justifiable, how different would that be from…
-- state sanctioned killing of criminals
-- the right to kill in self defense
-- the right to kill to protect one's home
-- the right to kill that results from engaging in wars

Not much different I suspect. We just need to use a gentler word than abortion, or simply change our attitude about it. After all, what could be more of an abortion than forcing a woman (*raped or not*) to bring an unwanted baby to term. One attitude about killing may be that it is ok when it is unavoidable, but that abortion is avoidable. Then who is to say that starting or entering a war is unavoidable, or that executing criminals is unavoidable? One person's avoidable is another person's essential.

The Right to Die

While we may all wish to die peacefully in our sleep at the age of a ninety or more, there are a great many who will not be so fortunate. Agony and unrelenting pain is the door that they must pass through first. Unless one is simply stuck on stupid, we should have real compassion for the anguish in those lives. No, not just an expressed sympathy for the victim or their relatives, but an activist's empathy for those who may be suffering an agonizing life.

One response to a harsh onset of death may be to offer some gem of wisdom like it is God's will, when in reality we have no clue as to what His will is or if He even has a will. In God We Trust should never be a principal for dealing with people's pain and suffering. How many of us would force a distressed animal to endure the same degree of pain that we condemn some humans to experience?

Several years back the government incarcerated Doctor Kevorkian because he facilitated the gentle suicides of a number of gravely, painfully ill patients. He was their angel of mercy, and our response was to unmercifully imprisoned him. As of this writing, just Oregon has a legal procedure for assisted suicide called Dying With Dignity. The fact that this is the only state with compassion for the terminally ill is a shameful reflection on man's inhumanity to man and those with the unsympathetic attitudes who behind it.

While there are the pitilessly who might let their loved ones suffer a horrific terminal illness, the rest of us should be more compassionate toward those who are enduring pain. We should allow them to die in peace, comfort, and dignity. But instead we permit the insensitive attitudes to prevail. We disregard people's agony in order to satisfy indoctrinations because our genetic-emotional brain is engaged on this subject. Talk about being self-centered in the extreme! Religion is both good and evil, and this is surely one of its more evil sides.

Religious Intolerance

The next time someone goes to the pharmacist for birth control pills or return from a trip carrying a bottle of Scotch from the Duty Free Zone, will they be discriminated against? It can and does happen in America. As you may know, some pharmacists have refused to fill prescriptions (*birth control and morning after pills*) that offend their religious beliefs, as if this interference with the rights of others could be any of their business. Some Muslim cabbies have allegedly refused to carry liquor toting passengers for their personal reasons as well. No one asked these self-appointed censors to pop a pill or take a drink. They just can't stand to mind their own business because for some bazaar reason we are their concern. Or perhaps they feel tainted by even a near exposure to "evil". Just how far can we permit this intolerance to go? Should the offended pharmacist not be...
-- in the same room with the birth control pills,
-- or the same building,
-- on the same block?

Should the Muslim who has a propensity to impose their religious beliefs on others not...
-- eat at restaurants that have bars
-- stay at hotels that have mini-bars
-- shop in grocery stores that have liquor aisles

Can this intolerance get any more ill-mannered? It is not their God or Allah given duty or their inherent right to impose their personal beliefs on others. But that concept does little to stop the thought-crusaders. For a few, the motivation to follow dogma is so strong that they will willingly risk their health, livelihood, or even their lives for it. Those attitudes have everything to do with beliefs that were instilled in them at an early age. Be it a cult or a religion, having beliefs that defy common sense is symptomatic of brainwashing. Those ideas should not be categorized as learning, education, honorable, or even their own. It is mind control, pure and simple.

Give me your child and I can create a saint or a monster

Are the two prior examples of intolerance too remote to have much impact to you? Then consider that there are authorities in this country with tendencies toward banning...
-- sex education for children
-- sexual counseling by school nurses
-- stem cell research
-- abortions on demand
-- the morning after pill
-- the right to die with dignity
-- marijuana for cancer patients
-- marriage benefits for same sex partners

Another sign of intolerance, though not so easily recognized as such, is the perennial, annoying complaint that is made about taking Christ out of Christmas, such as with...
-- the abbreviation Xmas
-- Christmas cards
-- the commercialization of the selling season

These people want everyone else to believe as they do, and they have the audacity to object when others won't. Say, aren't most these the same folks who purchase those Christmas gifts that ostensibly contribute to the conditions they deride? Their attitudes are both hypocritical and intolerant.

Some Jews do not escape a smattering of my derision for their continuing intolerance either. Their frequently repeated stories of the Holocaust persist some sixty years after the end of the war. And now this mantra is being taken up by younger Jews who were not even born when the war ended and who have no direct connection to the past suffering. Some time back I made an enemy of a woman who also was also not born until after WWII when I suggested that it was time to give up the chest-beating, as if only Jews had died in the concentration camps, or in the war itself. Time to move on, I suggested. She thought not. It offended her indoctrination, and she chose not to question who was pulling her strings, or why.

Now there are some descendents of Holocaust survivors who are suing companies in Germany for their suffering. Apparently this preoccupation with a horrific event that took place a lifetime ago is unending. So I would ask, is it about…
-- extracting sympathy from the rest of the world over evil deeds long since past
-- feeling good about a tired old cause
-- communal grieving that binds Jews together
-- using this issue to camouflage Israel's years of resistance to solving the problems with its Arab neighbors
-- all of the above

Curiosity of Belief

I think we can all agree that we are probably born without well-formed beliefs. They came to us from the influences that surround us, whether from communal interactions or from the observed statements of others. An inescapable conclusion should be that our beliefs are derived from sources outside of ourselves.

A commonality about people's beliefs in their religion is that they are situational beliefs. For the most part, the acceptance of a particular religion is mostly based on one's family, the people in one's area, or on the schools which one attended. It can even be based on borders within a small country if its inhabitants have been relatively stationary and have not been subjected to varying religious points of view. Some of these countries have been divided into distinct secular districts resulting from external influences, such as when a portion of a country was overrun by the inhabitants of another region.

In northern Iraq there are villages that practice a religion that is a combination of Judaism, Christianity and Islam because of years of population convergence. The illogic of this circumstance is lost on these people because they believe just as strongly in their religion as others do in theirs. In fact it is these same inhabitants who stoned a girl to death after she had converted to Islam. So people can be subjected to situational beliefs with the reason-awareness factor sorely lacking. By this I mean that the majority of us do not examine where our beliefs came from, and rarely scrutinize them for validity.

One of the precepts of Islam is to defend Mohammad against all who would demean his image or writings. Unlike other religions that have learned to co-exist with criticism, Islamists extremists would readily use force against a detractor. Freedom of speech is not a virtue to them, but is a conspiracy by those who ascribe to the falsehood of democracy.

Picking a Religion

Before anyone that is older than a child can adopt a particular religion they must be unaware of, ignore, or reject the tenants of other religions. It is not possible to hold multiple "truths" when they are in conflict with each other. In addition, believers must form the illogical conclusion that the religion they "chose" is the one true religion among the thousands that are being practiced around the world. So what are the chances that...
-- you picked the right one?
-- you had anything to do with its selection?
-- there is a right one?

When the Christians and Jews religions were first developing, no one knew exactly when Jesus was born. Various scholars came up with different dates based on their own calculations. Also during that era the Christian church was in competition with pagan religions for the hearts and minds of the people. To compete more effectively for a flock, they decided to usurp the date of a prominent pagan holiday as their own. That date was of course December 25th. Then this date was used to recruit followers from the competition, and it does not represent the actual date of Jesus' birth. A small matter you say? Accuracy is not important, you say? I grew up being taught that truth was important and not frivolous. Perhaps I was just indoctrinated.

Belief in a God

To understand the derivation of religions it is important to recognize where the concept of gods initially came from. It certainly did not start with Jesus. It began thousands of years earlier with the tribal medicine men and their bag of remedies, tricks and ceremonies. Because superstition was regarded as a legitimate substitute for an understanding of the world, the witch doctors used that attitude to their advantage.

A study by Northwestern University concluded that the belief in superstitions may have a common source. When people feel a lack of control in their lives they may fabricate or construe false patterns and meanings from chance events such as lightning, meteors, floods, eclipses, and the like. Superstitions offer them a sense of security when all they have is a provisional handle on the unknown.

In order for the witch doctors to remain in business they had to be effective by providing tribes with a reason to believe in them, their stories, and their interpretations of life events. Part of their magic was to learn simple things about the workings of the world, and then use those secrets to enhance their hold over an easily-impress flock.

Included with their practice might have come the employment of others who could be used to enforce a respect for power and to intimidate or punish nonbelievers. In time the need for using punishment lessened as people "chose" to conformed voluntarily because of indoctrination. In time, societies settled into the nearly universal belief that there was a single God, not one to be worshiped for every survival fulfillment. This evolving single-God harmony between faiths is what eventually led to…

-- a greater strengthening of religion
-- a common ground between believers
-- the creation its own legitimacy

Determining if there actually is a God who is the creator and caretaker of the universe, however, is an impossible proposition to prove because we have nothing tangible to get our heads around… nothing that does not involve folktales and exaggeration from which to make an evaluation. But those shortcomings do not mean that we can't make an effort to infer a supreme being using logic. Even though science can not directly test the existence of God, we might still be able to draw meaningful conclusions by studying the natural behavior of the universe. This empirical form of analysis is similar to the approach scientists used to learn about dark energy, dark matter and black holes, all of which cannot be directly observed either. It is in the details of how these entities exert influence in detectable ways that helps us to assess and describe their nature.

Similarly it is up to the logically trained mind to formulate reasonable conclusions about God from whatever we may find that constitutes evidence. One observation that could be convincing would be an uncontestable demonstration that there is not a perfect and endlessly repeatable order to everything in the universe. This condition might reveal an occasional capriciousness that would foretell a manager's hand at work… a very hot star that was red instead of blue, or a star that decelerated as it approached another, for example. But alas there appears to be no such telling proof, just unending cause and effect perfection. The closest we might come to a confirmation would be miracles if they could be proved to occur. This, however, is not likely because of our inability to distinguish between chance happenings and the so-called miracles.

Frank Lloyd Wright, architect: "*I believe in God, only I spell it Nature.*"

115

If I were to believe in God it would be for reasons that are far different from those that are suggested by the folktales taught in our institutions. I might believe because some aspects of life are too difficult to explain by any other reasoning, or that they may be so arbitrary in nature as to demand that there be a supernatural explanation. For example, I might be convinced because…

-- the path from elemental hydrogen to life is exceedingly complex, and is perhaps unattainable without having a game plan in mind
-- elements at the quantum level can manifest the characteristic of being (*so-called*) up, down, or both at the same time
-- light, sight and color perception are so fantastic that it is hard to imagine this was not part of a design
-- the subtleties of hue, saturation, reflection and refraction are extraordinary – and all from vibrations of photons which carry no intrinsic color at all
(It is thought that light bounces off objects in all possible directions, not just obliquely, yet light does not collide with itself, resulting in non-viewable detail. Since one of its aspects is its wave characteristic, cancellation and reinforcement of images must be at work allowing us to see clearly)
-- sound and hearing complexity fall into similar categories to light
-- of the water cycle upon which virtually all life depends for its biological functions
-- water expands when it freezes, making it lighter and causing it to float on the surface rather than sinking to the bottom, which eventually would leave no room for life to evolve
-- volcanic matter is lighter than earth's mantle and literally floats on top of it to form the continents - its hardness keeps it from rapid erosion, thereby separating land from the water for millennia
-- the diversity and usefulness of atomic materials are varied and seems to be requisites for the development of both life and advanced civilization
-- the physics of the universe fits together in an extraordinarily balanced manner with one event always leading to another, without ever getting out of control
-- the constants (*gravitation, speed of light, magnetism, radioactive decay, electron energy states, strong and weak nuclear forces, etc.*) appear to be fine tuned to permit the existence of matter and life - change any one of them and perhaps all hell breaks loose
-- of gravity (*try to make sense of that*)

The trouble with the above reasoning is that it was done by a person (*me*) with a limited understanding of the universe. If I had a more exquisite knowledge of the nature of nature I might not be in such awe of it. On the other hand I would most certainly not be inclined to hold a belief in God because...

-- fallible humans passed along folklore for many years

-- the retelling of history is never accurate, and is even more suspect when it is derived from the writings of a barely civilized people that were uneducated and superstitious

-- of social pressure to do so, such as with the prayers that are offered at the beginnings at some public events, or with funerals that are inherently religious in nature

-- of the near impossibility of getting elected to public office if one were reported to be an atheist or agnostic

-- it is inconceivable that He took thirteen billion years from the estimated beginning of the universe (*the big bang*) to create mankind (*did He have more pressing matters?*)

-- death, as far as anyone can prove, is final, even though there are those who say it isn't so, but without a shred of evidence

-- many of the worlds atrocities have been promulgated by the followers of religion - a situation which should never have been allowed by a so-called loving God

Richard Dawkins, writer: *"Religion is about turning untested belief into unshakeable truth through the power of institutions and the passage of time."*

Perhaps the most convincing argument that one can make against a belief in God is the unimaginable vastness of the universe itself. The edge of space, if there even is one, is far beyond the range of our strongest telescopes. Conversely, the smallest bits of matter are far beyond the range of our most powerful microscopes. Does all of this complexity exist just to provide humans with a home on a planet that represents an infinitesimally small portion of the universe? And then the rest of the universe is needed exactly why? Is it reasonable to think that God provided us with...

-- stars for their awe inspiration

-- ice ages to mold the face of the planet

-- meteorite crashes that altered planet life

There have been the major events throughout the ages due to natural reasons that have nothing to do with religion. Yet we fail to adopt a realistic viewpoint about the nature of our existence on planet earth. It is easier to believe in a fanciful God than it is to live with reality, relevance, self-reliance, and common sense.

Belief in a Devil

If God is the ultimate good, then logically there must be something that is the opposite, or the ultimate evil. In a similar fashion we are aware that...
-- light requires the alternative of dark
-- war requires the concept of peace
-- loud requires the variation of quiet

Our folktales tell us that the ultimate evil is called the Devil, and that it rules over a place called Hell. Furthermore it must be just as powerful as God because He appears to have no power to control it. Curiously and ludicrously though, we posses the power required to defeat the Devil all by ourselves. And this "miracle" is accomplished by engaging in good rather than evil. So are we stronger than God?

In our distant past humans determined that there were good gods (*which provided for us*) and bad gods (*that brought droughts, wars, pestilence, and suffering*). These false convictions took shape long before the Bible was created. In fact it was our ancestor's early fears and superstitions that were the precursors to organized religion. Then at some point the bad-gods were transformed into the Devil and the good-gods became God.

What is silly about the Devil is the church's necessity to have this imaginary character in the first place. Presumably it came about because if there were no devil there would be no need for...
-- an entity to forgive your transgressions
-- a counterpart here on earth to forgive your sins
-- Heaven and Hell

Belief in a Bible

It seems to me that if one believes in the Bible, they must accept it without reservations as being completely true, and therefore they would not have the option to...
-- pick and choose between the various stories that happen to fit their personal disposition
-- make assessments which do not conform to religious teachings
-- exercise the power to judge God's work by selecting only those truths that appeal to them

For example, those who believe that homosexuality is an abomination, as described in the Bible, must also willing to believe other biblical text that say...
-- it is acceptable for a daughter to have sex with her father in order to produce a child when there is a shortage of men, such as in war time
-- a parent is permitted to kill one's children if they are disobedient

If the Bible's teaching can not be accepted in their entirety, then how do we conclude that any part of the Bible is the Word of God? It can not be both true and false at the same time. The stories can not be factual, yet offer people the privilege of disavowing or "reinterpreting" those passages that may be in conflict with their ideology. Doesn't truth require some sort of consistency?

When the Bible contains passages that contradict its own text, or common sense, or current teachings, the true believer's response may to fall back on the construction of a labored justification to account for the inconsistencies. A "difficult" story may be portrayed as allegorical rather than as factual so that it doesn't violate (*really?*) the rule of truth. We have had years to master these convenient mechanisms to the point where they have become believable to the masses. The rationales are then accepted on faith for concepts which can not be explained, justified, or proved.

Belief in Attendance

There are people who attend a church, synagogue, mosque or other place of worship on a regular basis, and presumably believe that this repetitive attendance makes them more religious and a better person in His eyes. I gather that they also perceive a satisfying closeness to Him in order to explain this behavior. They may also fear that a lack of attendance is sinful. Even though I had been to church services untold numbers of times as a child, I was never able to discern a justification for what went on there since...
-- the Bible stories are endlessly repeated
-- the songs all sound about the same after a while
-- the benches didn't get any softer over time
-- most importantly, people didn't behave differently after their church experiences - in effect, someone talks, you listen, you go home unchanged

Wouldn't a belief in the Golden Rule suffice just as well as a guideline for improving our lives? Yet the tedious or inspiring (*depending on your perspective*) church-going ritual has managed to remain popular over time. One should really wonder how these repeated exposures to attendances would function to enhance the mind and soul. Or is it that we are slow learners and need repetition? The answer to this tongue-in-cheek question is undoubtedly found in our genetics which makes the instinct to be followers so powerful that we may not question it. And repetition becomes the cement for faith.

**Enhanced golden rule*: Do onto others as you would have them do onto you, or they may do onto you as you have done onto them.*

Belief in Heaven

When I think about Heaven as the great reward, I am perplexed as to how that would work. I suppose the true believers would be inclined to say that it just does. Anyway, my curiosity poses a number of unanswerable questions about the possibility of having this alleged eternal happiness, such as...
-- What would we look like, or don't we have any vision, just being body-less spirits

-- how happy would that make us to be just "thinking" ourselves around that universe?

-- If we are there with everyone we ever knew, what would we all look like… the same as when we died, when we looked younger, or what?

-- Could we imagine our appearance at our best time in life, and how realistic would that be?

-- Would we feel competent, clever, interesting, appealing, and successful, or do those feeling not exist?

-- Would all of our bad memories be wiped away, and if so, how could we still be the same persons?

When I was younger I tried to imagine what it would be like to be able to think like one of our pets. The problem with that prospect is that we could not be ourselves and also be the pet at the same time. That involves two incompatible brain statuses. As I see it, the same would be true in Heaven. How could we ever be ourselves and also be (*in effect*) another, totally happy person? Is it like a permanent high? If so, where is the reality in that? And if there is no reality, what is the point? After all, a high requires a low to be a high.

So for me the concept of Heaven has no common sense to it at all… but it needs to, in order to be relevant. The only reality about Heaven is that it has been used as an incentive by numerous religions for thousands of years to promote their cults and accrue believers.

Belief in Worship

Worship, to anyone with an open mind, is a carryover from our superstitious days when there were a variety of gods that were prayed to in a fruitless attempt to promote people's wellbeing. This patronage occurred as a result of our early fears and ignorance…

-- fears that the gods needed homage and sacrifice in order to provide for us because we were not fully aware of how to care for ourselves

-- ignorance of how the universe actually works and exactly what our place is in it

Since the above assessment will do little to influence people's belief that they need to pay respect to a superior being in order to be saved or change His grand plan, I have to ask the following...

-- What kind of God needs such deference and prayer anyway?

-- Do our wants and needs have to be verbalized to Him in order to get His attention? I thought He was supposed to know all.

-- Has anyone ever benefited from their display of adoration or beseeching, other than in their own mind?

-- Would any self-respecting God have the arrogant persona that we foolishly assign to Him?

Worship is a mechanism which permits people to imagine that they have a personal connection to God without demonstrable proof that such an attachment has been made

An interesting thing about prayer is that it has not been shown to have any effect on events. Positive stuff happens and negative stuff happens, all without any correlation to prayer. So here are other questions to ponder...

-- If it has not been shown that there is detectable benefit to prayer, what induces so many to indulge in the practice?

-- What should we deduce from the evidence that only a miniscule number of prayers even <u>seem</u> to be answered?

-- Why are not all of our prayers responded to if they are both reasonable and earnestly requested?

-- Is there any rhyme or reason as to which prayers are (*maybe*) answered and which are not?

-- Is prayer by the masses, having a common objective, more effective at getting God's attention than is an individual's prayer?

-- Why aren't people upset when a reasonable request is made through prayer and is not acknowledged?

-- Is God simply capricious?

Perhaps we should consider the placebo effect as a factor in people's attitudes toward religion and prayer. To a limited degree, if we believe that something is true, it may have a positive effect on our physicality, mentality and behaviors, at least in the short run. Hence repetitive church attendance. This brain mechanism is undoubtedly what permits people to promote their faith in God, and believe that something has actually been accomplished with their prayers even when it hasn't. It is only their faith that convinces them that there is something where there is nothing.

Ayn Rand, author (*roughly, as I recall from Atlas Shrugged*):
Churches will one day stand as a monument to the ignorance of mankind.

Belief in a Flag

This is at least as touchy a subject as religion is, with many of the same fervent overtones. It would not be a mistake to presume that there are a majority of people who believe that...
-- our flag is a symbol of everything that is good about America and consequently feel very proud of it
-- it represents a long history of struggles and successes
-- it symbolizes traditions that should be preserved
-- it is an honored covering for the caskets of our fallen heroes

Maybe it is used for too many duties. In addition to the above, waving and displaying the flag can be also used by some to...
-- subtly set themselves above others – as with the notion that they may be a better American than others
-- proclaim that one has made it in America – typically with the large flags flown by owners of grand houses (*did anyone think of rich Republicans while reading this?*)
-- contend that our country is better than all other countries – a thoroughly dumb-ass concept that we are indoctrinated with as children, and one that may not be wise to dispute in public
-- elicit respect for the displayers – such as when Presidents speak to the nation while surrounded with flags and banners – or during the red, white and blue balloon-dropping conventions that endeavor to portray politicians as worthy of respect by their association with respected symbols

We may profess a love for our country because of a childhood indoctrination or because it is mostly what we know of the world. This latter condition occurs because people are more comfortable with those things that they are familiar with, and are more inclined to discount those things and peoples that they do not know nearly so well. If one is realistic, we would know that virtually everyone (*including me*) loves their own country, without reservation, just like we may love our hometowns. But that does not make them the best, nor necessarily even better than any others.

Flags, banners and standards have been used as symbols for people to rally around for thousands of years. They are used...
-- during wars of rebellion to bind people together into a common cause... such as with the American Revolution.
-- as an enticing symbol for those who may be about to die, in order for them to justify their own deaths – some Muslims use the Qu'ran in this way
-- to symbolize of our power to other countries – which is why our flag is occasionally burned by protestors

 For those of you who do not agree with this thesis, I would ask you to come up with a single good reason (*short of a nice tradition that may bind people together*) for honoring a flag... one that could not be accomplished just as well without the flag. In order for it to be good, however, it must not be a reason that is used to...
-- justify dominance over others
-- enhance the herd instinct in people
-- express the idea of being better than others
-- promote an activity or group

Give up?

For me, a valid use of the flag is when it is draped over the casket of a fallen hero to show respect to the survivors.

During the 2008 election the press (*who are always on the lookout for salacious material*) asked candidate Obama why he was no longer wearing his flag lapel-pin. Regardless his answer, the question was as irrelevant as it was obnoxious. Does the lack of, or possession of a pin have meaning except to the pin-heads. The public was probably not aware of this "missing" jewelry until someone with an ax to grind, or a need for fifteen seconds of air time created the issue.

The flag is also used in conjunction with the Oath of Allegiance, but I'm not sure why people think any oath is necessary to affirm loyalty to a country that we already live in and love. It reminds me of the allegations that were made during the unconstitutional McCarthy hearings when everyone suspected of having socialist leanings was accused of being a Communist. On the bright side, McCarthy was voted out of office.

Patriotism Can Be Blind

From early on we have been taught that patriotism is a virtue, and it is an attitude to be admired. This training traces back to our earliest wars and religious campaigns where this incentive was used to encourage soldiers to give up their lives for a cause that was said to be greater than them and in the country's interest. And not too surprisingly this enticement was engendered by those leaders who were not in the front lines, or it was espoused by those political types with their own agenda.

Even today we have not acknowledged who is pulling our strings with this social imperative of voicing and supporting patriotism. While human nature normally induces us to resist participating in ones own death, that attitude may not hold true if a longstanding indoctrination or a national necessity intervenes. By "necessity" I am referring to self preservation, not just fighting someone else's war for their sake. And patriotism is definitely about war.

The leadership of this country has time and again led the population into unnecessary wars in order to satisfy their imagined needs, to right perceived wrongs, or promote their world view. Does Bush's attempt to democratize the Middle East come to mind? I'm sure it wasn't the citizens of Iraq who took down the World Trade Center, which was presented as one of the justifications for creating a war in Iraq. The alleged weapons of mass destruction was then a trumped up incentive for the citizens edification.

Only occasionally has the rationale for war been that it was engaged in for our own protection. When the Japanese attacked Pearl Harbor we properly took up the challenge. When a tiny Vietnamese craft was said to have attacked a US ship thousands of times its size, President Johnson was quick to rally Congress with this bogus excuse. And because patriotism (*supporting our President*) may have been imagined to be at stake, they took the bait, and thousands died for nothing. Behind closed doors, however, this "police action" may actually have been promoted because of Vietnam's oil potential or the chilly relations that we had with nearby China. But that did not stop the propaganda that was repeatedly fed to the public.

So wave or hoist the flag if that makes you feel like a better American than others. Just don't believe for a second that there is a shred of truth in it. I for one love this country as much as anyone, and have no great need to follow the patriotic crowd.

A gentler, kinder side of patriotism is the feeling of community that it induces in people. This is not a bad thing until it extends to thinking that somehow we and our country are better than others. That kind of discrimination is what makes a world community less possible. When we take sides (*ours*), we implicitly side against others, however subtly or intensely that emotion may be manifested. That can not be a good thing.

Why We Believe

It seems to be part of our human nature to look outside of ourselves for answers to difficult questions because of our innate willingness to be followers. But there is a downside to letting others make decisions for us. It reduces our capability to separate the self-serving behavior of them from those things that can be beneficial and practical. Rather than moving blindly in lock step with those who strive to attain power, we could gain lessons from...
-- studying human history and learn its implications on current behaviors
-- rebuffing the well-intentioned, but immaterial folklore that entices us
-- opening a kind eye to that which is different so that we can look for value in what we do not readily grasp

-- withholding judgments until we posses sufficient facts to make proper evaluations
-- appreciating those things that we can not change as long as they are not harmful to us and others
-- accepting that we do not have, and will never have, a lock what is right and wrong
-- treating each other with due respect to reduce personal tensions
-- discovering how destructive negative behavior can be for our socializing and our aspirations

Issac Isimov, author: *"If knowledge can create problems, it is not through ignorance that we can solve them."*

Is It God's Will?

One of the platitudes that we may hear when tragedy strikes is that "It is God's will". And of course this fable was taught to us by those lecturers who learned it from their instructors, who learned it from... So when we are told that something is God's will, what we are implicitly being told is that...
-- God intervenes in our lives without our consultation or consent
-- God must be capricious in His actions because we can not predict or always understand His actions
-- God is always right, and we should not question his alleged behavior or lack of deeds on the world's behalf
-- God allows evil to exist

Perhaps religion is His way of testing us (*as some may believe*) to see if we are worthy of entrance to Heaven. But it is far more likely that we are simply convinced by the false promises and exaggerated claims of religious leaders. This is the means by which people in authority maintain control of others who buy into their stories. And this speaks to the undeniable power that churches exert for the purpose of generating revenue and fostering subservience of the flocks. So logically we are left with three choices about what we might believe about God, which are...
-- He is not the loving God that we pretend He is
-- He is a loving God and we just don't get His logic

-- He takes no part in our world whatsoever

Benjamin Franklin: "God helps those who help themselves"

We have been told the above fable countless times. But perhaps we could put this in a more meaningful way… God offers no help whatsoever, so you had better do it yourself or it won't get done.

Attitude Adjustments

The Brain's Delay

An occasional cartoon shows a disheveled chap holding up a placard saying that "The end of the world is coming". This humor would be more poignant if the word <u>world</u> were replaced with the word <u>oil.</u> Our world's economy is excessively wasteful of, and is increasingly dependant on using vast quantities of this finite energy source, much of which is derived from potentially or actually hostile countries. But it is our genetic disposition that tends to tells us there is no real crisis until long after one is at hand.

In the distant past humans had only a few daily concerns, even though the ones that we had were critical in nature, such as gathering food, protection from animals, and avoiding the harsh elements. Those who survived those difficulties had learned how to cope with their environment, and in the long run this lead to constructive brain reprogramming (*instinct*). Successful solutions that were developed using trial and error eventually became translated into their brain wiring. However, going from problem recognition to hard-wired solutions takes time… a very great deal of time in fact.

Today we are confronted with a variety of dilemmas whose solutions have not yet been integrated into our brains… solutions which would allow us to adequately recognize and manage problems on a timely basis. It is our brains normally-important reliance on its previous programming that tends to interfere with recognition of, and derivation of solutions for new problems. We have a genetic imperative to reuse old solutions well after circumstances might dictate otherwise.

The world is changing at an ever increasing rate and we are terribly slow to keep up...
-- the first PC computer hard drive that I purchased for a client cost $12.000 and held 20 megabytes (*million characters*) of data | today we can get terabytes (*trillions*) of capacity for a hundred dollars or so

-- when I was a child, the DC3 was a spectacular airplane and could fly at some 200 miles per hour -| today our rockets fly in excess of 25.000 miles per hour
-- food, clothing and materials were initially derived from the environment | today these items can be conveniently obtained from stores
-- staying alive was an awesome task | today most of us do not have harsh struggles to provide for our daily comforts

It is a completely different world than it was a few tens of thousand of years ago. However, because our brain is not quickly re-wired...
-- our instincts have not yet evolved to manage some newer situations
-- we do not easily recognize the seriousness of potential disasters

We pay little attention to every day problems, such as...
-- the levee weakening in Louisiana, California and elsewhere that will cause devastation if they fail
-- the unrestrained growth of population with its impact on utilities, education and quality of life
-- people living far from their workplace and making long commutes
-- global warming and its repercussions for everyone
-- the lies that are told by our politicians
-- not exercising sufficient effort toward preventing future problems

In the distant past, energy was a precious commodity that could not afford to be squandered on frivolous notions. Today we do not plan for the future very well because our wiring does not commit sufficient mental urgency to that task. We prefer instead to react to situations, rather than to be proactive in their prevention. Evolution had taught us to live for today or you may not live into tomorrow.

Perhaps the least intelligent, head-in-the-sand mentality that is still being demonstrated by the global society is our dependence on imported oil. Yes, the US is stockpiling supplies in underground salt caverns, but this is primarily reserved for the militaries' misadventures and rare national emergencies. The majority of our daily oil is being purchased from countries that like our dollars but hate our politics, or even our existence. Some of them may be waiting for the time when they can damage our economy without having to devastate their own.

And if the religious radicals continue to gain control over these countries, they may not care about their own people's fate. One Iranian general related that his job was to drain US resources, and we are foolishly helping out in that cause. Just don't ask the radical leadership to become a martyr to their plans. They own the minds of thousands who are willing to become cannon fodder. Slowly but surely their power over the world's Arabs is growing.

For the radicals, life is about belief, not about living… their religion is rarely about people, but it is always about power

This country, as well as the rest of the industrialized world, needs to initiate an aggressive natural resources conservation policy in order to wean itself off of oil products, whether that source is foreign or domestic. As long as we can be held hostage to the mindsets of others we will remain their victims, with our lifestyle and liberty at monumental risk. We have had years of exposure to the impending dangers while failing to acknowledge the potential for disaster. It's time to pay attention.

World terrorism exists, among other reasons, in great part because of our oil dollars and our drug dollars

Without the petrol-dollars and the poppy-bucks that we supply to Arab countries, the terrorists could not easily afford to spread their havoc around the world. So why do we continue to support our own destruction? One answer involves the big oil companies who…
-- want to stay big
-- care little where their revenue comes from or goes
-- disregard the implications of purchasing oil because they profit immensely from it

Do these companies suffer during the escalating price of crude oil? Not at all! Actually they benefit nicely from the turmoil because their profit margins are a function of the retail price. The higher the selling price, the higher is their profit margin. Just check out oil's combined profits for 2007 of more than $125 billion if you are inclined to dispute this contention. As a consequence of big oil's comfort level being high no matter what oil crisis may occur, they have no motivation to change the equation between our wasteful consumption and the unacceptable risk of dealing with the oil producing nations from a subservient position. And our corporate-subsidized, election oriented, politicians acquiesce to this counterproductive plan because they are nicely compensated (*if you get my drift*) for that loyalty. Can these participants in America's downside be as witless, self-centered, and dysfunctional as they appear?

Does anyone not get that this unconscionable complacency regarding a fragile resource is due to the conspiracy that exists between big business and politics… a situation which is expediently mislabeled campaign financing? It is time to recognize just how detrimental this shadow government (*corporate lobbying*) is to this country and its future. Little is accomplished in Washington that does not have business interests and money as a motivating factor, with big oil being among the most dangerous to our way of life.

What we should be striving for is to use the genetic-rational side of our brain more often and use the genetic-emotional side of our brain less often… even though both can be valid under various conditions. Over the long run the inevitable re-wiring of our brains will catch up to the calendar. But in the mean time we have to exercise intelligence if we want to live up to our potential. We must…
-- be intimately aware of our evolutionary origins
-- know why our early genetic information is still with us
-- understand what to do to counteract its negative effects

Behavior Confusions

Attitudes are necessary because they enable us to make sense of and manage the events that compose our environment. Outlooks are not, however, derived from thin air. They are introduced to us in both conscious and subconscious ways from associations with the world around us. In addition we have genetic wiring (*propensities*) derived from our ancestor's evolution that adds to the behavioral soup. The attitudes we have and adopt make us who we are.

Col. Harlan Sanders, creator of Kentucky Fried Chicken*: "There is no bad weather, only varieties of good weather."*

The Selfish Gene

There appears to be a gene or two that are responsible for our having self-centered behaviors. No doubt they aided in our early survival because selfishness was not always a bad thing. Similarly, a set of genes appears to have developed into an instinct that allows us to generate the hierarchy-of-concern that we manifest toward others. This behavior, which is taken as natural, is that...
-- we care for ourselves first and foremost | though this can be temporarily set aside when we try to save the life of another, for example
-- we care somewhat less for those who are the closest to us
-- and so on down the line until we get to the many, who we may not seriously care about at all

While this attitude seems to be obvious and normal, it is not quite that simple. Evolution played a staring role in its development based on trial and error. In our early history we had successes and failures relating to who were the most essential friends for survival and who were not. This knowledge eventually led to developing a hierarchical attitude. This trait is acceptable today, not because it involves any sort of universal truth... it is just evolved pragmatism.

Theodosious Dobzhanshy, geneticist: *"Nothing in biology makes sense, except in the light of evolution."*

The curious part about defining who friends are is that it can be highly anti-social. If we are given the choice of saving the life of a loved one or saving the lives of a dozen strangers, it may be that the twelve would bite the dust. This is the emotional-selfish side of decision making, as opposed to the rational-logic aspect of our brain. Because we do not have the same connection with people that are not familiar to us, we do not have as strong an empathy for them or an overriding commitment to their survival. Rationally speaking, twelve lives are worth more than one, but we have not evolved to make that kind of judgment.

An example of rational-logic thinking (*for which no judgment is offered*) was expressed years ago by a social scientist. He suggested that feeding the starving people in Africa was counter-productive to their survival in areas with abject poverty. It was his conclusion that for every one who was kept from hunger and death, ten more will be born that might in turn starve to death. He believed that some Africans are on a counter-productive path, perhaps for a variety of reasons, in which more of them will starve each year. And if this lesson applies to Africa today, perhaps it is only a matter of time before it applies to the rest of us as we outpace our resources.

While our emotional-selfish thinking may have served us well during our tribal days, such as with the concept of protect your peers but not the strangers, it is not nearly as valuable a tool in today's world. Our social network has become so interconnected that we can no longer afford to have this perspective about who is a friend and who is not. Imagine what civilization would be like if we were not to care for others during natural disasters just because we do not know the victims. Very quickly people and countries could become pitted against one another in destructive ways.

An example of this kind of negative behavior can still be found with tribes of the Arabian Deserts that do not cultivate even rudimentary concern for their neighbors, instead preferring to exhibit aggressive behaviors (*perhaps due to sparse resources and indoctrination*) toward each other. Their lack of empathy has led to generations of religious confrontations and ethnic cleansing. They will occasionally kill the "others" because they can not tolerate competing religions (*even though they are similar*) in their midst.

Attitude Adoption

Making Determinations

It is natural to rely on our brain programming and education to resolve the answers to the questions that occur in our daily lives. At times we may also defer to others when we...
-- are unsure of our own judgment
-- respect the education of another
-- are under duress from intimidation
-- intend to please someone

Following the lead of others may be an adaptation that is similar to the imprinting function that is found in young birds and animals. For a period of time in our growth a temporary subprogram sanctions us to adopt the beliefs of others because there is too much information to evaluate on our own. These assumed beliefs can be reasonable or lack validity, but that may not matter at the time. In addition to this involuntary acceptance of ideas we can be susceptible to the ideas of others when we have confidence in the thought givers. What vested Catholic doesn't believe in the infallibility and proclamations of the Pope? People will sometimes construct reasons to believe in the unbelievable just because...
-- it is inspiring and makes them feel good
-- it offers a comforting explanation of the unknown
-- they put their trust in the information giver
-- it fits neatly into a philosophy that they have adopted

None of these reasons may be sufficient justification for believing in some of the assertions that are offered to us, yet it happens with some regularity. Critical examination of evidence is not always the first thought for us. It is easier to accept that those in authority are good and true, rather than to believe that we are being deceived on a daily basis. The reality is that there are individuals and institutions that are continually engaged in actions to mislead or misinform us. Knowing this propensity goes a long way toward our making informed decisions. It's called skepticism.

Henry David Thoreau, author: *"Disobedience is the true foundation of liberty. The obedient must be slaves."*

At a conference of young Arabs in Pakistan the organizer was attempting to dispel various false ideas about America residing with that group which he saw as detrimental to peace and harmony. There were many in attendance who believed that the CIA had been responsible for the planes that crashed into the World Trade Center and the Pentagon. While only a fringe element in this country would embrace that conspiracy theory, vast numbers of Arabs do. The unreasonableness of thinking that this was a pretext for invading their lands may do little to change their point of view. Being unquestioning believers in their religions is what makes them susceptible to those who voice this ludicrous propaganda. Authority rules! The big lie trumps common sense when it is not deemed to be a lie by the story givers!

Sheep and Wolves

Because of our history the majority of us are occasionally willing to tolerate the misbehaviors of others rather than voice our feelings about their actions. This code of conduct is so imbedded in our psyches that is has become an integral part of our unwritten code of etiquette. We willingly suffer the slings and arrows of offenders rather than be viewed as an offender ourselves.

It is interesting how the dominant leaders in history have been able to control the masses so easily, even when their self-serving dictates unfavorably affected them. A possible explanation of this conundrum is...
-- initially power is granted by the masses to those who they feel demonstrate a special ability to govern, guarantee security, administers a religion, or whatever
-- frequently an addiction to this donated power will turn those who are chosen into becoming self-serving

-- in more than a few cases the power of these leaders turns ruthless with the threat of suffering or death to those who dare oppose their authority
-- at the final stages of a power grab it may be too late for the oppressed to mount an effective defense of their liberty
-- by then the authority has been consolidated into the hands of a few and against the masses who were the original power givers
-- additionally there are the thugs and their generals (*who also crave power*) who are employed to maintain order

Do you ever wonder how it is that the police and troops of a dictator state can mete out the harshest of punishments onto their fellow citizens? Surely they do not all agree that the dictator is deserving of the position that was given long ago. And not all fear retribution if they do not conform because mutiny is always an option. The answer must be that they crave the little bit of power that they hold over others.

We have an undeniable tendency to grant power to those that we are subsequently controlled by

There may be penalties meted out to prevent rebellion, and this oppressive environment can last for decades or hundreds of years until dramatic events change that cycle of control. The Chinese Dynasties which began thousands of years ago are to some degree still in effect. In the case of Stalin, he was so ruthless that when he died that no one has been permitted to wield hist level of power again. Even in the first minutes after his death, comrades were paralyzed with the fear that he was just feigning death in order to trap an imagined enemy. You may recall how many of them were purged on the slightest suspicion of being an opponent.

Eventually an anathema to state oppression overwhelmed even the staunchest Communists as the USSR broke up and limped toward democracy. But power has a way of regenerating itself, as witnessed by the backsliding of freedoms under Russia's Putin, or with the suspensions of constitutional liberties by leaders in other countries, in their quest for more and more authority.

Collaborating politicians also crave power, the favors it provides, and will generally support the person who provides them with those benefits. This last scenario is not all that far distant from the political system which we employ in this country. Concern for the populous by essentially all of our politicians is only a secondary consideration at best. And if you examine their political power structure, there is an undeniable incentive for those at the top to take advantage of those who farther down the ladder.

Make no mistake - virtually no politician makes the effort involved in seeking public office in order to benefit the people

As I have observed, power is initially given by its victims. This occurs without the use of force in this country because we…
-- pay little attention to what it is that our political leaders are engaged in while we "sleep"
-- don't know who they are taking money from or why
-- are not aware of their voting records or whether or not their votes coincide with their public statements
-- remain foolishly hopeful that politicians have integrity
-- may harbor a belief there are no good choices (*true*)

What people do not seem to grasp is that voting for the lesser of two evils is still voting for evil.

It takes too much effort for the population to become informed, not because they may not wish to know, but because the information is difficult to obtain from the candidates or the press. And the downside to this situational apathy is that the masses tacitly bestow their power onto those who may deserve it the least. How many of those people who have run for public office in the past would you really have wanted to be elected?

Abraham Lincoln, President: "*Nearly all men can stand adversity, but if you want to test a man's character, give him power.*"

The result of government power being consolidated against the populous can be unrest and potential revolution. For generations the kings and dictators in the Middle East have siphoned off their countries' wealth for their insider clique and themselves. Then they suppressed the population to stay in power. Finally in 2011, enough was maybe enough as the Arab Spring began in one country after another, which was helped along by social networking (*the Internet*) allowing the rebels to mount coordinated resistance.

Aggressive Behavior

Ancient humans struggled on a daily basis to find food, retain their meager supply, and thereby survive. Part of the process was getting to sources before others did… a fresh carcass for example. There was also the need to develop the skills that permitted the retention of food once it was discovered or killed. Success demanded this. As a result of engaging in these difficult circumstances over long periods of time, valuable survival technique became hard-wired into their brains as instinct. This intuition allowed successive generations to acquire the knowledge of their forefathers and have the motivation to do what was necessary to succeed without the need to go through a protracted learning process.

Our manifesting both aggressive and cooperative behavior is the result of adopting those actions that functioned best in particular situations, which gives us the term: survival of the fittest. Because of competition with animals and other humans, there was a need to develop workable behaviors. One of these traits would be the act of cooperation in hunting, food gathering and its preparation. Another would have been the use of aggression, selfishness, deceit, and lack of sharing in order to protect one's food supply and mates. Apparently we had good reasons to develop both of these traits since neither by itself would have been sufficiently successful.

An example of our propensity against sharing is demonstrated by children's tendency to hoard their possessions. They are none the worse off for sharing, but this behavior does not come naturally. It must be learned, and their genetic dispositions toward selfishness overcome. In recent times we have concluded that cooperation can serve us well. But having this adaptation constructively re-work our brain wiring may take thousands of years to become instinctive.

Illogical Behavior?

In rational human beings, behavior is not technically illogical regardless of how it appears. It is each person's response to outside stimulus which is based on their initial wiring and subsequent rewiring. It is their personal logic. When that programming is defective, the output can be equally faulty. I mention this because it may be the best way to explain deviant behaviors and incarceration recidivists. We all have, to some degree, an ongoing tug-of-war between our good and bad dispositions. Those of us with more positive role models to emulate will incline toward the good. Those with darker experiences will gravitate toward the negative side.

The tendencies of our progenitors evolved from circumstances in which their most effective behaviors tended to supplant their least effective behaviors. But being effective does not imply that the behaviors were charitable. Since nothing succeeds like success, our genetic wiring has been cast in the direction of what had worked best over long periods of time. Sometimes harsh or unforgiving behaviors were required to manage the day. At other times generosity and caring would have won out. The result of these adaptations to circumstances is why we have become somewhat skillful at living with both ends of the spectrum.

During our tribal history there were times when difficult decisions were made to advance the welfare of the group or an individual. For some Eskimos, children who were born without their first teeth were put out on the ice to die because of their superstitions. Tribes with offspring that had disabilities may have sacrificed those lives for the benefit of the group as well. That these attitudes were based on ignorance was of no matter because of the nature of ignorance itself. Simply put, if you don't know, then you don't know. Because compassion was eventually deemed to be more socially rewarding it came to dominate in most cultures.

Our tendency toward malevolence, while generally suppressed, is not completely repressed. If we are cast into the right circumstances our personality's negative side of our can assert itself. And this can occasionally surface with unusual force. Just look at talking head Hannity's excessive diatribes directed toward those he doesn't agree with, as a modern example. He gets paid for this attitude because there is a ready audience for the dark side.

In an experiment at Stanford University a group of students were put into a simulated prison scenario as either guards or prisoners. The unrestrained guards became so ruthless toward their fellow prisoners that the researchers had to cancel the test after only a few days. So is it any wonder that we have the expression that power corrupts and ultimate power corrupts ultimately?

The lesson about behaviors is that we need to be vigilant of the propensity for mischief by those who are holding power, whether they are…
-- a companies' president
-- our country's President
-- or people of lesser status

Because the attainment of power can so easily unleash the evil of corruption we must assume that this behavior is both natural and frequently occurring, and that we must act vigorously to constrain it. This is why the framers of the Constitution formed three independent branches of government in order to provide the necessary checks and balances on each other's tendencies. The result of their insight has generally been to prevent any one branch from becoming too powerful (*read uncaring*).

On the international front, the mania about retaining power for some Arab leaders had been so strong that they apparently believe that they might remain power long after they had gone into hiding. Gadhafi was found hiding in a drainage ditch in his home town. Hussein was found hiding in a "spider hole". Had they been willing to relinquish power, they might have lived out their final years rather comfortably with the money was no-doubt stashed. But the addiction to power warped their common sense, and they paid the ultimate price for that obsession.

Our Indoctrinations

We can not easily predict the future except on occasion by looking at appropriate examples from the past. Even then our programming may prevent us from making intelligent assessments of what may likely occur or how we should react to it. The world, for example, had been engaged in wars since before recorded history, and we are unlikely to change our aggressiveness in the foreseeable future. The root of this continued belligerence is because the brain has that tendency imbedded in it, and we become fairly ineffective at re-education somewhere in our youth. Once we have an idea locked away in our heads, like the belief in God, bigotry toward others, or winning at all costs, there is little chance that logic and persuasion will be effective at disrupting that prior education.

We all have negative inclinations that are not generally acted upon because most of us get the fact that having restraint can keep us out of trouble. But the offenders of this principle suffer from a failure to absorb that education at an age when it was likely to sink in. They may even believe that doing the crime and doing the time is their karma.

While incarceration is often thought of as the solution to civil disobedience, the rate of jail overcrowding and undiminished rate of crime would suggest otherwise. Therefore we must try to discover more effective methods for controlling this behavior and not just lock it away with its prohibitively high costs. After all, do we care how antisocial one might potentially be if that negative side is never manifested. One solution might be to develop a school program that convincingly explains the downside to students about antisocial behaviors... one that denigrates to the concepts of gaming the system and of winning at all costs.

Defining Anger

Perhaps the best way to view your anger is to recognize that one is often angry with one's self, regardless of whom or what is the object of that expression. This perspective, however, does not correspond to the thoughts that people invariably attach to the emotion. But putting anger into this new light can be more productive than our propensity to blame others for our feelings. When getting angry we are actually indicating that we are not capable of dealing with a situation, and we don't like the reaction our coping-inability has generated by that experience. We simply may not possess the proper tools to manage the situation, and that is really what makes us angry. So whose fault it that?

No one makes you angry – you do it to yourself

There is another aspect to anger which can be the result of a learned response to problems or difficulties. If your parents approached their problems using anger, it is likely that you will use this technique in your own dealings. Anger may then be viewed as an appropriate solution even though the outcome is seldom favorable. My father was apparently raised with a strap, and at times he used the same solution on his children. While it left no scars, physical or otherwise, it did demonstrate his indoctrination. As a result of that early education I needed to rethink my approach to dealing with pet issues. Thanks to my wife I began using the affection training that she had learned as a child, and found it very productive.

Hatred And Anger

As children we become aware of this thing called hate. It is occasionally expressed by parents and peers, but was always something of a mystery to me. Yes, I probably said that I hated creamed cucumbers or hated being teased, but that's not the same emotion as the hatred of others. There are people that I don't care for and may choose not to associate with, but my feelings never reach the level of hate that some express. It makes me wonder if there is not a genetic component to hate that I was fortunate enough to miss.

I suspect that hate is primarily, but not exclusively, related to the lessons that we learn in the home. Parents can manifest strongly negative attitudes about ideas, things and others. Then it is likely that the "legitimacy" those feelings will be passed on to their children as parents transfer these emotions to susceptible youths.

Like anger, hatred indicates a lack of coping skills. It shows how easily we can assign negativity to others while ignoring our own involvements or failures. We may even rationalize that if others are the negative party then we had little or no material contribution to the event. In the final analysis though, hatred harms the hater. Having the understanding that your anger and hatred is all about you is a good first step in dealing with its root cause. After developing this appreciation, more appropriate responses can be formulated.

Nature of Delusion

Before delving into this topic it might be appropriate to agree on the definition of two terms in order to get on the same page...
-- Ignorance is a lack of knowledge on some subject. We are all ignorant about the vast majority of details in the universe. This is nothing to be overly concerned about except in those cases where we may be purposefully ignorant... such as in not keeping up with laws, education, or events.
-- Stupidity also infects us all. It is the failure to draw reasonable conclusions or exercise appropriate judgment even though one is aware of the pertinent facts. Stupidity can also be a denial of facts because they do not fit into one's particular philosophy or belief system. For example, it is stupid (*in my opinion*) to avoid medicines that cure just because they may not be holistic or because one does not believe in doctors.

Don Wood, author: *"Stupid is forever, ignorance can be fixed."*

Occasionally our decisions about life and others are based on a combination of both ignorance and stupidity. We may be somewhat aware of the adverse affect of a potential action yet choose to execute it anyway because we have not fully considered its implications. Insisting on having one's way with a mate is an attitude that ignores the long term negative effects.

Two major areas in which ignorance and stupidity are fundamental are with politics and religion. It should be abundantly clear that both institutions have their share discrepancies and deceit, but there are multitudes that ignore the obvious. Indulgence in our delusions occur when we believe the real world to be false or the false world to be real. Having unwavering support for politicians and religion characterize this confusion.

In the real world it is reality that should count. Fantasy and wishful thinking should not. Self delusion is also a mechanism which we may call on to comfort ourselves when we imagine that a belief in a more accurate reality is untenable…that a dear friend is dishonest, for example In this case we may choose to adopt a convenient or comfortable fallacy about the person, but that does not make it true or productive. Being aware of whom others are, as well as what their motivations, capabilities and shortcomings may be is better than living with a deception. Delusions only serve confuse us and support those who would take advantage of us.

Natural Law

In 2010 and beyond, the United States took a warning shot across its bow. The financial crisis came about by, among several reasons, the US and other countries living beyond on their means. The prevailing fiscal delusion was that countries could manage to get by forever with an ever increasing debt load… a massive liability that will be passed on to their children's children. While there are still voices that say it is not as bad as it seems and the sky is not falling, the facts beg to differ. The chickens are coming home to roost. Having misguided optimism is no substitute for skepticism and a directed responsibility.

The predicament of America today can be loosely compared to the fall of the Roman Empire. Their demise has been attributed to…
-- nothing much being accomplished without resorting to bribery and raising taxes
-- not being accountable to any one for living beyond its means

-- a military with troops in too many countries, pursuing too many wars

The parallels in the above history lesson about Rome and that relationship to the US are…
-- a Congress that has little interest in solving America's problems because they have been corrupted by the bribery that has them doing corporate bidding instead of ours
-- a destructive spending battle between the Republicans and Democrats, with both side have little taste for raising taxes to insure fiscal integrity
-- a flagrant lack of controls on Wall Street that led to a financial meltdown in several sectors of the economy (*especially in housing*) with virtually no one being held accountable
-- administrations that keep playing the military-industrial-complex card long after its fruitlessness has been established in the regional wars that we have no business pursuing

The parallels are unavoidable. While things might change for the better, our political inertia says it won't.

What is Truth?

Is it Debatable?

An insight into our chronic inability to faithfully record historical events for posterity has its roots in the truism that history is written by the victors. Even if an author were determined, it is not easy to represent events accurately and dispassionately. We each have our initial wiring and a lifetime of re-wiring to contend with. That contributes to making accuracy improbable in the extreme, and reasonable accuracy difficult. I am aware that with my writing I have an agenda to present, and I will not characterize opposing viewpoints as kindly or effectively as they might deserve… certainly not as passionately. After all I am here to present my perspective and let you judge it on its merits.

Rewriting History

Our formal education is based on the teaching of history… because it didn't just happen, did it? And history can be represented by people who are fallible (*with good intentions*) or unscrupulous (*with intentions to mislead and distract*). Just listen to the opinions expressed on any political talk show if you want unrestrained examples of the latter. One doesn't have to be informed of a guest's affiliation to glean what it is.

We should all be aware of how political "facts" are routinely rewritten to promote an agenda, to present an undeserved image, or distort the truth. The torrent of spin that is used by those who have distortions to promote has become such a common feature of the political landscape that we fail to call it by its correct name of lying.

Politicians occasionally revert to their childhood behavior of denying facts as if that will make them false. Sadly that diversionary tactic works far too well when dealing with the ill-informed public and the hapless press. In addition to lying, politicians may use the technique of answering a question that was not asked, rather than the one that was. This method of distraction can be so effective a practice that the original inquiry goes unanswered as reporters refrain from being impolite by repeating the question.

The downside of people's telling of history is that they can indulge themselves in misrepresentation of the facts to satisfy a personal bent. The particulars surrounding our country's culpability in the big and little wars of history have routinely been distorted to the point where we tend believe ourselves to be heroes, semi-invincible, and having no culpability that contributed to the events. As an aside, remember that all wars are started or entered into for…
-economic gain (*you have what I want*)
-conversion (*you believe what I believe*)
-power (*I want your allegiance*)
-or some combination of the above

These are not honorable motivations and we should not pretend that war is ever honorable, even in the rare case where it may be justified.

As the generation go by, history is retold with multiple changes in attitude. Established facts may be discounted or ignored if they interfere with the viewpoint of the teller. At times older version of "the truth" may even be rediscovered. These changes in perspective are usually subtle, and are especially evident with the biographies of Presidents and other famous people. This occurs because the degree of reporting accuracy resides with the person writing the document, along with the fact that positive attitudes sell better than negative ones.

Misstatements and dishonesty are also evident when it comes to the school text books where many of the US's historical negatives are ignored, expunged or glossed over. Because of this tendency toward dealing with anticipated censorship, pundits may wonder how history will depict a particular President after his departure from power or his death as if future biographers would have special insight into a person that the current biographers do not have. What they are really asking (*perhaps without knowing it*) is which aspects of the person's life will be more interesting to future writers and thus become more popular. And which of the less interesting aspects (*though still potentially important*) will fall by the wayside. History is a popularity contest with in-vogue ideas making the grade while others may not.

Historical detail has to be interesting for it to survive into the future

It is not just history that is written by the victors. Textbooks that we use in our schools and colleges can be promoted by one group or other with their own take on how history should be presented. Committees that evaluate what our students read as part of their curriculum might not have open and independent minds. The books that they approve may not accurately represent facts or even an academic consensus. Nor might they reveal how much of the author's opinion is couched in the writings.

Fair and balanced reporting is becoming ever more unlikely as the writers and talking heads take increasingly polarized positions on everything political. Facts be damned, full speed ahead to promote a particular conservative or liberal agenda. This makes both ends of the idea-promoting spectrum frequently illogical, annoying, and sometimes unsafe. Does anyone remember the killing of an abortion doctor which may have been inadvertently encouraged by the religious right's identification of that person?

Even outright lies do not pose a serious problem for the rigid purveyors of attitude and hate. As those "reporters" are no doubt aware, they are more believable when there is a shred of truth mixed in with their propaganda. That well-known technique makes it easier for an anxious-to-believe audience to accept the attached lies and distortions. Most of us are not terribly adept at separating truth, from exaggeration, from fiction. So the spin goes on without serious interruption.

Replaying History

Hundreds of years ago Europe went through a period labeled The Dark Ages. While I am not a particularly good student of ancient history, my interpretation of that period is that civilization (*freedom*

149

from oppression) had run amuck, with those who had power (*status, soldiers, horses, armor, weapons*) victimizing those who didn't. This was more than just minor confiscation crops or livestock. It was the wholesale destruction of villages and cultures, as well as the carting away of their metals, women and foodstuffs. Resistance to these rampages might be punished by torture and death. Sometimes the slaughter of hundreds of people was used to send a warning to the next village of victims. Today we may sense that this extreme level of barbarism could not be repeated, but that attitude is a dangerous complacency. In Syria, for example. Madmen are at large in numerous countries because the human brain comes wired for aggression...

-- children can be extremely cruel to each other
-- youths (*as with gangs*) can be ruthless in their treatment of outsiders, as well as their own
-- adults with even greater means at their disposal start wars to satisfy their need to dominate other cultures or to secure their natural resources (*sound familiar?*)
-- dictators around the world routinely suppress opposition with force to assure the retention of power for themselves and their minions

What we should know from history is that we are capable of serving up great injustices on each other. This innate behavior is also manifested in smaller ways, such as with homeowner-meeting arguments, civil court confrontations, and aggressive drivers. This behavior is most dangerous when whole groups ascribe to achieving gains at the expense of others.

When we compare the behavior of Japan prior-to and after WWII, one has to wonder how they were able to make such a dramatic transition to peacefulness from their highly aggressive, cruel, land-conquering, people-oppressing mentality. The only answer I can come up with is the fire bombing of their cities and the atomic bomb attacks. They were such a shock to their invincibility that they were forced to rethink their attitudes about themselves, their leaders, and their place in the world. They were presented with a price that was too high to pay, and they thankfully learned from that lesson. The Japanese culture of warriors became one of <u>peace</u> and prosperity instead of <u>war</u> and prosperity. Just don't imagine that prosperity for the people had ever been the motivating force behind Japan's war mentality. It was the acquisition of raw power for the benefit of those who were in control.

Follow the Crowd

How it Started

Because we do not have a strong sense-of-self at an early age we are susceptible to the influences of the good and bad ideas that surround us. This means is that we will likely adopt a submissive position to those who are more experienced and forceful than ourselves... at least initially. We may even maintain that behavior for a lifetime. An example of people being influenced by charisma and false message, rather than substance, would be the various hate based and quasi-religious cults. They have become adept at capturing easy believers. If you think this crowd following mentality has not a serious problem, let me remind you of Wako TX, Jim Jones (*Jonestown*) and Charles Manson.

We may not have been born with an ego, but we are hardwired to develop one, regardless of how diminutive or overblown it may become. And this ego is what allows some of us to become leaders. On the other side of the coin, being a follower involves having trust in those who are perceived to pose no threat or that may offer something of value which you may not be able to acquire on your own. This was an important evolutionary step that helped society to form stable groups and avoid chaos.

The nature of growing up is that some of us may aspire to leadership, but many more will become content with lesser roles. Those who settle for less may subsequently admire those who are able to attain that higher stature. In looking up to these people we might assign positive qualities to them that go beyond what they warrant. We may even develop the belief that the rich and famous do not put their pants on quite like us. Because of this embellishment of others that we do not know well, followers can create heroes and the overly respected out of ordinary people.

Inappropriate respectfulness toward leaders results, to some degree, from the civic lessons that we were taught in the early years of schooling. What curriculum for youth would show disrespect for our founders, civil servants, or country, that is, prior to a more enlightened high school, college, or real world education? Apparently we prefer that our children are fed nice-nice stories rather than having them deal with a harsher reality. As a result of this early bias in our education we exaggerate the ordinary merits of leaders and discount or ignore their shortcomings. School teachers may privately hold their contrary opinions, but their classroom books present the more attractive and occasionally false version of our history. How many of us are aware that...

-- at least half a dozen Presidents carried on sexual affairs while they were in office

-- virtually all politicians use their public office for private aggrandizement

-- the vast majority of our government's business is carried out in back rooms with little concern for apprising the public of these activities

-- Congress has bestowed super-premium health insurance and retirement plans on themselves while accomplishing little for the average citizen's needs

Misattribution

When I was very young, my class was told the story of George Washington (*GW*) and the cherry tree. Without having any basis in fact this tall tale was repeated to show GW's worth as an honorable man and his value as the father of our country. It didn't seem to matter that the story was fictional because it satisfied a need to present him as a super-hero. The same is true (*although it's false*) about the story that GW commissioned Betsy Ross to sew the first Stars and Stripes flag. The lesson here may be in how easily we believe the stories that are told by people in positions of authority.

GW himself contributed to the illusions that we have about our first President. He was known to have manipulated the fledgling press to his advantage, and sat for dozens of sculptures and paintings that, at his insistence, featured dramatic poses and a square jaw that he didn't have. As a result, most of his likenesses are more flattering than accurate.

Today we honor GW as the great father of our country, rarely acknowledging that had his boss General Lee not been captured by the British, GW might have been relived of his command because of a string of defeats and retreats. Is that news to you? I don't remember details like these being brought out in any of my history lessons. Nor do I recall information about the secret societies that our founding fathers were members of. Among the carryovers from England were those societies that were crafted to cater to the indulgences of the powerful and avoid the scrutiny of the common folks. Hellfire and Freemason were among them. Some of these societies were created specifically to cater to sexual interests, while others were about indulging in food and drink. Still others were created for the surreptitious manipulation of government.

Another oft-repeated story that could benefit from the light of day is the one that gives credit to President Lincoln for freeing the slaves. While he did issue the Emancipation Proclamation as our Commander-in-Chief, its primary purpose was to cause economic hardship to the South rather than to offer freedom to the slaves. This came about because...
-- slaves were deemed to be property
-- the South was our enemy
-- the President has the authority in times of war to deny property to the enemy, making the blacks a pawn in the civil war

Lincoln did make the statement "If slavery is not wrong, then nothing is wrong". But the Emancipation Proclamation was designed to free the slaves in the South and not in the fence-straddling Border States. Emancipation was used selectively as a concession, and the lack of it was employed with some states to keep them in the union. It was not until the states passed the 13th Amendment to the Constitution that the ownership of slaves was abolished... and that was after Lincoln had died.

Celebrity Obsession

Our creation of heroes generally results in the promotion of people in a way that is disproportionate to their contribution to society. The esteem with which some of us hold undeserving politicians is an example of this inclination. They were selected by the temperament of the day or perhaps by being in the right place at the right time. They seldom demonstrate greater leadership skills than others who might have found themselves in the same position. They just made the right statements, cultivated the right people, became willing patrons of the powerful corporations, and received the necessary votes. So if this is true, then our leaders are elected as much by good fortune and guile as they are for their professional talents. It then follows that the political arena is merely a playing field for the rich and powerful and a crap shoot for the rest of us.

With the expression that the position makes the man we have the implication that there are a many people who would have been comparable leaders had they found themselves in those situations. Another implication of this saying is the recognition of how ordinary politicians actually are… something most of us do not get.

Those Who Aspire

The problem with our election process is that the traits that are required to meet the challenge of elections and fund raising are not suited to those who might be an honorable candidate. How else would you explain the propensity to…
-- make promises to the electorate that are then dishonored
-- carry on sexual affairs with apparent impunity
-- vote on bills that they have not read
-- cater to the lobbyists who feed them money
-- accept strings-attached gratuities from corporations

If you have any doubts that politicians are all about money, go to the following website…
    opensecrets.org

Corruption succeeds when good people doing nothing to stop it

Ditto the Media

Nowhere does inappropriate and excessive admiration for individuals hold truer than with our media stars. Their every word, no matter how silly or pointless, holds us in the rapture of their celebrity. The result is that…
-- successful movies and DVDs that are virtually all profit to the stars and backers, with the participants being paid outrageous salaries
-- thousands of dollars are offered for first pictures of the magic couple's baby
-- we want to know how stars dress, who they are dating or dumping, where they party, who is in rehab this week, as if we knew and should cared for these people
-- we are still trying to procure pictures of Diana's car crash
-- being an alcoholic or drug user is not necessarily detrimental to one's career
-- killing one's wife or ex-wife does not necessarily mean doing jail time
-- substance and talent have been supplanted with cosmetics, dress, and outrageous behaviors

The media creatives unabashedly work to manipulate us day and night. One method used for this purpose is having one staged ceremony after another. A partial list of these award ceremonies includes the…
-- Oscar
-- Emmy
-- Bammy
-- Grammy
-- Golden Globe
-- Critics Choice
-- Screen Actors Guild
-- New York film Critics
-- People's Choice
-- Country Music
-- Billboard Music
-- MTV Movie

-- Kennedy Center
-- Walk of Fame
-- Betty Davis lifetime achievement
-- various Hall of Fame ceremonies
-- celebrity roasts
-- and hundreds of invented honorariums that publicize and enrich the award giver as much as the award receiver.

The above list, if you include the numerous lesser and local awards, is nearly endless. And there are some who never seem to tire of this self-serving charade. Are the star's repetitious thanking of God, co-workers, and family all that interesting? Do we really care that much about them?

Perhaps the most recent, inane, trumped up award is for the Young Hollywood Stars. Since these aspiring finalists do not have anything remotely approaching star status (*except perhaps with teeny-boppers*). The possibilities for their gratuitous selection are perhaps some personal connection with the show's producer, or simply a random selection of wanna-be types to fill out the numbers that are needed to make the show seem legitimate. I can hardly wait for the Baby Hollywood Stars honorarium.

So who are the major supporters of this outpouring of hero worship? Certainly it is the people who are being honored. Their billing rates may go up as a result, along with our ticket prices. But it is also the organizers of the events who benefit. These are the thousands of ancillary people who concurrently make big bucks off of their calculated elevations of everyday persons to stardom.

When I was younger and more immature I thought that the Academy Awards was run by impartial folks, and that the winners were actually the most deserving. The reality about this false assumption is that there is a massive promotion of various stars by their publicists and managers utilizing connections, coercion, and billboards in advance of the ceremonies. Because this promotion has gotten out of hand, in 2011 the Academy has banned the gala endorsement parties that have been run in a near time frame to the awards.

I am no longer naïve enough to wager one red cent on the outcomes of this rigged affair. If it was not rigged, how else would anyone in their right mind imagine that an obnoxious, annoying-sounding song about whores (*for 2007*) could win anything but ridicule, much less the Academy Award for Best Song? Well this must surely have occurred because the previously-ignored category of Rappers was on top of the Whose Turn Is It Next list. The Academy was desperately trying to show that in spite of their declining ratings, it is hip, cool and relevant. Gag. The reality is that they were appealing to a more diverse audience in order to prop up their diminishing TV ratings, which does not necessarily have much to do with celebrating talent.

The honoring of long passed-over actors was the impetus for the Academy's adoption of its Lifetime Achievement Award. Those who have received this acknowledgement had been repetitively ignored by the voters for reasons other than their lack of talent. As a result of this failure to honor a few deserving stars, the "oversights" were becoming an embarrassment to the members of the Academy. Those who became Achievement winners apparently did not have enough good-ol'-boy buddies to score an Oscar in the first place, which is all about the ability of politics to trump talent. And if this is true, how can we ever expect to witness an unbiased ceremony?

In 2009 the Academy decided to increase the number of candidates for Best Picture from five to ten. Ostensibly this was done to give more movies a chance at winning. Logically this increase should not change which movie wins just by adding a second tier of five also-rans. Undoubtedly it was done to have more of their TV time focus on movies rather than awards like "The best gaffer in a foreign comedy about wine and food purging" which are manifestly boring to the audience.

Also in 2009 we were subjected to a massive outpouring of grief for Michael Jackson. Weeks went by without much letup in the media-orchestrated hype which conveniently helped sell millions more of his albums. Since Jackson was one of the most talented individuals to reach stardom, there is no dispute about his immense skill. But when the Al Sharpton/ Jesse Jackson bandwagon blatantly maneuvered to elevate Michael to near sainthood at his memorial, it showed how cynical these pontificators were, as well as how easily the populous might be manipulated by well known individuals. Clearly their agenda was also celebrity-by-association for these two.

The fascination that we have with stardom points out one of our less productive brain wirings... being followers. We tend to respond to people who are hyped by the media and ignore those we are not. This amounts to reliance on name recognition and the recommendations of others rather than on our own judgment. We permit those who are respected to tell us who is better and who is not. But to the contrary, we do not ordinarily let others tell us which food we like or which automobiles we like. So why allow others to make entertainment judgments for us?

Star-Power's Draw

Before his death Cary Grant became a celebrity spokesperson for a company that he had no real connection to, other then for his presumably impressive paycheck. To the public he appeared to be a likable, talented actor whose charisma was meant to rub off on product being hawked. Successful media personalities may lend their names and persona (*goodwill*) to those products and companies that are willing pay the price... a fact that has nothing to do with product quality. Yet we fall for these phony endorsements as if their star magic could somehow contribute to enhancing our lives. The reality is that it works for some not-so-deep thinkers, which is enough to justify the corporation's costs.

Then there are times when even Hollywood goes too far in its promotions. I refer to the poor judgment of letting Tom Cruise loose on the public airwaves in 2008. His nearly fanatical devotion to a mind-numbing cult became too much for even his most ardent devotees. Eventually his studio bosses severed relations with him to save face.

The next time you watch one of the awards programs think about how you are being manipulated by the media and their red-carpet, star-creation business. You may assume that it's ok... in which case it is for you. But perhaps it is not just the stars that make good movies,

159

but also good scripts make good movies. And if this is true, shouldn't we be a bit more attentive to the writers? The trouble with this last proposition is in how movie scripts might to be made in the first place...
-- potentially a non-writer may come up with a movie idea – perhaps in the well-known 25 words or less
-- someone with more talent fleshes out the story line
-- a screen writer polishes the dialog
-- a director makes running changes
-- the actors may be creative as well

In this scenario the guy at the top of the list may not even recognize the final movie. Some movies are generated from popular books, with the same results. Take the movie "Clan of the Cave Bear" as an example of manuscript-gone-astray. It barely resembled what was an excellent book by a top author. As a result of these movies-by-committee, films begin to look like the incoherent 1949 Studebaker... fenders by Joe, hood by Fred, windows by Sarah.

Another example of the failure to correspond to an original story would be the difference between the Broadway version of "Mama Mia" and its pathetic movie version. The screenwriters perhaps did their best to duplicate the excellent concept of turning a series of hit songs into an mildly interesting story. Then, I assume, the powers in charge abbreviated the musical sequences (*the whole point of the play*) in order to make room for a flood of amateurish, over-the-top "acting". They further ruined the script by employing actors who could barely sing. What were these pinheads thinking? The movie became another Hollywood bore that was targeted at a teeny-bop audience, or at those who might be enamored with the cast and not offended by the silly writing.

Logic May Not Rule

A Little Philosophy

At times I have advocated several of the relationship strategies listed below. My wife and I have found this advice to be invaluable in working out our connection with each other. They are...
-- The person with the greater need should prevail <u>unless</u> that person always has the greater need
-- Create the best history that you can with your mate now, because it will be with you for a long time
-- Having fun and seeing that your mate has fun brings great rewards
-- A counselor may suggest what mates can do to improve on their partnership. Let me suggest that this line of reasoning is backwards. I would advise that they concentrate on what they shouldn't do. If you eliminate the negatives and irritations that can degrade a friendship, the rest will take care if itself.
-- The understanding of a mate's wants and wishes goes a long way toward creating harmony. It also comes down to giving as much as you get. Can that be a bad thing?

And if I still have your attention, here is a poem about relationships that you might appreciate.

Careless...
Our friendship, shattered like a crystal bowl,
lies on the floor between us, while we stand,
Knowing that neither time, nor skillful hand,
nor all our sorrowing will make it whole.
But only yesterday, it was a wonder:
So clear it was, and delicately wrought;
I set it on the mantel of our thought-- -
to see it broken by a moments blunder.
Careless, I placed it perilously high;
Carelessly, you made a clumsy move,
which sent it crashing to destruction in the grate.
Oh, we have both been careless, you and I,

like children, playing with an ornament,
who do not know its worth, until too late.
Janet Graham

Backscatter Backlash

In an effort to make our airports secure, the Transportation Safety
Administration (TSA) purchased a technology that can see through
people's clothing for the purpose of detecting weapons. The catch is
that the scan in its normal state is semi-reveling of one's anatomy.
For their part the TSA does use electronic filters to obscure facial and
genital features. Even if these machines are used for more than
those travelers who fail a standard screening test, what is the
problem for its critics? Apparently there is a small but vocal group
(*who take their showers in the dark*) that are opposed to these
devices as an invasion of privacy, as if that is more horrific a problem
than is a downed aircraft or a terminal filled with bodies. Such a silly
little people.

I can't help but relate this sexually repressive attitude to our religious
and social teachings about the body. For some, sexual expression in
any form must be avoided no matter how irrational the reasoning.
Even sex education for their children is anathema to a few.

Social Networking

What can be said about the people who are willing to ware their
hearts on their sleeves and wear their thumbs down to the quick?
The thought that comes to mind for me is: get a life. But it's not as if
these folks have no life at all. They may just think so. Or perhaps it
is that they do not invest enough effort at making and keeping real
friends.

Apparently the brain is wired to get a high from exercise, sex, food,
and even (*no kidding*) from talking about ones self. This is why some
of us turn out to be braggarts, and others bore us to death with those

endless stories about their lives, pets, children, co-workers and relatives. Who cares! As it turns out, they do. And they think that the rest of us are somehow interested in that trivia.

The vast majority of social material that is posted online almost definitely falls under the not-very-damn-interesting category, but it perpetuates this medium because the readers of these postings can then feel free to add their dullness's to the "wall" and feel better when they get their mild high.

Social etiquette used to dictate that we keep our personal lives to ourselves rather than imposing them on others. With the advent of smart phones and the Internet, the rules have changed, and not for the better. Now anyone with the requisite digits can feel important without actually accomplishing anything significant.

Finding an old school buddy (*that they may not have liked all that well, and who may not have liked them all that well*) can become an interesting task for some. One of our friends had one of these long-since forgotten acquaintances fly across country to stay a week. After the initial catching up period (*for maybe an hour*), what do you talk about with a near-perfect stranger?

With students, one has to wonder how much of their time is diverted from their studies in order to keep in touch. Can this be a factor in this country's low scholastic scores? Well, duh.

Impersonal Internet encounters have turned into a video game for some, with the consequential loss of reality. This posting and blogging openness has a tinny ring to it. For some participants, it is little more than a contest to see how many "friends" they can accumulate. Friends? I thought forming a relationship required an occasional face-to-face encounter. This new method of making friends has become as thin and tenuous as the ether.

Then there is the issue of Internet anonymity. Those youths who are most desperate to make friends may end up being subjected to those nefarious few who are only interested in taking advantage them… usually sexually. The skill of common sense that is required to deal effectively with this issue is located in the frontal cortex of the brain.

And this area does not develop fully until we reach our 20s. That can make them a prime target for pedophiles and other predators. Parents need to adopt openness with their children and insist on having access to their emails.

As it has failed to accomplished with vast amount of Internet spam, the government does very to attack this problem. Until such time as a horror hits home with the child of a politician or major celebrity, the beat will go on. Our evolution has dictated that we do not learn new tricks easily. Apathy rules.

On the Smartphone Front

What is becoming common is not just distracted driving, but also distracted walking. The statistics show that the reported injuries from this so-called sleep-walking activity have doubled for each of the last two years. One woman walked off of the end of a long pier and had to be rescued. Another person walked into traffic and was killed. Lamp poles in London are now padded because there have been so many "accidents". How important can a phone call or web surfing be that people are willing to risk their safety? Maybe this is another example of nature's impetus toward survival of the fittest and improving the gene pool.

Suckers for Scams

Now that computers and email are nearly universal, Internet scams reel in thousands of surfers and emailers on a daily basis. Then for those of us who do not want our in-box filled with the resultant of junk, an industry has evolved to limit that nuisance. So some pay for the phony offers and links, and the rest of us pay for their stupidity. One possible solution to spam might be to report it to the feds. Their address is spam@uce.gov. I can not verify the effectiveness of this "solution".

It's not as if the problems with spam and scams haven't been exposed uncountable times in publications and on television. For those who want to avoid this scenario there is a simple solution... don't ever respond to any email ads. But natural curiosity, naivety, and thoughtless avarice rule the day for these self-made victims. That is what makes spam and scams worthwhile for its purveyors. If only 1/1000th of 1 percent were to take the bait, the sheer volume of emails makes the bad guy's efforts pay off.

For some time now I've sent the following email to friends who forward attachments to me. You may want to copy this notice to a word processor for your own use.

To our friends
Excuse us, but we do not open any attachments and links that are not created by the sender. Bad guys use enticing attachments to enter and poison computers. If you are inclined to pass them along, please don't.

As for using Websites without concern, there is software that attaches to browsers which will rate websites as safe, unsafe or questionable (*McAfee Site Advisor, Goggle and others*). There is also software that will notify a surfer that a Web site may not be what it pretends to be (*a counterfeit*) in an attempt to obtain your personal information (*called phishing*). The easy solution to this last problem is to <u>never</u> supply sensitive data to an Internet inquiry, no matter how legitimate it may seem... because they never are. If you must provide some information, use the phone, and then only when you initiate the call.

I received an email addressed to Dear Customer (*note that a name was not used*) that was ostensibly from my bankcard company. It warned me that there was a problem with my account and to click on the (*legitimate appearing*) link. Knowing that this was a common scam, I phoned the company to ask if they were responsible for the email. "No" came the reply. "It was a scam".

Articles informing us about scams appear regularly and there is no excuse for ignoring these warnings. And don't take the bait by completing contest forms that promises a chance at a vacation, car, or whatever. This may be a companies' primary method of targeting you for future sales promotions, or it may be a spammer's way to verify your email address. A free gift is the price some companies will pay (*maybe*) to get your information. Even if they are legitimate, your chances of winning are zip, anyway. So why subject yourself to promotions for that one chance in a million.

For those with elderly parents who may be more susceptible to enticing come-ons via Internet, mail, or phone, try to monitor their activities. Request that they pass along all offers for your review before acting on them. If that fails, taking away their computer may be the only solution, if that is possible.

Scams that make the rounds with every spike in the price of gasoline are the (*drum roll*) mileage enhancers. Hundreds of these devices have been tested by the EPA over the years, and the few that did work had such limited benefits as to be not worth the purchase price. On the other hand, rational driving habits are free, and they produce far better dollar results… that is for those people who actually care about gas economy. Another side of this is that there are far too many of us who can't make the connection between a thoughtless driving style, their bloated vehicle choice, and the downside of excessive consumption. So what would I describe as thoughtless? Here is my A through D of foolishness...
-- Accelerating up to stop signs, and lights
-- Being unnecessarily on and off of the gas pedal
-- Continuously driving in oblivion and not looking a half block or more down the street to judge when to back off on the accelerator
-- Driving too fast toward the slower car ahead, and having to apply the brakes unnecessarily… may I say like a damn fool?

You can use your **brains** *or use your* **brakes**, *the choice is up to you. If you choose the later, don't whimper about the price of gasoline*

Conspiracy Theory

One of the more important aspects of the brain is having the ability and incentive to formulate answers to questions, even when they

prove to be illogical. Without this faculty we could never have survived the journey from early existence because survival required the development of solutions to daily problems. The downside to this skill is that it is not always be well connected to common sense. We may not spend sufficient time evaluating the answers that we come across, especially if we are effected by…
-- previous indoctrinations
-- a faulty education
-- the inducements of other
.

Throughout the years there has been one theory after another that satisfies the conspiracy buff's need to have colorful explanations for seemingly unusual events. Two of these stories that will not die are about an alien spaceship located at the government's Area 51 in Nevada, and the other about there being a second assassin in the killing of President Kennedy. Even some supposedly intelligent people will ignore the undeniable logic that it would have required dozens or hundreds of people to be involved in the cover-up of an alien spaceship and the Warren Commission's findings.

Coincidence is just what it portends to be, and does not imply or require that there be a nefarious or religious explanation to what has happened

So how should one evaluate whether or not to believe these conspiracy buffs? Well the answer is actually much simpler than one might think. Just take a look at the Watergate break-in for an insight into this. A few experienced criminals broke into an office building, got caught, and all the power of the Nixon administration was unable to keep the White House involvement a secret. Why then would any reasonable person presume that the previous "conspiracies" would have any better chance of remaining clandestine? While this logic may not answer every sensational explanation of the unknown, it likely covers nearly all. We possess the genetic imperative to create occasionally-fictional explanations in order to manage what we do not or can not know. Again, isn't this the genesis of religion?

Emotional Fixation

There are a proliferation of television talk shows that deal either partially or primarily with the seamier sides of human nature. The Jerry Springer Show has reached what must surely be the epitome of yellow TV journalism with its endless series of mentally crippled guests who bemoan one disturbing, unresolved agony after another. Why anyone would give this group their fifteen minutes of shame is a commentary on our lack of sophistication and a need for listening to prurient details. These guests are not in control of their lives, and they have no positive examples for the rest of us to learn from. So what is this bazaar attraction to the bazaar?

One talk show host admitted that she couldn't stand to <u>not</u> find out why the parents of an abused boy had deposited him on the Oprah show. Really? Weren't these the same parents being irresponsible once again? Why then would Oprah want to invest her show's time and energy on such defective guardians? The answer is because there is a ready audience for it. Stupid is as stupid does.

If one must have an over-developed sense of curiosity about their fellow human beings perhaps they would consider putting that energy to good use in discovering what our stealthy politicians are doing behind the closed doors of government. They are closed you know. Or they might contact their local newspaper and ask why they have mostly spotty reporting about politicians, yet can dedicate volumes of newsprint to cover every mind-numbing sporting event on the horizon. Shedding the light of day on the activities of our elected officials might actually lead to something productive, and not just to pointless, childish hero-worship.

Emotional Reactions

A recent medical breakthrough has resulted in the provisional development of a vaccine to counter the spread of some sexually transmitted diseases (*STDs*). Instead of having universal praise greet this medical effort, there were ever-present voices of ignorance and disapproval. So what was their stated objection? It was that if medicine were used to prevent sexual disease, teens may consider this a green light to have sexual encounters. Yep that is what was said. So the dubious logic from this unfortunate element is that we should punish rather than protect our children who experiment with sex, presumably because this is what God would want. Really? On the other hand we should remember that...

-- nobody knows (*just pretends to know*) what God might want... or if He even has any wants (*which is unlikely*)

-- our prohibitions regarding sex are derived from the possibility of pregnancy among those who are least able to manage it (*sex is not inherently evil, dummies*)

-- sexual prohibitions are a relatively recent event in our history thanks to the manifestly unattractive Queen Victoria having been so up tight (*if she wasn't getting any than neither should others*)

-- sex is enjoyable for a very good, genetic reason, which is the pairing up of the sexes for both pleasure, sharing of workload and procreation... and that basic instinct should not be and can not be denied

-- allegedly good intentions, such as promoting the sexual abstinence of our youths, does not make for good outcomes when it leads to their underground activities

-- dictating what is sexually appropriate for others is not for any stranger to say

A sexually repressive mentality based on dogma rather then concern for people is typical of the religiously indoctrinated. These people presume that they have a grasp of what is good (*abstinence before marriage*) and evil (*abortions*), and would readily impose those beliefs on others given half a chance. And they probably do not even know where the prohibitions against sex (*which have not always existed*) came from, and they doubtless don't much care. They know in their hearts that it's wrong, and that is what counts.

Not too surprisingly, a television report indicated that the conservative states have more pornography searches (*per person*) on the Internet than did the liberal states. The undeniable conclusion to this is that sexual repression creates a stronger sexual interest. And like the classic statement in the movie Jurassic Park, nature will not be denied. Even if the adverse problems surrounding sexual activity were resolved tomorrow it might be many years before our thinking would catch up with the new reality.

Good and evil are the fabrications of civilization, and they are not universal truths, as some our "insightful" leaders would have us believe

Orientation Reactions

When I was a child I thought that there was something wrong with gays and lesbians because that attitude was the consensus in the small town where I grew up. While I didn't meet anyone from this group until after high school, my peers somehow understood that they were to be derided for their unconventional lifestyle. That ignorance, which was no doubt derived from the attitudes of others and not from experience, ruled the day. While I grew out of that mindset early on, it became apparent to me that many others had not. Upon revisiting my hometown a few years later, I took notice that my old classmates were still engaged in the occasional verbal gay and lesbian bashing and other tough talk. A positive status was clearly attached to expressing negative and macho attitudes.

A number of people with an anti-gay bias will happily point to the Bible as their justification for their vilification… something about man not lying down with man. Others may offer the unsupportable conclusion that homosexuality is not a natural behavior. They might even suggest that it is a conduct which can be unlearned. This of course flies in the face of reality if one chooses to examine the real facts about gayness, rather than repeat the false statements of those who have no clue. Let me offer an insight here that may help these people get their heads straight. Natural is what happens naturally, whether we like it or not. Not being able to accept this truth is the result of indoctrination, not education or intelligence.

According to a survey, up to eight percent of all lambs are born gay and will attempt to mount other males. Similarly, one of our male cats will occasionally mount his male womb mate. On a waterskiing trip I noticed two male ducks that were taking turns mounting each other. The reasonable conclusion that should be derived from this conduct is that…

-- gayness is not restricted to humans
-- it is not a learned behavior for either animals or humans
-- there is no harm done by being gay, only what is imagined by those who have been too indoctrinated to think rationally

If these conclusions are correct, then what is the point in condemning gays and lesbians? The answer is that we may believe flawed ideas that have been put forth by poorly educated people who have chosen to perpetuate their ignorance toward others.

There was a time when the Greek and Roman cultures took being gay as being natural (*which of course it is for some*) and socially convenient, if you take my meaning. There are other cultures today that do not express the mindless anathema toward homosexuality that American's do. Our prejudices and ignorance are among the attitudes that label us so negatively on the world's stage. We are not, however, the worst of the bunch. It appears that Arabs take far greater umbrage.

An interesting event took place with the government of Largo Florida when its City Council suddenly voiced the need to terminate its long-time City Manager. The announcement was made shortly after giving him both high marks for his skills and a pay raise for his dedicated service. What was the reason for the dramatic turnaround? It was that this middle-age, married man had decided to have a sex change operation in order to get his body in sync with his brain. He was uncomfortable enough with being a male that he chose to expose his decision to the public.

While his preference probably distressed his wife of many years, she opted to support him in his choice. Even the Mayor of Largo was willing to back him. What is interesting about his story is the change in the attitude of the narrow-minded City Council, with some of the vitriolic expressions that were used to condemn the City Manager. Perhaps the kindest of their comments only incorporated the phrase "lack of trust". Try as I may, no public trust issue comes to mind, only small minded bigotry. As for the residents of Largo, they should be embarrassed by the behavior expressed by politicians who clearly don't know how to keep their unfortunate opinions to themselves, and who are not well steeped tolerance.

Apparently the 11th Commandment is: Impose your religious beliefs on as many people as possible whenever the opportunity arises

On balance, was there really any harm done to the city or its citizens from this person's choice… that is once you exclude those from the bigoted, religious right.? We spend far too much energy condemning good people just because they may violate dogma. As I have stated, religion is both good and evil, with the evil side going virtually unchecked in this country. In many ways some are as rigid in their code of belief as are extremist followers of Mohammad. And look where that has gotten them. They would rather hate, kill and die than question the validity of their beliefs.

The bar against gay marriages has been affirmed in a few states recently, as well as the pressure to end gay adoptions. One of the arguments against this latter practice is that there is alleged evidence that a mother/father based home makes the best family environment. So even if this assertion happened to be true, does it mean that…
-- all male or female couples are not as good as any mixed sex couple?
-- children are better off living in foster homes or orphanages than with same-sex couples?

Isn't it likely that those who make these judgments have had their shallow opinions colored by indoctrination, and that their beliefs have virtually no foundation in reality?

It Is My Right…

The above subtitle might be the beginning of a refrain that ends with "to have as many children as we want and then raise them as I see fit". Few of us would go out of their way to rue against that statement. Many might see this attitude as being extremely unwise, but that would be about the extent of their criticism. Throughout history we have celebrated the birth of children. In some places, procreation has been elevated to a badge of honor, especially with the production of male children in the Americas to the south of us. This mind-set may even include those who wish they could still display the much-ridiculed "baby on board" signs without embarrassment… a subtle way of their saying that I am better than you.

There is no longer a rationale for this overly baby-centric attitude. It evolved in our past in order to prevent populations from dying out, but this is hardly a concern with the planet approaching the seven billion persons mark. While our genetic attitude about children remains relatively unchanged, the world is rapidly becoming overrun with people who will eventually tax its natural resources beyond the breaking point. And if you don't believe that this downhill scenario has already started, consider the following…
-- One presumably-thoughtful study suggested that the earth can support perhaps eight billion people as long as the weather does not become extreme.
-- If it did take a turn for the worse, that number might drop to as little as two billion.
-- The population is increasing rapidly, and the resultant global warming may be causing weather to be headed into the toilet.

Those who made the study are no longer talking about running into difficulty hundreds of years down the road but perhaps only decades. In another study the verdict was that the population will reach a point of using twice the world's natural resources by 2030, not exactly light years away. That amounts to cutting down two trees for every one that is grown, or using twice as much raw material as we can mine. And given our penchant for disposing of commodities in landfills rather than recycling, it's not a pretty picture.

We may do nothing to help our children's children because we do not know them… one of our less charitable, genetic-emotional traits

The world has a limited amount of land that is suitable for the production of food, and this is being eaten away by new construction to the tune of thousands of acres <u>per day</u>. The rain forests are being decimated by those natives who use this surprisingly poor quality land to raise meager crops. They plant for the single year that the soil can provide nourishment, then they move on to clear (*devastate*)

more land the next year. As a result of these pressures we are on a perilous path that will result in mass starvations for third world countries (*perhaps reaching as high as 90%*) and food productions difficulties for the rest of us. In addition, the oceans are being over fished at a rate where large numbers of previously common seafood are no longer on the menu. The once popular Coho salmon, for example, is categorized as being virtually extinct. It is increasing difficult to find Petrale Sole. The oceans are becoming more and more polluted as well...
-- which can lead to die offs of marine food stocks
-- which can lead to the extinction of species
-- which can lead to...

The as-we-see-fit attitude with child rearing mentioned above can occasionally result in children having only a minimal education in social graces. Then they may grow up to instill their negative values and inept life strategies on their own offspring... a process that can be repeated for generations. What may not be taken into account in the parent-child relationship is twofold... children require discipline and parents need respect.

As for discipline, children need to be taught how the real world works so that they can learn...
-- how to make friends when they enter society
-- how to avoid making enemies
-- that they are not the center of the universe, in spite of what some thoughtless "soccer-parents" think
-- that success comes from both effort and perseverance
-- that failure can be a life-long burden

Without respect, parents can not hope to make headway against their children's innate wiring and the peer pressures that they encounter. The parent's role should be to instill a positive education into their children, and not make the mistake of assuming that they will be able to obtain these lessons elsewhere by osmosis. We must work to prevent...
-- schoolyard and life-long bullies
-- liars, thieves and cheats
-- children without a sense of self-worth

-- children growing into adults only to work the system and then think that they have achieved something
-- neighborhoods that perpetuate crime because it is seen as the only way out (*even at the risk of death*)
-- generations of families surviving in the dole system

It is nearly impossible to be in a public place where there are not undisciplined children imposing their misbehaviors on others. The reality is that their parents bare sole responsibility for these traits due to inadequate rearing. A child's deficiency in social adjustment is particularly apparent and irritating when flying because the rest of us can be a captive audience for long periods. This makes flying in less than first class a serious hit and miss proposition. The parents of these annoying children (*who must have known that a problem would be at hand*) tend to sit idly by, which amounts to teaching the child that antisocial behavior is ok. Is it any wonder that petty and felonious activities become a way of life for so many who are raised without discipline? Or are you under the impression that there is no correlation between a lack of training as a child and their behaviors as an adult?

At some time in their future these children will be required to find and maintain viable employment and refrain from behaviors that are unproductive. They need to be prepared for the difficulties of the workplace. It is the parent's role to see that training takes place, both in the school and in the home. Their frequent giving in to what a child may want can be detrimental to their adjustment.

Perhaps we may need to punish more parents as a result of their raising disruptive or criminal children... and no I am not kidding

An Affair to Forget

There are people in this country who see it as their duty to exploit public events for their personal gain. Reporters may be at the pinnacle of this list, but there are also the self-appointed pundits who are also eager to have their voices heard. To some degree I respect the objectives of reverends Sharpton and Jackson. But at times they have been known to go over the top on issues… particularly Jackson with his unconscionable support for O.J. Simpson.

Their assessments of the ill advised statements made by Don Immus a while back would be another example of this excess. While no one should defend the racial slurs he made about the Rutgers women's basketball team, we should show a modicum of intelligence and let the punishment fit the crime. Some sort of reprimand was clearly called for. However, having Don's radio program terminated seemed a bit heavy handed. Perhaps the initially devised two week suspension would have been sufficient. Interrupting one's livelihood was overkill in this case. His transgression, though serious, was just not that serious. It appears that the two networks which fired Immus may have caved in to pressures, or they found a convenient excuse for terminating his contract. Who knows?

I'm not an Immus supporter or detractor, but I do know that he cares for needy children on his ranch in Montana. That generosity alone should qualify him for a break, along with our recognition that people are not all good or all bad. We are not talking about an evil person, regardless of how misguided his words were or how forceful the condemnation has been toward him. What this event demonstrates is the widespread intolerance that we readily show for others. We are taught this nasty habit early on as children by the holier-than-thou who preach against some lifestyles. As a result, people have learned that they don't need to…
-- be charitable to others
-- try to understand each other's point of view
-- and especially, mind their own business

So it comes as no surprise that this mean-spirited mentality would carry over into our adulthood since we are constantly having the behavior reinforced by religion and other negative examples.

The downside for the African American community in this episode may be the message that was broadcast by some of its leaders. They were saying, if I got the story right, that blacks can be victims because the white man has the power to demean them. Don't think so! And nor should they. Within days of this event hitting the fan, the women's team was on the TV talk show circuit with their story. They were deeply wounded and told reporters that they were beginning the healing process. Healing? Really? What happened to the perfectly adequate cliché of sticks-and-stones? There could be one or more of the following thoughts in play with this incident…

-- the women came to believe the exaggerated press reports (nothing new here) about how awful the insult was to them

-- they bought into the Sharpton/Jackson scenario that the white dude needed to be punished

-- they were participating in their own 15 minutes of fame

I can't know what was in the minds of these women, but their helping to turn this event into a three ring circus also bordered on shameful. I do, however, assign most of the blame for this out of control incident on the press with their relentless, vicious, coverage. If a story is emotional, they will surely beat it to death, knowing full well that the sensation-hungry public will eat it up. I don't recall Sharpton being crucified when he made his public remark about <u>hymie</u> New York Jews sometime in the past. Most of the press let that blow over because it was not seen as an ongoing diatribe. Perhaps that level of restraint would have been good advice here as well.

While I'm not excusing Immus, I am aware of how easy it is to say something that you regret when one has to do a lot of talking to an audience. In an effort to say something that is new or different, unintentional mistakes can be made. And those mistakes may not accurately reflect a person's true beliefs.

History and Logic

Las Vegas dearly loves gamblers that play their betting systems because they know that there can be no system that defies the odds. Math is math, and mathematics rules. The more players play, the more the average loses will seek their natural level. The gaming tables are set up to take advantage of the odds, and the house will always prevail over the player in the long run. When I was younger, I lived in Las Vegas where I met a fellow that…

-- used a pre-Rogaine concoction on his receding hairline to prevent baldness - unsuccessfully

-- played a complex system that kept track of winning and losing hands at Blackjack – unsuccessfully

He was a believer, and none of the pit bosses minded that he used pencil and paper to log his play results. He penciled in his win/loss annotations on multiple columns down the page, and would stay on a winning column until he lost a hand or two, and so on in a semi-complicated, pointless fashion.

In another case my brother suspected that he could beat the roulette table with a clever betting system (*I'm guessing he was not the first to try this*). Basically it involved waiting until red or black came up eight times in a row and then he would place a bet on the other color (*sounds like more waiting then betting to me*). If that bet was lost, the next bet would be doubled on that same color (*to recoup the loss of the first bet, coming out even*). If the first bet won, he was ahead of the game. Sound good? This scheme worked for a while until one day the table limit (*$250*) was reached and doubling was no longer an option. Then a big loss overwhelmed the many small gains as the law of averages took over. Now you know why there are table limits in casinos… to relieve you of as much money as possible.

The principle which may not be grasp here about betting is that the odds on any event do not care in the least about history (*previous bets*). It does not affect the future when probability is involved. If someone flips a coin once or one hundred times, the odds are always 50-50 on the next flip. No string of heads or tails, no matter how long, can ever change that.

Generally attributed to Yogi Berra, baseball player: *"It's tough to make predictions, especially about the future."*

A similar logic mistake may occur when people are deciding whether or not to sell a stock. They will be inclined to take their purchase price (*history*) into account when making the decisions. Once again, history should never be considered. What may matter is…
-- do you want the money now
-- is the short term prospective negative or neutral for holding onto the stock
-- are there other stocks that you expect to appreciate faster

Decisions that are based on the purchase price are as irrelevant as those that are based on a coin flip. They provide no transferable information from the past to the future. Not selling a stock because it would mean taking a loss can sometimes be a guarantee of taking additional losses. I assume a number of readers have engaged in this money-losing strategy.

Insufficient Concern

A few years back a survey indicated that nearly three out of four people who were intending to buy a new car said that they would be interested in purchasing a vehicle that has better gas mileage then their current model. Allowing for those who were just being politically correct in the presence of a questioner, the actual number of those who were seriously interested in fuel economy was probably less then half of what was reported. Higher gasoline bills are the price of supporting their macho vehicle habit. As a result of this apathy, trucks and large SUVs have little mileage advantage from one year to the next. So who are these people really kidding? In 2007 the Toyota Tundra outsold the Toyota Prius. Further questioning in the study revealed that about half of the people were interested-in diesels or hybrids, which is a long way from being serious-about them. That was so long as they wouldn't have to compromise on size, power and pricing. Well where did they think the economy was going to come from... some sort of black magic? When we pretend to want something that we aren't willing to pay for it's called hypocrisy.

An unrevealing commercial touted a Chevy truck that had more power than the previous year, yet had better had gas mileage. What, a mile more per gallon? GM didn't disclose the numbers in their advertising, but they took an opportunity to mislead the public about their commitment to fuel economy.

One city made the nightly news for initiating a four-day work week in order to reduce city expenses. As a result of that policy the employees had one less day of commuting, sitting in traffic, and wasting gasoline. They interviewed a woman who drove ninety minutes in each direction to hear that she was thankful for the reduction in her fuel bill. So why do I mention this? Well because she was being interviewed while sitting in her full-sized SUV, that's why. Apparently there are a number of people who find it acceptable to squeeze into tight parking spots, tilt around corners, and guzzle gas with a 7000+ pound vehicle in order to bring home a few groceries. Are you one of them?

Then there is the inherent danger in owning one of these top-heavy, high-powered vehicles, which, when overcorrected, can lead to life-threatening rollovers. This hazard potential is still a fact of life even though the press seems to have forgotten about it. Maybe they believe the auto industries' propaganda about the effectiveness of stability control packages. The single-car accidents that I read about are mostly truck and SUV rollovers.

I live in a town where some revere trucks as a driver's ultimate status symbol. For me they are uncomfortable, mostly ugly, noisy, gas guzzlers. But no matter since the driver's feelings about their ride can be everything. When I drove a convertible to softball, no one paid attention. But one day when I arrived in an upscale, rented SUV, it drew a small crowd. Go figure! Some people just can't learn a new trick while they still have a dollar in their wallets. And don't kid me that those construction workers with empty truck beds really need the cargo space. They just need to be viewed as macho no matter what the cost.

Sure there are a number of people who absolutely, positively have to own a large truck or SUV for their occupation or their family needs, but what about the other 90 percent who drive them? When gasoline peaked at over $4.00 per gallon, some of people seem to get religion as the sales of more energy efficient cars surged. Time will tell how long that new vision lasts. After all it was the forth energy crisis in forty years, and we seem to have learned zip from the first three. Owners with a lead foot just have difficulty transitioning to "unleaded" driving.

Wealth and Greed

Just how much money does it take to have a comfortable life anyway? Apparently there is never enough for some people. While I am not privy to the standard of living that is available to those who have multi-million or billion dollar estates, I can make an educated guess about their attitudes based on their lifestyles. And while this speculation is not necessarily a blanket indictment of everyone in the wealthy class, it probably covers most of them. So here is my idle speculation of what they may believe in...

-- having the most marbles is its own reward, regardless of whether or not they can all be used

-- houses, yachts, jewelry, cars, travels, or whatever can never be too extravagant

-- inequity of gross wealth in conjunction to gross poverty is not a thought process that is entertained with any sincerity

-- privilege is earned from meritorious behaviors, and the wealthy deserve the excesses that they have attained

-- having poor work ethic is what drives people into the lower classes

-- the poor do not deserve more than they have... especially if has to come from the rich

-- government that should not force the wealthy to support universal healthcare because they already have and can afford theirs

Herman Melville, author: *"Of all the preposterous assumptions of humanity over humanity, nothing exceeds most of the criticisms made on the habits of the poor by the well-housed, well-warmed, and well-fed."*

Has anyone noticed the daily ads for high end watches in the WSJ? Apparently their more wealthy readers are sucked in to the look-at-my-watch mentality. It can't be that they keep better time than other watches.

As we may believe, competition within reason is good for society, but unrestrained competition can have negative results. The wealthy appear to be in competition with others in their class for more money, more privilege, more prestige, and doing whatever it takes to get it. They simply care little for those on the outside.

The top end of the federal minimum wage scale is set at about $16.000 <u>per year</u>. The income of the CEO of Goldman Sachs is about $16.000 <u>per hour</u>. A thoroughly disgusting statistic in my mind. Over the last few decades the disparity between rich and poor has widened with the result that the middle class slowly disappearing into the lower class. This trend will probably continue unabated until the have-less contingent makes an effective effort to attain a share of power that is commensurate with their numbers. Let's hope it does not take a revolution to bring that change about.

While power does not come from the barrel of a gun in this country, it does reside with those who we elect to represent us. So until we insist on ending…
-- the political corruption by lobbyists
-- secretive Super-PAC campaign contributions
-- obscured voting records
-- corporate backing of sweetheart bills
…nothing much will change.

In the mean time those with the power of money will continue to see that their greed prevails. Who do you think pushed through the tax cuts for the wealthy during the Bush II administration that are still in effect. His faulty use of economics did convince enough people to quell any riot.

James L Buckley, politician/writer: *"I am persuaded that in the case of elected officials, the overwhelming temptation is to conclude that it is more important for your constituents that you be reelected than that you deal honestly with them."*

Dumb Business Tricks

What Were They Thinkin'?

Power is not inherently evil, or is it? Ordinary people who have great power visited upon them through their efforts or happy convenience may become changed for the worse. They are no longer ordinary to themselves. Their inner voice tells them that the rules that other live by no longer apply if breaking them is done with stealth. The devil on one shoulder speaks to them more forcefully than the angel on the other.

People in positions of power may revert to their childhood behavior of wanting to have all of the toys, to the point where they will do virtually anything to get them. Having <u>some</u> is never quite as fulfilling as having <u>more</u>. Multiple, expensive objects can be the object of intense desire, and the exposed examples of this behavior are too numerous to mention. This need, far too often, leads to unethical, immoral, or criminal activities in their business dealings. One might think that the number of these miscreants that end up being exposed or land in jail would act as a deterrent to others with insatiable desires. But that appears not to be the case. Apparently great power, like drugs, dulls the wit.

Fleecing a company or the public should not remain a secret for long if we are paying attention to overt manifestations of wealth. One possible conclusion about this lack of exposure is that others who are also at the top of this game are playing in the same ballpark. Perhaps they are keeping their own secrets and respecting those of their peers. Crooks do not rat in other crooks.

They Auto Do Better

What may be one of the most pathetic businesses in America has been our auto industry. It once had a half dozen thriving manufacturers and is now down to 2½. They have gone from producing virtually all US vehicles to producing only a fraction of them. In 2011 GM and Ford's share of the market was less than 20% each. It's not as if this sorry condition beset the industry overnight. The downhill slide took some fifty years of arrogance to accomplish. That means fifty years of not minding the store while the executives were drawing salaries and bonuses. How did the industry let this tragedy occur? There are several factors that took place over time...

-- several smaller (*that are now out of business*) manufacturers thought that they could get away with building poor quality cars just because the Big Three did

-- when times were good and there was not yet competition from Japan, the manufacturers gave away massive future profits to the unions by granting excessive benefits packages, on top of good salaries

-- the sales model for Detroit was to build bigger clunkers, even while automobile demand was inexorably changing toward higher quality and greater fuel efficiency

-- billions of dollars were spent (*wasted*) on marketing to the diminishing number of Americans who still believed in Detroit's "bigger" line

-- lobbying congress to keep the automobile mileage requirements in check to permit the greater profit margins on the sale of their oversized slugs

-- ignoring the flood of high quality, imported cars until it was too late to mount an effective counterattack – and it may be too late (*short of some miracle*) for Detroit to convince us that they do know what is expected and will perform accordingly

Prior to a modest recovery, the government had an opportunity to provide a long term solution to Detroit's financial problems by...

-- temporarily taking over the auto companies with bailout funds and debt repayment provisions

-- firing the incompetent top executives and boards of directors

-- replacing these people with executives who have demonstrated an ability to manage corporations efficiently

-- forcing the unions into making reasonable concessions to limit the blood loss

-- insisting on building quality cars that will compete effectively with those coming from abroad

Dumbthink is of course not restricted to automobile companies. In what must be one of the lamest decision by corporate America, Pfizer Inc. decided to commit more than $87 million toward promoting their previous cash cow, Lipitor. Now this may not seem too outrageous in the high finance world of the drug empire, but this judgment was made after their patent had expired in the fall of 2011. I guess they thought that they could become the "Kleenex" of this particular segment of prescription drugs. With new generic replacement coming onto the market in the near future, this was a risky call.

Airline Cattle Call

Let me suggest what might be among the lamest of decisions adopted by the airline industry in recent memory... the Airbus 380. You know, that huge double decked aircraft that can tote a megaton of people and their luggage half way across the world without having to refuel. Apparently the developers and purchasing airlines felt a pressing need for their airplanes to live up to the name <u>bus</u>. It surely can't be that people want to embark/debark a plane with several hundred more people than now, and have even more lost bags. Talk about catering to the bottom line rather than to the comfort and convenience of the passengers. But this is the direction that our air carriers have been taking for years. They have made air travel anathema to most of us and an experience to avoid whenever possible. When my wife and I used to fly to of San Francisco (*which is some twelve hours away by car*) we experienced the...
-- transit times to and from the airport
-- security screening
-- waiting for the plane to be given a gate
-- waiting for boarding to begin
-- waiting for the plane to fill
-- waiting for takeoff clearance
-- the length of the flight, of course
-- waiting at baggage pick up
-- taking ground transportation to a hotel
-- other holdups

With all of these delays, air travel to SF can take about the same amount of time as it does by car, or about twelve hours. So why fly and then have to suffer the additional expense and delay of renting a car? Even with the high price of gas, the cost of driving is still less than air fare for two. And it immensely more enjoyable if one has the endurance for long distance car travel.

No Class First Class

It has been some time since first class travel on the US airlines has resembled its previous level of comfort and attention. While the seats are about the same, catering to the passengers has fallen off sharply. On an early evening flight last year our meal consisted of multiple bagged snacks and free drinks. This was, however, much more than the single bag that was offered to the economy seat patrons. The justification, according to the attendant, for no meal was that it was past their dinner hour. Sorry, but it was our normal dinner hour. And of course they did not take into consideration that we were traveling without food to the airport and waiting a while to board during their dinner hour.

Now in 2012 the airlines are planning to reduce the number of first class seats because 75 percent of them are occupied by full mileage point passengers or those who upgrade to first class using points. That is a mostly non-revenue scenario that hurts the bottom line, and that leaves the carriers with a limited incentive to provide this comfort. Forget that the airlines doled out or had sold points for flying in their planes or using their credit cards. Their contracts to provide seats to wherever is mostly hot air unless you fly at off-peak times, on circuitous routes, or manage to book one or two of the few seats that they allocate to points passengers on a seemingly random basis. Of course you can usually get a seat if you cough up two or more time the normal number of points. And this outrage is well known to the government which does nothing to rein it in.

Personal Competition

If you are a Creationist you may not have relevant arguments about the nature and derivation of the behaviors that are exhibited by modern (wo)man because we were all created at the same time as our fingernails. But if you examine evolution, it can be useful to give meaning to our social and anti-social traits. The behaviors that we have developed conspire to make us what we are today, like it or not. One of these negative traits involves competitive behavior. This is a attribute which would normally be deemed to be positive. Whether it is when we are participating in sports, business, or mate selection, some degree of competition is a given, and it is usually constructive.

But competition did not materialize out of thin air or by the grace of God. It became hard-wired into our brains during the search for and the retention of mates, food and security. Those who were most adept at finding and protecting their resources influenced the rest of us by having those beneficial behaviors passed on to successive generations via their genes. If there was no success, there were no successive generations. It could not be more straightforward. So this is a genetic imperative that has been handed down to us even though we have moved further away from the difficulties that led to its development. Today we continue to view competitive behaviors as being as asset, and will sometimes overlook its adverse side effects because of our conditioning. For example, what could be more unacceptable than...
-- dog or cock fights
-- drinking contests
-- bar altercations
-- road rage
-- professional boxing
-- phony wrestling
-- assault hockey
-- basketball as a contact sport
-- the escalating number of fights in the sports parks and arenas

So not all competition is productive. The negative side of this activity can also be observed in the widespread and lightly reported use of illegal drugs in virtually all sports. Since winning is the only thing (*to paraphrase Vince Lombardi, the late Coach of the Green Bay Packers*), cheating is a big part of that everything.

Business Competition

Competition rightfully exists in business, but the fight for consumer dollars can lead to amoral, unethical behaviors in that undertaking such as…
-- making secret, anticompetitive deals with other companies
-- solicitation of insider information
-- concealing cost saving alterations to a product's formula

This last item is common way to make a buck by deceiving the public when it is accomplished by reformulating a recipe so that it…
-- may appear to have been improved
-- can legally be claimed to be new and improved
-- uses fewer and less expensive ingredients without a corresponding reduction in price

Every now and then a company announces that a product contains a 10% (*or whatever*) increase in some valued ingredient. More than when exactly? Did they also reduce that particular ingredient over the last months or years only to be able to tout a contrived improvement? The answer to this question is occasionally yes. How many time over the years have we heard that the same candy bar now has 10% more chocolate? If this were true, with out incremental reductions, the bar's weight might a pound by now.

The food industry commonly reduces the amount of an ingredient in a product when wholesale costs escalate… all without informing the public of any change to the product, unless they use the phony new and improved claim *(a quality that may rest in the pen of the creative since the feds make no effort to verify it)*. This lack of meaningful disclosure of a change in ingredients is simple deceit, and has been businesses way of doing business for years.

Since non-disclosure occur with some regularity, one can assume that my negative interpretation of business practices has validity. It would be helpful to see a regulation put in place that would require companies to reveal when an alteration to formula has taken place that significantly alters a product. If their recipes are proprietary for valid reasons, they should not have to disclose the exact alterations, but a mandatory notification of some sort might alert the public to any unconstructive change.

Years ago a chocolate drink powder was introduced using a puffed-up formulation which permitted quicker mixing with milk. Since the objective of the new chemistry was not done to con the public, the puffed-up mix came in a rather large jar at a smaller jar's price. Once its success in the marketplace was recognized, the chemistry was adopted in a preexisting drink mix. Within a short time, the original product was dropped from the store shelves and the newly-puffed product was packaged in its original, smaller jar for about the same price as its previous powder. So instead of using two tablespoons to make a glass of chocolate milk, it took three or more… a significant increase to the consumer and profit to the manufacturer.

Eventually the manufacturer returned to what appears to be the original formula packaged in what looks to be the original jar's container size. Apparently there is not a sucker born every minute as they expected. Consumer price resistance was probably a factor in this turn about. Score one for the good guys.

In a similar fashion to the chocolate caper above, we should be aware of the puffing of ice cream to the point where in most cases it is essentially frozen air… no exaggeration, more air (*sometimes 60%*) than liquid. This ingredient weight reduction practice started more than fifty years ago and has continued unabated ever since, with just a few notable exceptions in the super-premium (*real ice cream*) sector. With regular ice cream, chemicals such as edible "glue" have replaced cream as the primary thickener. And law makers have permitted this reduction in quality to exist without intervention.

FYI - Did you know that low fat ice cream may contain more sweetener and calories than regular ice cream in order to offset the less desirable taste of what should no longer be labeled ice cream?

We can thank the efforts of the dairy industry for getting legislators to support their deliberate program of putting less and less of a product in the same size container. Because ice cream is sold by volume, not weight, replacing the solid portion of the ice cream with air does not require a reduction in the container size. Over the years, efforts by consumer advocates have failed to get ice cream sold by its weight (*as it rightly should be*) due to industry lobbying (*bribing*). Can you imagine a can of peaches sold with more juice than fruit and the manufacturer getting away with it? Well if that wasn't enough of an assault on a staple, the half-gallon (*2 qt*) cartons have been volume-adjusted downward to the current 1.5 quart standard in two stages to help obfuscate the change. Apparently the manufactures shamefully figure that the public does not pay attention to product sizing, and they are not far wrong.

If one looks around with a critical eye it is possible to see similar actions being taken industry wide across a broad spectrum of products, and to what good end? When virtually all companies conform to a new, smaller size, or they similarly convert their product to less costly ingredients, they are all in the same boat, competitively speaking. What the chemical industry (*who may be the biggest benefactor*) supplies to one manufacturer, they can supply to all.

Logic might indicate that this sizing and ingredient modification behavior is actually a stimulating, competitive game, and that businesses enjoy it just for the fun it provides. It certainly can't be that they get off on retooling their production lines from time to time, for no long term advantage. What ever happened to the effort to get all products delivered in standard sizes anyway? On the other hand, what resizing and other dodges do is to pump up the potential profit margin so that the corporations can indulge in the all-to-common practice of having the discounts that are so attractive to consumers. In industry-speak it is called "high/lo pricing". To put it another way, companies end up with bloated margins in order to have impressive sales price reductions on some sort of predetermined schedule. But with competition being wide spread among manufacturers, everyone is basically on a level playing field, and no one gains any lasting advantage. The winners are the newspapers who get to broadcast the weekly sales with their multi-page ads. The losers are those who receive inferior products or end up paying higher prices in order to support the advertising cost of the recurring discounts.

FYI - When a chef from the Food Channel was asked which olive oil she purchased, her response was "The one that's on sale – one is always on sale". You might do the same for the products you buy.

I suppose there may be a slight advantage to having bloated list prices among those shoppers who are more impressed with their "savings" than they are with their expenditures. Wouldn't you think that they might get a clue when there are frequent clothing sales of 70% off or more? Do they think that these businesses are in the money losing trade?

When I was a kid, the large potato chip box was 16 ounces in weight from virtually every vendor. Gradually, so that few might take notice, the size of the inner bag was reduced ounce by ounce. Eventually when the smaller bags looked silly in the box and became too small in size to be convenient for the homemaker, a colossal, new 1 pound box was introduced. This downsizing and upsizing has happened many times over the years because so few pay attention to, or object to the consumer manipulation.

At one time the 14.5 ounce can of vegetables was 16 ounces. And why is it 14.5 ounces anyway? Well do the math. Actually doing the math is the problem because this odd sizing game makes price comparisons more difficult. The conversions to obtuse sizing have become so flagrant that grocery stores may include a cost-per-ounce listing on their shelf labels for those with the inclination to use them. Do we need more proof than this that manufactures are working to obfuscate their pricing to the public?

Then there is the cosmetic industry. This is a large group of companies that have taken prevarication to new lows. Recently it was the essence of avocado that did wonders. Before that is was milk and botanicals. Then it was mushrooms. Oh no, not any ordinary mushrooms, but Portobello mushrooms… presumably because they are known to be a gourmet treat. We can only hope that it will not be garlic's or cabbages' turn next.

Business Rip Offs

In 2010 it was reported that several insurance companies had taken advantage of the relatives of deceased soldiers. They managed the death benefits, earned some 5% on these accounts, and then paid out about 1% in interest to the relatives. The retained difference amounted to nice windfall for this handful of companies. A class action suit was eventually initiated to recover these ill-gotten gains. This is only one example out of many on how big business can be corrupted by its quest for ever greater profits.

The home/small-office printer and ink cartridge business is an excellent case of an all-too-clever business plan with their: set prices low now, get large profits in the future scheme... one that we should all be aware of. There are many other companies that function in this devious way. Basically the game is to price the non-disposable part of a product near or below the cost of manufacture to encourage sales, then make up for the tiny profit or initial loss with the highly profitable, disposable items that are used by these products. Printers and ink cartridges are a part of this notorious business plan. In a few cases these printers are priced below the cost of their replacement printer cartridges. In one particular case a new printer was priced at about 30 percent less that its individual cartridges.

For my printers I have chosen to purchase cartridges from a third party supplier at a significant discount. The potential downside to this method can be the loss of warranty (*who cares*) and products that may shorten a printer's lifespan. I have experienced a few faulty cartridges that were replaced, but have not yet had a printer problem.

In 2013 Anheuser-Busch was accused, in a $5 million, false-labeling, class-action lawsuit, of watering down its beer. Their labels state 5% the alcohol content for the regular beer, while some light versions are said to be 4+%. However, it is alleged that the alcohol content has been reduced by 3 to 8% with the addition of water to the batches after normal brewing. Since the manufacturing tax fees vary based on the amount of alcohol in a product, I wonder if A-B notified the government of the change to reduce their taxes... not likely. More likely is it that they were just happy having to brew less alcohol.

Absence of Standards

As a beginning programmer I was expected to learn the coding standards for software so that the end-user would not be required to guess or research what to do next when running a program. For the most part, our community has improved on these techniques over the years. As a result, software usually functions in a similar, reasonable way from program to program. When using a program, if I am required to read the instructions before running the software, I know that the programmer or analyst had not done their job well.

Other industries are another matter. Perhaps the most glaring absence of standards is with the electronics industry's remote control units, whether for the DVD player, surround sound or the TV itself. Those who are employed to design these devices apparently lock themselves in window-less, phone-less rooms without meaningful contact with the outside world, except during bathroom breaks. The result is what one might expect. There is little rhyme or reason to the button layouts from one manufacturer to the next. And remotes do not function with other manufacturer's products.

What must surely be the worst case of remotes-out-of-control are the TV/DVD controllers which can be found in hotels and resorts. Even with my background in electronics, using these devices is anything but simple. I imagine that the hotel's engineers are driven crazy explaining the function to guests. To a lesser degree, the automobile industry functions in a similar mode. Driving a different car should not mean having to retrieve the operating manual or suffer minutes of concentration before embarking. Yet being an occasional rental customer I know this expectation is a flight of fancy.

It's not as if having a product designer who is trained to observe the consensus of standards were an insurmountable process. It just requires a little communication and compromise with others in the same industry. But companies behave like the political parties do... the other guys are their mortal enemies. It's a worse than silly position, and their attitude makes it our loss.

Another absence of standards revolves around the way that items are rated. Years back this problem surfaced when companies stated the size of computer video displays. Eventually a universal, diagonal measurement was settled on after disgruntled consumers played the lawyer card. Today flat screen television sets and monitors are another example of a standards issue. One of the measurements of quality resides in the contrast ratio (*the difference between pure black and pure white*), but not all manufactures use the same testing algorithm (*mathematical formula*) to calculate this. One company's stated ratio of 25.000 to 1 may be better than another company's ratio of 50.000 to 1. And it is not as if the one with the deceptive rating does not know what they are doing. But because the government does not oversee this process the manufacturers feel free to fudge the numbers without fear of retribution… until someone plays the lawyer card.

Excessive Promotion

If I were to identify the one business that is the most corrupt from a consumer aspect it would be the cosmetics industry. Virtually nothing that they tout to be miracle skin rejuvenation products is even modestly effective, but this does nothing to stop new remedies from regularly being added to their advertising budgets. When the initial flood of purchases dies off and they become uneconomical to promote, it's on to the next name in this name-game scenario.

Every now and then one of these companies (*usually of modest-size*) develops an aggressive business plan that is intended to take it into the big leagues. A few years back a cosmetic company created its variety of products for consumers. Then they went on a spending binge with an immense advertising budget and unsubstantiated claims to capture a share of this large segment. A research article indicated that this company was spending 85% of its income on advertising and only 15% on their products, company administration, and debt. Based on how little they allocated to R&D it's likely that their products consisted of easily purchased ingredients and did not represent cutting edge anything. The advertising blitz went on for a few years, and then just as quickly as they came on the scene they dropped off of the map, probably when too many consumers discovered that their wares did not live up to the hype.

Recently members of the automobile insurance industry have begun engaging in this same breakout tactic… massive, dishonest advertising to obtain a bigger slice of a large pie. But since huge budgets are being directed into these campaigns, how much can be left over for filling auto claims fairly, or for the rate savings that are so stridently claimed. And how can they all be cheaper than the others?

Deceitful Promotion

The propaganda surrounding advertising has for some time been used to promote their industry as being beneficial to the consumer. It alleges to introduce us to new products and exposes us to what we might need to know. Without advertising, so the story goes, many good ideas might languish in the minds of their creators, and not become known to the public. Unfortunately the bad comes hand in hand with the good. This is because there is only minimal government intervention into the deceptive practices of business. Corporations are free to extol the nonexistent virtues that they assign to their products without fear of contradiction or retribution. In some cases this deception takes the form of its packaging graphics. That is, the paper and ink package presentation of a product which may have little connection to the contents inside. Some foods use manicured "serving suggestion" pictures on the outside of the box, or they may offer the equally deceptive "enlarged to show detail" statement in their ads. How these images relate to what is on the inside a package or what is the actual sizing of an item must reside in a purchaser's imagination. In a similar vein, a soup manufacturer was discovered putting clear marbles in bottom of its televised soup bowls so that the solid ingredients would sit near the surface and look more substantial. And what was the punishment for this unrealistic display? It was a cease and desist order. That's all. Not exactly a stinging rebuke that might deter the next company from perpetrating such a fraud.

Years ago the milk industry came up with a slogan for an ad campaign that promoted milk as "Natures most nearly perfect food". This advertising ran for months before the misstatement of fact was forced off of the airwaves. Later they were back with the catchy phrase of "Good for every body", and again they were required to retract their ads. More recently, milk had been promoted as having a beneficial effect on dieting. And again they were required to delete these commercials because of having no evidence to support their dubious contention.

These ongoing efforts by industries do not surprise me because there is virtually no economic downside to these calculated misstatements of fact. Their message can be removed from circulation, but the public may remember it and never realize that it was nothing more than a clever marketing phrase with no scientific support, or that the misstatement of fact had been forced off of the airwaves. So the FDA issues their directive, and that is the end of it. No public rebuke, rarely an order for corrective advertising, generally no fines or other penalties, just a brief interruption in business as usual.

One extremely rare exception to the slap on the wrist was a "juice" packager that made misleading claims about their products. They were subsequently required to purchase a substantial amount corrective advertising. So what did they do? Did they have to explain that they had lied? No. They were permitted to advertise that their juice had a percent of real fruit juice as if that was an advantage to the consumer. After a run of these "corrective" ads and a loss of consumer interest, this particular item dropped off the map.

Excessive and fraudulent commercials is more evidence of how the government is run by big business.

A government/business promotion that dwarfs much of industries' advertising is the elevation of corn to rock star status in the search for sustainable energy sources. Yes…
-- like other many grains it can produce ethanol
-- we still have some suitable land left that can be used for additional corn production
-- we do need alternative sources of fuel if we are not going to reduce our dependence on foreign energy

-- it would benefit the farmers (*especially the already prosperous corporate farms with millions of planted acres*)

But almost no one tells us is that...
-- ethanol has a 30% less energy content than gasoline (*to be fair, ethanol is 113 octane, and if cars were specifically tuned for this with a higher compression and more substantial plumbing, the energy output would become equivalent*)
-- the energy in a gallon of ethanol is only marginally more than the energy that is needed to produce it (*a study by Cornell University stated that it takes 1.3 gallons of oil to produce 1 gallon of ethanol when every aspect of production and delivery is considered*)
-- the price of corn, corn products, and corn fed for livestock has escalated as corn's new demand moved it from corn-the-food-crop toward corn-the-energy-crop
-- the agribusiness corn producers are the big winners
-- politicians benefit from the massive amounts of money that are diverted from the loose pockets of agribusiness
-- demand for oil and all of the ills that accompany it goes on virtually unabated

If the above is not convincing enough, consider that a full sized SUV requires 450 pounds of corn in order to yield enough ethanol to fill its tank. That is 450 pounds of a crop that can not be of benefit to us elsewhere, including foreign exchange. And this use of corn has driven up the prices of feed animals and the consumer products that rely on corn. Proof of this is that in the fall of 2011 the price of corn had risen 16 percent over the previous year. Have you noticed beef prices lately?

Deceitful Representation

From fast food to frozen food, figures don't lie, but liars sure can figure. According to news reports, these industries are well known for underrating the calorie counts of their products by as much as 30%. The government may require posting this information on a label or a wall, but apparently they have no inclination to verify the results. Perhaps they figure a close call is sufficient for consumers to make "informed" judgments. Or more likely it is that they assume their going through the motions of industry oversight will keep us off of their backs.

What could be more dishonest than the blizzard of phony claims and intentionally misleading statements that are made on a daily basis by the food, cosmetic and other industries? Quasi-terms and labels are invented to sound meaningful but have no actual basis in English or in any facts that they might imply. Perhaps the most abused word is natural. There is no legal definition to this word, but it is freely used to impart the illusion of goodness to many products. Have you ever bought a natural hair spray? What exactly could be natural about hair spray? Is there a hair spray plant somewhere that I don't know about? Virtually every ad on television is laced with some degree of sounds-impressive-but-says-nothing verbiage to deceive consumers. A buyer's judgment that if it sounds good it must be good is nothing short of a fool's logic. More likely is the fact that if it sounds good it is probably a prevarication.

Mark Twain*: "Get your facts first, and then you can distort 'em as much as you please."*

As one example among many, a cosmetics company uses an invented word in their advertising that is similar to regenerate. According the dictionary <u>their</u> word means… oops, the word is not in the dictionary. It was created for the illusionary effect that it could produce in the mind of the consumer. A product with regenerative qualities must surely accomplish something, right? A number of companies use this type of faux-word technique because of the gross gullibility of consumers and that recognition of this by advertisers. In recent years there have been a number of new ice-cream-like names that are used for what we might assume to be real ice cream, but are not. These invented, cutie names are used so that the label does not have to disclose something like: this product does not even come close to being real ice cream.

An often-abused word is fresh. It may or may not mean what you think it does, and reaches the zenith of obfuscation with the term fresh frozen. So is it fresh or is it frozen? Is it frozen while fresh as apposed to being frozen after rotting? Many of us will recognize the dichotomy of juxtaposing these two words, but this does nothing to prevent food companies from utilizing advertising doublespeak to influence those who are easily misled.

Another deceptive uses of words is to describe a product using the term made <u>with</u>. This widespread and misleading phraseology works to a manufacturer's advantage because the average person will assume they are being told that a product is made <u>of</u> some ingredient or material, when in fact they are being told no such thing. Made of means composed of a single ingredient. Made with carries no such denotation. It only means that it contains some of an ingredient.

One restaurant chain claimed that their burgers were made with three, desirable cuts of prime beef. And of course they do not say how much of each is used. Is it 3% or 33%? We don't actually know because the intention of the ad is meant to mislead, not inform. These folks rightfully figure that people may assume that there is some sort of even ingredients split in the burgers. The ad further suggests that their burgers taste better than those that are made from other (*and perhaps just as tasty*) cuts.

Then there is the breakfast syrup that is no longer made with butter as its name implies. When it first came out it specified having 2% butter on its ingredients list. Now that the consumers may have become aware of its butter content, that component has been reduced to 0%. So did the manufacturer disclose this significant change, other than its absence on the ingredients list? Did they remove the word butter from the name? Nope. Instead it now claims that the product is buttery, in its ads. So apparently a claim of being buttery and not actually containing any butter is ok with the manufacturer and the feds, even if it may not be with the rest of us.

Many of the products that we buy have a similar, cavalier attitude toward the dispensing the truth. Misleading the public, it seems, is not against the law, as witnessed by the fact that there are so many corporations indulging in this practice.

Another fine product has also succumbed to the shrink the size rather than raise the price strategy. I picked up a "quart" of mayonnaise at the grocery and discovered that their standard jars are now only 15 and 30 ounces in size. Can 13 and 26 ounces be far away?

On the soft drink front, a small soda carrier holds 6 bottles or cans. The next size up holds double, or 12, as we might expect. With this established progression in mind, one would not be blamed for assuming that the next larger size would contain 24. Nope! It holds only 20… 4 short of doubling the previous size. At first glance the large case might even look like it holds 24. This is probably what the vendors would like you to think when you try to compute its cost per bottle or can. Let's see… if 12 cost $4.95 and 20 cost $8.49, quick - which is the better value?

An area that seems to be on the move is "store brand" pricing. While most of us would expect this to be an area where bargains can be found, it may not always be the case. Apparently the chain stores are finding this to be a better profit center for them then by increasing their prices. In addition there may be some deception involved in the packaging. I noticed that one stores pasta boxes were the same size as a popular brand, but the contents were 12 ounces, not the normal 16 ounces, making the cost per ounce higher for the store's product during the frequent sales of the name brand box.

An article in a scientific magazine alleged that the holistic or health formula industry had virtually no products that were, or could be proven to be either safe or effective. But you wouldn't know this from looking at the health-store shelves that are packed with "cures and remedies". Because these formulas are not drugs (*they are legally foods*), the government does nothing to regulate their implied (*or explicit by the sales clerks*) benefits to the consumer. I wonder. Could the Justice Department, the FTC or the FDA ever consider false advertising as sufficient justification for prosecution? It is easier for these agencies to ignore the billions spent by the easily-duped public then to stop consumer fraud through law enforcement. I don't suppose that lobbying has played any role in this charade.

Why is it that we are forcefully disposed to restrict those harmless activities that offend some people's moral compass, but are unwilling to deter the every-day white-collar criminals? Surely we can not believe that false advertising is victimless, or that those who are duped deserve what they get.

In one particularly egregious case of advertising, a company's package wording <u>implies</u> that it prevents colds from airborne contagions. The problem is that implying is not the same as a direct statement, and it can not easily be litigated against as a false writing. Their original packaging entreated us to "Take at the first sign of a cold symptom or before entering crowded environments". This is not exactly a promise for it to accomplish anything, is it? Then in print so small that you may not be able to, or are interested in reading it, they say "This product is not intended to diagnose, treat, cure or prevent the common cold". So then what is it? Well it's one hell of a money maker, that's what. Then in an attempt to turn their product's liability into an asset, the packaging shouts that it was "Created by a second grade school teacher" as if this tidbit of information should be convincing to anyone with more than a second-grade education. Perhaps this female creator had assistance in developing the product from her scriptwriter (*no kidding*) husband.

To date, there is no cure for the common cold and apparently no cure for the common sucker either

In the not-really-saying-anything department, commercials may start with a statement talking about how consumers want to save money. One would not be faulted for expecting that the subsequent dialog would have something to do with savings in the following seconds. But a lack of follow-up information on that subject happens far too often, and we are left with a savings-implication that is less than worthless.

Deceitful Incentives

A product commercial on TV may include the stipulation that it is available for only a limited time. Infomercials invariably express the condition that their offer has a short duration. Oh sure. That's why these same commercials run over and over containing the same time restrictions. They apparently learned this false enticement style from auto salesmen.

This may not apply to your airline mileage card, but it did to ours. The bankcard's advertising claimed to provide a coach class ticket to anywhere in the US with an accumulation of 25.000 points. No blackouts, no holiday restrictions, virtually all cities. So far, so good, right? Well there was a downside that must be tucked away in the fine print of their contract (*you know, the details that nobody reads*)…
-- if the ticket is for a short hop that an airline carrier may normally charge 15.000 points for, you still pay with 25.000 points
-- tickets are dispensed from the airline's class of least desirable seats with departure times like 6:00am and 6:00pm
-- if an early or late departure is an unacceptable burden, the flyer can pay extra fee (*we experienced $90 in one case and $150 in another*) per person to receive a more favorable departure time
-- apparently the bank that we had our card with would purchase the cheapest tickets in the marketplace, so our flight from Phoenix to New Orleans went through Atlanta with a long delay

Then there are the catches incumbent with airline-specific mileage card programs. I attempted to book a flight to Hawaii using points six months in advance of the trip. Initially I was told that those seats were not yet available, the agent didn't know when they would be, and told me to continue checking back. What, every day? On contacting customer service I was told that the 35.000 point seats had been available for 240 days before the flight date and that they had been sold out. However, I could fly for 70.000 points per seat if I wanted… on the same flight and date. The moral of this story is to plan your holiday well in advance to obtain the few seats that are allocated to mileage-points redemption.

In attempting to book two mileage points flights to New Orleans the following year, I started checking for availability 240 days out as I had previously been instructed. As you might guess, there were no seats available on any flight in and around my preferred departure and return dates, much less a convenient time of day. After a few days of surfing their web site, a phone call to customer service informed me that those seats are freed up based on a proprietary algorithm (*mathematical formula*) that looks at how fast the plane is filling up.

Big demand for seats equals few or no mileage seats. However I could book a 25.000 point flight for 60.000 points each, or more than double the nearly fictional seats. On further checking I discovered first class accommodations to our location were available for 50.000 points each. A no-brainer for me.

Deceitful Banking

If you have been paying attention you may have noticed that there are a proliferation of TV ads for checking account debit cards. I'm not quite sure why anyone would want one of these cards unless its sole purpose is to limit a child's away-from-home spending to the amount allotted to their account by the parents. Short of that kind of control, I must be missing the point. Don't credit cards work in basically the same way without theses particular limits? Maybe people get debit cards because they have no credit. A bank's financial justification for the costly promotion of these cards can have only one purpose, and that is to increase revenues. Ordinarily that might not be a negative scenario, but a portion of the additional revenue is achieved by expecting cardholders to mistakenly overdraw their bank accounts and incur penalty fees. Something like one third all purchases are now made with a debit card. Knowing the average consumer's proclivity for misjudging their account balance, a bank's income must be substantial. In addition, some banks do not permit consumers to opt out of the included "overdraft protection" plan to eliminate insufficient-balance coverage and penalties. As a result the cards can be used until denied, regardless of their negative balance. Nice! And of course some of these same practices apply to checking accounts. Overdraft fees can range from $10 to $35 or more if the balance is not brought up to date quickly.

One particularly egregious revenue-generating aspect of the bank's overdraft procedures can be to pay the incoming checks beginning with the largest ones first when there are several presented for processing on the same day. What this does is insure that the client incurs the maximum number of bounced checks. In this scenario a single large check could cause several smaller checks to bounce when only one check needed to bounce if the largest were considered last. When questioned about this policy, the bank's rationale was that large checks are probably more important to the customer and should be paid first. Sure.

Note: This practice is now illegal.

Banks should be in business of protecting their client's assets, not to plundering them with high fees and other harmful practices

Another way the banks bilk the consumer is with changes in the interest rates that they charge. You may qualify for a nominal rate, say around 8-10%, and then have it changed to a much higher rate because you applied elsewhere for an additional credit card or two… perhaps for the sole purpose of receiving a 10% discount on first-day purchases at a department store. So taking advantage of those deals can be very costly indeed. Sometimes it results in the doubling or tripling your previous interest rate for no legitimate reason. Receiving additional cards extends your potential debt and is a warning flag (*or is it a target?*) for the banks.

Be aware that potential debt can be assessed as negatively as is actual debt by both the credit reporting agencies and by the banks

To compound matters, banks appear to be ratcheting down a billing cycle's grace period to twenty-one days… down from what had been the industry standard of twenty-five days. And the banks may be in no big rush to get your statement in the mail. We have seen ours take up to ten days in transit from its closing date. So it's not enough that the credit card companies make a healthy fee on transactions, but they want more, and will think up new ways to get it.

In addition to questionable banking practices, there are the unfair policies of…
-- double cycle billing in which lenders calculate one month of interest fees based on two months of activity the first time that a less than full payment is made
-- allocating customer payments to the charges that have the lowest interest rate (*assuming that the account had been charged different*

rates at different times, even if the higher rate came first) and therefore earn more from the higher interest rate

Let us say that you pay off your credit card debt on time each month. Then you inadvertently pay one dollar less than the full amount that is due or are one day late due to slow mail delivery. The following month you go right back to paying in full. Any reasonably intelligent person would assume that there would be an interest charge for just one month. Wrong. The banks will charge interest two months in a row – potentially doubling your interest rate for that period, and it's all legal. This is patently unfair, but there is no one on your side to stop it. If you have a $5000 balance at 9% interest rate and then accept a teaser rate of 0% on a $7000 balance transfer (*which converts to 18% in six months*). Payments will be applied to the $5000 portion of the indebtedness that is being charged the 9% interest. This may sound reasonable at first but the effect is that the interest on the $7000 is coming ever closer, and is at 18%. This becomes an interest landfall for the banks, otherwise why would they offer the teaser?

Note: *In 2010 a law took effect that addressed bank policies. While this went some distance toward fairness, it was hardly circumspect. Even before the regulations became law, the banks were busy inventing new ways to enhance their revenue, such as by increasing interest rates on those who do* not *have a payment problem. In addition, those who pay their balances off every month may be subjected to an activity fee, or those who do not use their card regularly, to an inactivity fee. I imagine that this is going to be a hit against American Express as cardholders shed those excess cards that are not universally accepted. There may also be reluctance to waive any first-time overdraft fees or late charges. In 2009 the banks made $39 billion on this service, and it's likely to increase.*

One item that missed the 2010 law is how credit card credits are handled. American Express reduces the balance owed on telephone of online transactions as soon as the credit has been processed. Visa, on the other hand, does not consider your incoming credits until the next billing cycle. What this means is that you have to initially pay for those items that were returned in one cycle, and then wait to have your statement credited on the next cycle. This is a major windfall for

Visa when you consider this huge amount of monthly float as an interest free "loan" to them.

In 2011 the Federal Reserve was assigned the task of setting the rates (*card swipe fees*) that bankcard processors could charge for their debit and credit transactions. The idea was to have them more closely reflect the cost of processing. Fees typically ran 2-3 percent for credit cards and 1-2 percent for debit cards, and the cost to the consumer (*indirectly*) had grown to $40 billion dollars in 2009. For years merchants have been complaining that the rates were too high, and forced prices up to cover them. When the Fed proposed limiting bank fees to 12 cents per transaction, the lobbyists got into high gear. One of their claims was that retailers wanted the consumer rather than themselves to foot the bill. To which I would have to observe that they already do with higher product pricing. In what may have been posturing, the financial institutions said they might have to stop issuing these cards. Because of the lost income, several banks said they will begin charging debit card holders a monthly fee. So it appears that consumers may not win the fight for fair fees no matter what the feds decided.

In 2012 a consolidate set of suits against the credit card companies shot down the provision that vendors who accept their cards could not charge customers less for paying cash. Now they may do as they please, and we will see how that plays out for consumers. It will be a difficult decision for the vendors because so many people use credit cards, and they may not have an appetite for increased costs.

It turns out that Bankcard companies don't just do the banks bidding. They also play unfairly among themselves. MasterCard and Visa were required in 2008, via settlement of a lawsuit, to pay American Express nearly $4 billion dollars because of their antitrust violations. AmEx had accused a credit card processor of conspiring with MasterCard and Visa to discourage their client banks from issuing Amex cards. This shows how fierce competition for the dollar warps the perspective of big business and encourages the sleaze to come out of the woodwork.

We should note that no individual from Visa, MasterCard, or the processing company was fined or sent to prison. Perhaps AmEx concurred with the court that this is <u>just business</u>, like lines from the Sopranos and other Mafia works. Bankcard companies also play fast and loose with the credit card's business customers. When they are paid with a credit card, the transaction debits their account immediately. But what about paying the seller? They may not get their money until three days later, which amounts to an interest windfall for the bankcard folks. If you tally up how many transactions occur per day and multiply that by an average transaction amount, then total that for the three days that they can invest the vendor's money, interest revenue is significant. And of course it is not shared with the seller who has to wait for his money.

Another way that banks work against people with debt is when they are permitted to manipulate interest rates at their discretion. In the distant past there were usury laws that limited the amount of interest a lender could charge to a borrower to 24%. Now apparently all bets are off because rates in the high 20s and occasionally in the 30's are not uncommon because revolving credit is not considered a loan. Really? And with debt at an all-time high, this has become a big bonus for the lenders. Wouldn't you like to borrow money for less than 5% and lend it out for 30%? Who needs loan sharks when we have bank sharks?

Banks also use the "subject to change" disclaimer to alter your credit card contract at will. And of course this is done without your advice and consent because they know that you might not agree. Going hand in hand with rate obscenity are these contract rules that few of us ever read, until it is too late. For example, if you are late with a car payment, an <u>unrelated</u> credit card company may have the right to double or triple your interest rate on your account with <u>them</u>. The same might be true if some other credit history that you have is not perfect. Imagine that you have $10.000 of debt on a credit card and inadvertently miss the due-date on some <u>other</u> payment. When this is transmitted to the credit reporting agencies, your credit card company is also privy to that information, and they may invoke their fine print rule #999 where they can arbitrarily increase your interest rate, even though there was no credit offense against their institution. If this happens, the interest burden that you may have been able to manage on the $10.000 debt might now become unmanageable. This is all because the credit bureaus can transmit your information freely (*ok so far*) and the banks can use it as they see fit (*not ok*), and all with virtually no oversight from the government.

Censorship Express

I have taken the position that censorship, short of not being able to scream "fire" in a theater, is not productive, and it is not for anyone to promote or impose. But there are those who just can't stand to mind their own business. In 2012 PayPal, the major Internet transaction processor for the credit card companies, dictated to Smashwords, an Internet publisher, that they must remove all of the books from their inventory that deal with incest, bestiality, and rape, or they would be denied PayPals payment transfer services. This threat carries a lot of weight because of how important their services are to publishers and independent writers. While the credit card processors that are behind the PayPay initiative were not disclosed at this time, it is likely, according to Smashwords, that it was probably all of them.

One has to wonder at why restricting the publishing of legal books would be on the agenda of these companies. How is it that they feel the need to interject themselves into this arena? Aren't there enough pressing problems in this country without big business putting their religious noses into legitimate writings? Censorship is an obscenity that should not be tolerated by any society. And if these business' win this battle, where does the war end. Didn't we learn a lesson from the book burnings in Hitler's Germany?

On the good news front, a few weeks after the fallout from their decision hit the fan PayPal saw the light (*emails, letters, editorials, phone calls*) and essentially reversed their decision.

On the bad new front, there was a very public book burning of piles of three books in an author's series that included a good deal of very hot sex. One of the males interview over this event complained that the books made it impossible for men to live up to the new expectations, as if these novels had become a woman's bibles. My take is... how do meatheads like this ever get their 15 seconds of fame? Oh yea. Its that sex repression thing again.

Getting Back To Banks

The bankers lobbied congress a few years back to dramatically tighten the criteria for exercising bankruptcy because of their own loose credit and debt transfers policies? So have you homesteaded your home in those states that allow it? If not, do it **now**! This is a consumer protection feature that prevents institutions from attaching a specified amount (*up to 100%*) of the value of your home to service your debt, should you exercise personal bankruptcy. You may have $100.000 or more in home equity dollars that are exempt from credit company seizure. Once the bankruptcy proceeding are over, you could sell your home, recover the equity, and the greedy lenders can not touch it.

Disclaimer... *since I am* **not** *a lawyer, you are advised to seek appropriate legal council in order to verify my understanding of the law.* **Ok**? *And don't you just love it that I have to say this for something so straightforward?*

One final indictment against the banking industry. When the financial institutions were consolidating and misrepresenting the risk of their predatory (*insufficient homeowner income*) loan packages, the banks were complicit by selling them forward (*and taking commissions*) to Fanny Mae and Freddy Mac (*FM/FM*). Then some of them they took bail-out money from the feds to stay above water when the housing collapse occurred. In 2011 the Federal Housing Finance Agency (*FHFA*), with the jurisdiction to oversee FM/FM, sued seventeen major banks which were instrumental in some $200 billion in losses. Their suit alleged that these banks broke state and federal laws with their loan package sales. The FHFA alleged that these home mortgage backed securities (*derivatives*) had been marketed with registration statements and prospectuses that "contained materially false or misleading statements and omissions". Regardless of the outcome, my bet is that none of those culpable in this scandal will be required to enter into the restitution by returning their commissions, or by facing jail time. Wait and see.

Going hand and hand with the housing crisis are the incredible lines in the sand that have been drawn by mortgage banks. Rather than renegotiate their high interest-rate loans, they have mostly chosen to turn out owners who could have managed their debt if the interest rates had been lowered. So instead of promoting good relationships with the communities and maintaining a steady flow of income, these banks saw fit to evict people and shoot themselves in the foot. In some cases where the homeowners made an effort to negotiate their monthly payments down, bank policies prevented them from even talking about doing a deal unless the homeowners were delinquent in their payments. Yep! Talk about self inflicted wounds. While there are reasons why the housing crisis occurred, this ongoing foolishness has exacerbated the problem rather than resolve it. And those of us who were not part of this difficulty have seen their home values plummet as well.

Whistleblowers would not be needed in government or business if there were not rampant, corrupt practices going on

I suppose for the elite there can be made a case made for excessive executive compensation. They are in the upper echelons of business, and feel that they deserve to be there. In addition, they believe that their contribution to the organization far exceeds the small fraction that they receive… i.e. a small piece of a much bigger pie. Maybe you even buy into this self-serving philosophy.

As an aside to the above, one of the primary CEO missions is to disseminate the company's programs to upper management and to receive back information on how policies are working, to make valid corrections as needed. Quite often the problem with having this procedure function optimally is that those who are doing the uplink reporting may wish to put the best light on problems to protect their own positions. Or a CEO's position may not be made crystal clear. In this event the staff is not to be faulted.

For most of us, our permissiveness with corporate selfishness has led us to circumstances where we sit quietly in the shadows while the business executives make (*not earn*) thousands of times what the government sets as the minimum wage. Lehman Brothers, in one particularly egregious case, paid a consultant nearly $1.000.000 <u>per</u> <u>day</u> for 17 days just prior to their receiving $billions in a Fed bailout.

Along the same lines, Goldman Sachs Group, Inc (*GSS*) seems to have become a breeding ground for unrestrained corruption with their all's fair in business attitude… a concept that inexorably flows down from the top of the management ladder. And these deficiencies in fair play are not isolated examples. Executives at the top pay scales have historically shown little regard for their worker's compensation in comparison to their own. The disparity between one's actual worth to a company and their good-ol'-boy network of inflated salaries has been getting more egregious over the years.

In 2013 once again, an activist group has tendered a shareholder proposal to have GSS adopt an independent Board Chairman who has not had affiliations with the bank. GSS's traditional response in these matters has been to ask the SEC to exclude the proposal from its proxy. The subject of chairman independence has become a hot topic among corporation investors these days, but their success rates have been mixed. GSS, with its efforts, has managed to beat back a series of these proposals to date.

Merrill Lynch is reputed to have remodeled its executive's office a while back for an incoming CEO to the tune of $1.2 million. This included chairs for about $15 grand each, a $35 grand toilet, a $1.4 grand trash can. This is more than the average price of five homes in 2007 dollars. And we haven't touched on the golden parachute, country club membership, chauffeured limousine, executive jet, stock options, and, oh yes, base income. The chauffeur service alone ran some $230 grand. Ain't life <u>grand</u> at the top?

Insider Trading Deals

In 2010 Rajat Gupta, a director at GS, was charged with leaking secrets about the bank to a hedge fund. One of his insider tips was that Berkshire Hathaway was about to shore up GS during the financial crisis. In 2012 presiding Judge Rakoff said that this was "disgusting in its implications" and "a terrible breach of trust". So

211

what was the sentence handed down for such a heinous crime? It was two years (*probably to be at some clubhouse jail if the sentence is upheld*) and a five million dollar fine (*which is chump change to people at this level of banking*).

Since 2009 six former SAC Capitol Advisors (founder Steven A Cohen) employees have been convicted of insider trading. Four are now cooperating with the government, and a seventh was indicted in 2013, thanks in part to information provided by an un-indicted mole. This seventh person, according to a criminal complaint, was involved a conversation with Cohen and in the selling $700 million in holdings of two drug companies. This sale took place just one day before a negative drug-trial announcement was announced. Draw you own conclusion on this.

When criminals rip off the money markets for their own gratification or in some cases for playing the big shot role to their friends, it is not just about the money that is illicitly made. It is also about the money that others either do not make or actually loose as a result of that action.

Executive Misbehavior

In separate GS cases with judges, lawmakers, and regulators it has been suggested that the bank ignores their conflicts of interest and sells investment to its clients that it knows are weak, all in the pursuit of a profit. In 2012 in a very public resignation, one of their bankers in London wrote an op-ed article for the New York Times saying that the GS sells financial products "that they are trying to get rid of." He went on to remark that "It makes me ill how callously people talk about ripping off their clients".

While we are on the subject of ripping off. Morgan Stanley (*MS*) had been sued by the American Civil Liberties Union (*ACLU*) for violating civil rights laws by encouraging a lender, New Century Mortgage Corp (*NCMC*), to push risky loans in black neighborhoods in Detroit. The ACLU and others file the lawsuit on behalf of the homeowners who took out these loans from NCMC. The corporation was a sub-prime lender that has now gone out of business. The lawsuit claims the MS pushed NCMC to make the risky loans because MS took a profit at the start of each loan process, and then sold the loans before they could go bad. That left others who were down the "derivatives" line holding the bag. As you may know, many of these bad loans ended up in Fanny May and Freddie Mac portfolios, which are insured by the federal government (i.e. us).

In 2012 a portion of the Dodd-Frank package on financial reform, which has been labeled an "internal equity provision", obligates board members to take into consideration the differential between their executive's pay and the average salary of the companies' employees. In recent years, executive pay packages have been rising faster than the inflation index. I guess even the Republicans have had enough of this out of control trend. Of course, looking at an issue is certainly no guarantee that these boards will act to change an outrageous ratio for the reasons discussed later.

How Are *You* Doin'?

Just how much was or will-be your retirement settlement worth? $250.000? Nothing at all? Perhaps you are in the wrong business. The place to be is in large corporation management. Apparently there is a you pad my wallet and I'll pad yours scheme in play at the expense of stockholders and employees. Boards of Directors are aware that the more money they bestow in executive compensation, the more that they are likely to receive for their limited duties. In an example of the limited part, Condoleezza Rice was able to both head up the State Department and remain on an oil company board at the same time, thereby demonstrating how little work may be required of figurehead directors. And if she was not devoting sufficient time to her board duties, what do you think she might be getting being paid for by the company? Do I need to spell it out?

There is also a system in place where some executives go from corporate, to consultant, to director, to government, to corporate positions, and they benefit from these round-robin journeys because they are very good to others (*reciprocity in action*) in their fraternity. Not to mention, they can collect multiple (*double dip*) paychecks.

This vies-a-vie may not be a subject that is publicly spoken of, but the players have learned how this corrupt system works. As for these executives, how could there be any other rational explanation for their inflated pay other than reciprocity? Certainly it would not be that they deserve it. So when one in this exclusive club benefits, they all benefit. I have not heard of a board member ever being confronted, dismissed or prosecuted for conflict-of-interest or fiduciary infidelity.

This high level fleecing of companies occurs when stockholders don't make the connection between management rip-offs and lower dividends and stock prices. Shareholders with very large portfolios may also be part of the problem when they do nothing to correct the situation with their voting rights. This "arrangement" is somewhat analogous to the small city in California where the city managers voted themselves and their college's outrageous salaries for doing very little work on the cities' behalf. They were, however, busy putting their friends and relatives on the payroll for non-existent jobs.

Another aspect of executive pay revolves around their perks. Personal travel on corporate jets has become commonplace... and not just for the execs, but for the directors that approve this expense, as well. A shareholder of Chesapeake Energy Corp. has accused this company of understating the cost of personal travel on their fleet of jets by as much as $10 million per year. The suit alleges that there has been substantial use of this perk, along with the circumvention of public reporting rules. These aircraft expenditures are generally calculated on variable costs such as fuel. It excludes the fixed costs like pilot salaries, maintenance, and the cost of the aircraft. Wouldn't you like to take your next vacation and only pay for your portion of the fuel that is consumed?

The shareholder also alleges that the amount of personal travel involves such a "high proportion of the total use" that the fixed costs should be included in their compensation reporting. The fact that variable costs at this company do not count is an outrage to all shareholders. Do we need any more evidence that the company directors and executives have a cozy reciprocity arrangement when it comes to benefits?

***The wealthy make the regulations that benefit the wealthy – Is
this coming as a news flash to you?***

How much are we talking about in excessive executive compensation
anyway? An example would be the Home Depot's (*HD*) golden
parachute to their relatively short term CEO. According to the news
reports, after just six years of mediocre performance and much
grumbling from the stockholders, he abruptly quit(?). As a result, his
severance package was $210.000.000. That's hundreds of millions
of dollars folks. Can you imagine what they might have paid him for
doing a good job? It is hard to believe that a company even as large
as HD would not miss that kind of money. I'm sure the stockholders
and lower paid employees would if they understood the implications.

Now this executive has taken the helm of another large company,
presumably with another extravagant severance package. And this is
far from being an isolated example of excess. Packages that are in
the hundreds of millions of dollars are more common than you might
think. I read about one that was somewhere north of $400.000.000.
That is more than $1.000 per day in the average person's lifespan,
seven days a week, diapers to diapers. But not every CEO who is
terminated is treated quite so well (*a bit of sarcasm*). In 2011 Sara
Lee Corporation dumped its chief with a pay package valued at only
$11.000.000. That is not all that shabby for being fired. If you were
let go from your job, you might not even qualify to collect
unemployment insurance?

Then there were the unceremonious departures of the CEO's of
Fanny Mae and Freddy Mack in 2008 who were also given golden
parachutes. Despite their corporations being deeply involved in the
packaging (*reselling to investors*) of high risk home mortgage loans,
these two received over $30.000.000 in severance pay. That's a nice
reward for running their businesses into the ground to the point where
they required massive government bailouts.

A survey in 2011 by the Public Affairs Council found that the public
had a good opinion of business in general but not of its leadership.
And this is when there are very few people who are intimately aware
of the extent of good ol' boy networks and how corrupt the executive
compensation is in these exclusive clubs. I will spare you the details

of the numerous examples that cross the business pages on a
regular basis.

Delaware Connection

It turns out that there is a third component in influencing executive
pay, and that happens to be the state of Delaware. In return for the
revenue that it receives from the incorporations of large businesses,
the state's laws and regulations (*according to a statement made by
Carl Ichan*) coddle the directors that coddle the executives with their
excessive salaries, bonuses and golden parachutes. Delaware also
makes it illegal for shareholders to bring a legal action that would
move a corporation out of the state. So for their pieces of silver,
Delaware allows the unhealthy director-executive connection to
function unfettered against the interests of the employees and
shareholders. This is the same type of venue (*flag*) shopping that is
done by foreign shipping companies so that they are not subjected to
stricter US rules.

According to a survey more than 60% of the population believes that
the rich are responsible for creating wealth and jobs in this country…
apparently ignoring the fact that the middle class has been shrinking
for years while the upper class is becoming ever more wealthy. And
this percentage of true believers has not deviated significantly in the
many decades since the original polling on this subject. So the
propaganda that is espoused by the rich has been thoroughly
effective. The rest of us just can't seem to get with a rational blame-
game to account for people's shrinking income. Most of us don't
even pay due diligence to those billionaires who freely admit that their
class is grossly under taxed. In the mean time the sheep are led to
the slaughter, and they go along willingly.

Competition Reduction

If a company is limited in the prices it can charge the public due to
competition, and is therefore limited in the profits it can make, the

solution sometimes lies in eliminating their competition. No, not like what Standard Oil did in the early days of automobiles when it…
-- reduce the price of fuel in locations where there were other gas stations until that competition went out of business
-- then they raise their prices where they eliminated the competition to make up for the losses

Today the answer is to buy out the competition with stock, like smaller Air West's attempt to buy out larger Delta Airlines or US Air's proceedings to buy out American. Here is one formula. First, make an offer to issue stock to cover the cost of to-be purchased company. One might think that this dilution of a companies' stock might serve to distress the investors, but not in always. What the buying company and its stockholders get is the other company and all of its stock, so the acquiring companies' stock is not really watered down. After the purchase occurs, which results in less competition in their field, the acquiring company is in a better position to do several things, such as…
-- terminate or lay off redundant employees
-- raise prices with less concern because of diminished competition
-- acquire the other companies' technology and brain trust
-- reduce worker's health or retirement plans if appropriate
-- increase profits through economies of scale

The consequence for the consumer can be higher prices and reduced innovation. Reduction in business competition is seldom good for the consumer or the economy.

Oversight Reduction

We should be aware that professional groups such as doctors, veterinarians, lawyers, real estate agents, appraisers, etc. are allowed to establish their own oversight committees which function as judge and jury over their members. When someone violates a guideline, sanctions can be applied. So far, so good? What you may not be aware of is that these societies are self governing for the purpose of protecting their members against government regulations

and the public. They can then set up guidelines to limit members of their professions from…
-- being witnesses against each other
-- contradicting each other
-- counseling each another's clients/patients

Because of self-regulation these societies can act as good-ol'-boy networks which then can work against the interests of those who utilize professional services. It also means that the members can be subject to the whims of the controlling bodies without an appeal through normal civil channels. Can you imagine what the building industry would be like if its contractors were allowed to police themselves? Because the aforementioned groups are generally white collar, organized, and have money for lobbyists, they have been granted special privilege from the government that others are not so fortunate to receive. While this is not always a bad thing, it can and does lead to abuse. Without going into detail, when we looked into using a veterinarian oversight committee to sanction a vet for malpractice (*nearly causing the death of a pet*), we discovered just how uncooperative and protective of their group they can be. The same was true, of course, for the vet's insurance company.

White Collar Crime

One last thought on how we under-prosecute white collar businesspersons when they commit non-violent felonies. This is a problem that is not always recognized by the-world-according-to-Republicans who may foolishly believe that businesses are self-regulating. The numerous complaints that were made to the Security and Exchange Commission (*SEC*) about the Madoff scam, for example, seemed to have fallen on deaf ears. And where are his co-conspirators? Can one man really steal over fifty billion dollars and not have help from dozens?

Investment bankers who created the real estate house-of-cards passed on the derivatives risk, eventually to Fanny May, Freddie Mac and others. This con may have been a low-risk/high profit scheme for

the bankers, but it created extreme hardships for the millions of homeowners who…
-- shouldn't have been qualified for loans in the first place
-- lost their homes
-- lost equity in their mortgages

To date none of these traders has yet to pay back a penny of their ill-gotten commissions, which in some cases ran in the hundreds of millions of dollars. Just let Joe blue collar and try to shoplift a shirt at a department store and stay out of jail. We put our foot down on that kind of behavior.

White Collar Stupid

In 2010, 29 men will killed in the worst US coal mining disaster in decades at the Upper Big Branch mine in West Virginia. In 2011 a jury found the security chief guilty of lying to the investigators who were probing that explosion. He was also found guilty of disposing thousands of security-related documents at the Massey Energy Company mine. So rather than being a help with the investigation, he earned a date with a sentencing hearing.

In 2010 the Gulf of Mexico experienced the world's worst oil spill. It substantially exceeded that of the Exxon Valdez in 1989 which ran aground (*apparently thanks to an inattentive captain*). BP, the owners of the drilling rig that failed, has been rightly accused of several well-duhs when they…
-- drilled far below the 18.000 foot depth that was permitted
-- had not installed the blowout prevention device that should have been located 200 feet in the seabed (*they reportedly saved about $50.000 by skipping this device*)
-- installed only one switch that could stop the oil flow, and that may have been located where the explosion occurred, leaving the remaining crew with no options
-- tried to encourage the fishermen who were voluntarily helping in the containment to sign waivers of liability against BP should something go wrong

-- made an effort to lay the blame for the spill on the company that operated the rig
-- claimed that their liability was limited, after endlessly repeating that they would take full responsibility for the spill

Thanks to Vice President Chaney's assurance years earlier (*you may recall that he and President Bush came from the oil industry*), the oil companies were guaranteed that their blowout liability would be limited to $75 million... an incredibly tiny amount when compared to the Gulf of Mexico's cleanup price tag that ran into the billions of dollars, or compared to BP's $5.6 billion profit for the quarter in which the spill occurred.

It should come as no surprise to anyone that major companies would play fast and loose with their liability. Corporate America's first responses to misdeeds are denial and subterfuge. It does not much matter that it was BP which was the responsible party in this case. Other large corporation might have pursued the same course of action. Their business integrity revolves around the bottom line for the executives and shareholders (*which include the executives*). On top of this tragedy you have the deep-thinker Rush Limbaugh taking sides with BP. I wonder if that was because he is also big business and empathizes with others in that class.

By mid 2011 only a few billion of the $20 billion cleanup fund had been allocate to those who suffered damages. On the other hand, the law office of Kenneth Fienberg was receiving $15 million per year to oversee BP's disbursements while the victims struggled to receive any or full compensation in time to save their businesses (*I would have done Fienberg's job for a whole lot less*). All along, BP was repeatedly voicing the propaganda that they were doing everything they could to help those in need. On the surface it seems like Fienberg's concerns for the little guys also appears to be minimal. Or perhaps it is just one more situation where big business gets special breaks from those who are part of or sympathetic to big business.

In 2012 BP began a major ad campaign telling us how well the clean-up and recovery of businesses the Gulf States was taking place. No real examples, just verbose blather. And the press seemed to be in any great hurry to dispute the claims. So in the two years we should believe that everything is back to normal. Sure.

Undeserved Credit

It has taken years to overcome the technological problems and business reluctance required to begin producing a low sulfur diesel fuel. As frequently happens, Europe is ahead of us in the areas of conservation and pollution control because they do not permit the oil companies to dictate policies to them… as least not as much as we do. They are concerned with the environmental impact of excessive use of fuels. But as soon as the mandated European-style reformulation of the fuel for cars sold in Europe was completed in the US, the oil industry creatives were prepared with their self-promoting ads that took credit for this achievement. There is just no hint of integrity with the oil companies because their oligopoly status insures that there will be a lack of veracity and responsibility to the consumer.

Deserved Discredit

While most of us believe that there is sufficient evidence to support the CO2 connection to global warming, there is a vocal minority that is intent on debunking that theory about the cause of the current warming trend. Among them is a major oil company which has for years funded a company-line think tank dealing with this subject. In their efforts to distract the public from the peril, they offered a fee to any author that could make (*make-up*?) a case against the idea that global warming is man-made. The industry's attempt to deter the public from the notion of our planet being in environmental jeopardy is similar to the tobacco industries' campaign in the 1980's of trying to convince us that their products were not hazardous to our health. You may remember that each tobacco CEO swore under oath before Congress that they were unaware of any <u>credible</u> connection to cancer and other health concerns. This level of deceit is now being practiced by big oil with their employing several of the tobacco industries' techniques, such as…
-- funneling money to sympathetic Congresspersons who have no integrity (*I guess that covers just about all of them*)

-- engaging in disingenuous and attention diverting advertising
-- providing financial support for disinformation articles and speakers that pretend to be unbiased
-- sowing doubt wherever possible

The problem with consumers is that their apathy toward self education lends them to being easily manipulated. Their listening to what the experts have to say rather than paying attention to conscienceless promoters and politicians is not happening.

Invasion Of Privacy

Many Americans take for granted that we have the legal protection of personal privacy. They might be surprised to learn that the Constitution offers no such specific assurances. Yes, the framers did include a Bill of Rights with related provisions in this area. Among them are…
-- privacy of beliefs (*1st Amendment*)
-- privacy of a home against demands that it be used to house soldiers (*3rd Amendment*)
-- privacy of a person and possessions against unreasonable searches (*4th Amendment*)
-- privacy of personally held information… aka privilege against self-incrimination (*5th Amendment*)

As for this last amendment, we may mistakenly construe that our personal information is protected by the force of law. Nothing could be further from the truth. While no one can compel us to reveal our secrets (*except by granting immunity or the threat of contempt*), this is exactly what we do "voluntarily" on a routine basis. Revelations can come about when our personal transactions take place in the public domain, such as through banking, borrowing, purchasing, using the courts, and the Internet. And nearly all of them are recorded by those companies who make this information their own business in order to sell that data to a wide range of interested parties, including the government. These data capturing companies maintain records on virtually all of us, and their databases include the billions of public transaction that take place. It is collected, collated,

and served up to the buyers who may glean, among other things, what are our...
-- home address and phone numbers
-- religious preferences
-- buying habits
-- mortgage debt
-- family structure
-- court history
-- individual and family income
-- offenses that we may have committed

Ever since George Orwell's classic book dealing with the perils of big brother government there have been occasional, dire warnings from a handful of citizens as to the adverse consequences of having power concentrated in the offices of a few. For years we have been warned of this encroachment into our private lives, and the warnings have gone mostly unheeded. Sure, there are a number of fringe groups that extol the evils of the state, but they too are largely ignored. That is unless they address their grievances with violent or illegal action. And with their paranoid comes the imagined repression which serves to fuel their extremist beliefs. Need I mention the initials NRA as a group loosely falling into this mindset?

Who would have thought that it would be our businesses and criminals, rather than our government, who are leading the assault on our being left to live in peace and quiet? Forget for the moment the malicious hackers that try to inflict harm for their monetary advantage. Business ads and click-tracking on the Internet are pervasive, and it is trending ever more in that direction. When you browse on the net there is software everywhere that wants to know what you are buying and what your surfing habits are in order to target you for future screen invasions.

When I joined the Air Force many years ago I was surprised to learn that they were aware of a traffic ticket that I had received. Now if this information could be so easily obtained by some entity before computerization took hold, what do you think today's snooping capabilities are? A big-brother expose' revealed that Google has kept a record of every inquiry ever made by every person who has used their search engine. While they claim that they have no nefarious motive for this failure to delete, they are not spending millions of dollars on data storage for nothing. It is only a matter of time before they decide to sell this data to those companies who will use it to pigeonhole our activities for whatever motives they might have. And the folks at Google had the brass to lobby (*successfully*) to have their company excluded from a privacy protection law.

In 2011 MasterCard and Visa announced their intentions to tie their vast databases of credit card purchases to each cardholder's online experiences for the purpose of targeted advertising. These product connections would then be sold to companies so that they could provide ads that reflect our implied interests. For example, if you subscribed to an automobile magazine, you might be subjected to receiving car ads on your browser. While the details of this new form of database mining had not been worked out as of this writing, the handwriting is on the wall. Back in 2011 Fair Isaac (*the folks who brought us the FICO credit scoring*) announced that they are branching out into the new area (*for them*) of understanding human behaviors. This is not an intellectual quest, but rather it is being done to determine ways to predict our actions in order to sell that information to those companies which will use it to their advantage for advertising purposes. I suppose there are some who will not consider these probes into our lives to be much of an invasion of privacy. Perhaps they can even be viewed as being an improvement on the annoying, pointless ads we are now inundated with. Count me out on that score.

When I receive an offer to upgrade an installed piece of freeware, I wonder how much of the new coding is devoted to improving the product and how much of it is directed at nagware (*popup solicitations to upgrade to a **pro** version, or worse*). One piece of anti-malware has reverted to issuing several-times-daily nages about upgrading, in contrast to their previous monthly or reboot schedule.

Another piece of freeware (*Ad-Aware*) repeatedly tried to install a toolbar even after I un-clicked the box to permit it. When this toolbar popup failed to go away I uninstalled the software. When that did not get rid of the nagware, another piece of software that I use came on the screen telling me how to rid the computer of this persisting annoyance. Fortunately my computer background allowed me to understand and follow their technical instructions and clear the last remnants of the software. I imagine that other, less trained users just go nuts.

If one is not circumspect about paying close attention to each new version during its installation, it may download an unwanted toolbar, change your browser's home page, change your browser, and add other pieces of software that are either unwanted or unsafe. More than once I have had to uninstall offending software to rid my computer from attached nuisanceware. Sometime the software is embedded so deep into the computer's innards that highly specialized, counteracting, products are required to get the job done. Fortunately for me, I have thirty plus years of dealing with computer ills to fall back on. My sympathies to those who don't. Still, once in every few years or so I have to completely flush the computer and reinstall all of my software in order to get back to normal… a very time consuming process.

After updating one freeware product I immediately began receiving junk mail that continued in spite of reporting it to a government site. Trying to unsubscribe to these senders of garbage only serves to guarantee that you will receive even more junk mail in the future because you have now verified your email address to the bad guys. This well-intended but pointless action will likely result in having your address sold to other bad guys. If your browser has an auto ignore option, that is a useful feature. If not then your best option may be to abandon the old address and create a new one. Hopefully your contact list is up to date so that you can notify one and all about the change.

I received a series of "no subject" emails from a neighbor, which I immediately deleted. Later he sent out a warning message to those in his address book that he had been hacked. My reply to him (*as politely as I could*) was that this problem occurred due to some action he had taken, and that he may want to hone in on the cause so as to not have it happen again. It is rare that his situation would be the result of someone else's poor computer judgment, a stolen email list is one for example, but possible.

As I have advocated forever, never click on any links at unknown web sites or on links of any kind sent to you by friends. The chances of infecting your computer with this action are substantial. The only exception to this rule might be an attachment that you know was created by the sender... such as photos. But then you can never be positive of the contents in advance without contacting the sender in advance of opening the whatever.

Those of us who buy books at traditional shops can expect anonymity from those interests who may want to profile us. But this is turning out not to be the case with the increasingly popular downloaded books. The purveyors have our email addresses and selection tastes to use as they see fit because the government has yet to protect us with any meaningful extension to privacy laws. Now it is unlikely in the extreme that this data will be used in a nefarious way. However, it will certainly contribute to the flood of spam that reaches our inboxes or ads that pop up on our browsers. Then it is only a matter of time before our data is marketed to others for their own purposes, just like our public records now are. Computers have the capacity to store and collate trillions of pieces of information, and they are being used for that exact purpose.

Of course we have all read about/heard about the profusion of identify theft cases. By now we should all know about shredding our documents rather than trashing them. In spite of this there are millions who want every detail of their lives broadcast over the social networks. Undoubtedly this is because we receive a mild brain high (*no kidding*) when we talk about ourselves. But no good act goes unpunished. The bad guys have taken to extracting and using this inside information to impersonate the blather-er to their older relatives, using horror stories about needing emergency money. Then they asked to have the money sent ASAP before the story can be verified.

Dumb Political Tricks

From My Perspective

I suppose politics has always been a dirty game, played by those with power to gain and little substance to offer their constituents. It's not that they don't have the skill set to provide positive guidance and improvement for the rest of us. It's more likely that they lack the incentive to fight the system that they are ensconced in. After all, it provides them with a level of benefits that you and I could only hope for, if we were to wasted time doing so.

Our political government has been structured to provide a degree of luxury and job security beyond what is deserved by the participants. Over the years a seniority system has been developed that gives those at the top rungs of the ladder great control over those below them. Equality among Congresspersons is merely a figment of the imagination of those without a clue. As a result, little gets done that does not play into the quest for power.

It has been said that politicians are interested in four things - **Power, Perks, Pork and** (*the polite version*) **Privates**

The 2-Party System

System is an appropriate descriptor for the manner in which politics is pursued in America. It permits candidates to start with a roughly fifty-fifty chance of being elected to office, which is not too bad for persons who have few qualifications beyond oratory.

The logic that justifies our electoral process may be that a time and money consuming, three-party run-off is not required. The person with the most votes is not forced to negotiate a platform with multiple parties, as is the case in other countries. A downside to this method of selection is that platforms become inflexible since money flows to those platform positions that are of interest to big business. In other words, party positions become rigid to avert an interruption in their campaign financing. The result is that important issues for the voters may have little chance of receiving a fair hearing.

So what is this fixation that voters have with party affiliations anyway? Am I missing something important here? Is one side mostly mistaken with their particular platform while the other side mostly correct with theirs? Is it our herd instinct in play?

Friedrich Nietzsche, philosopher: "*Insanity in individuals is rare - but in groups, parties, nations, and epochs it is the rule.*"

To top off this unrealistic state of mind, some states require voters to have party-designated registration prior to voting. Then there is the ill conceived but convenient option of for voting a straight party ticket, which only perpetuates the silliness. Why should people vote for a bunch of candidates that they are not familiar with on philosophical grounds? Why should we believe in a black and white political world when life is cast in shades of grey? How did we become to be so myopically one-sided in the first place? Well perhaps it is the herd instinct.

Mark Russell, humorist: *"You've got the brain-washed, that's the Democrats, and the brain-dead, that's the Republicans!"*

Bill O'Riley (*of Fox News*) said to his credit during the 2008 campaign that he did not care about the parties. He just wanted to know the politician's positions on the issues. Unfortunately both sides were, as usual, short on specifics and long on pandering platitudes and disingenuous sound bites. Getting away with this self-serving, anti-voter conduct can partially be attributed to people's lack of ability to assess what is being told to them. If one is continually being deceived by irrelevant, convenient arguments, who is at fault…those who are the frequent liars or those who are allowing themselves to be lied to?

George Orwell, author: *"In a time of universal deceit, telling the truth is a revolutionary act."*

I was at a luncheon when one of my friends pulled out a local absentee ballot, and asked others at the table if they knew some of the people on the ballot. One attendee asked if this ballot was for just one of the parties. The answer was "Yes". Apparently my friend had no fondness for anyone from the other party or for their platforms. Shouldn't we consider that both parties have a few decent ideas to offer and more than a few ideas to reproach. So why is it that so many of us are adamant about supporting a single party? I can account for possibilities in support of this peculiar behavior. It may be that people…
-- became interested in a particular party as children when their acceptance level was high | a form of indoctrination
-- grew up in an environment (*rich or poor*) and related to those interests and the party that was most intimately linked to their pocketbook | a form of it's all about me
-- became involved with a party that was popular with their social group or their campus mates | a form of follow the leader
-- they researched the differences between all of the candidates and made informed judgments | a form of intelligence

What are the chances that the last possibility is the one that leads to most people's party affiliation? Slim to none I expect. If due diligence were involved in approaching these decisions it would be impossible to align one's self with a single party on all issues. Being an independent that decides matters on their merits makes more sense. But then we do not always use logic as our guide to forming opinions. Mostly we are persuaded by influences (*good and bad*) that we encounter and find enticing.

James Bovard, Civil Libertarian: *Democracy must be something more than two wolves and a sheep voting on what to have for dinner.*

On the positive side, in 2011 it was reported that 40% of us consider now themselves to be Independents. This is a far cry from the 10% just a few decades ago. It shows a significant disaffection with the polarization that has been demonstrated by both parties. In 2012 the satisfaction level with federal politicians was reported to be 9 percent. The decades of political nonsense may finally be coming home to roost, but I wouldn't hold my breath. I suspect it will be years before the politicians truly get the message from a mostly silent electorate.

On the Larry King show in 2010, Jesse Ventura, ex-professional wrestler and ex-governor of Minnesota, suggested that the main problem with the politics is that we are "subjected to the Republicans and the Democrats". He went on to say that their staged antipathy toward each other is accounted for by two things. They…
-- are both phony, like professional wrestling (*politicians do socialize in private*)
-- and they act against the best interests of the country (*by putting their own interests first*).

John Adams, President: *"In my many years I have come to a conclusion that one useless man is a shame, two is a law firm and three or more is a congress."*

Mother of Deception

There are beliefs that can be beneficial, and there are those that work against our welfare. One of the counterproductive ideas is that our country is being governed by the politicians for the benefit of their constituents. Even a cursory examination of their political behaviors and lack of effective governing should make these failures evident to all but the most indoctrinated or disinterested.

The reality is that our leadership has long since given up their autonomy to the interests of major corporations and their collection of lobbyists with deep pockets. How politicians vote on any issue has been subjugated to a desire to be reelected to office, which means accepting whatever campaign funding that they can lay their hands on, regardless of the attached strings. Knowing this fact of politics, corporations willingly subsidize reelection efforts with contributions to both parties, while at the same time exacting a toll of loyalty. Could their making political payments to both sides be any more telling about their motives?

Political decisions, policies, and laws are not being made based on concerns for the interests of the public. If they were, we would not be…
-- the last industrial country without an decent healthcare system
-- encouraged to buy massive SUVs and trucks for routine use
-- traveling to Canada or Mexico to buy drugs and healthcare at reduced prices
-- constantly being misled by the flood of false advertising, which now occupies about one third of television viewing time thanks to deregulation years ago (*early regulations permitted stations to have six minutes of commercials per hour*)
-- wondering why there is so much cancer while eating contaminated foods, and permitting corporations to pollute the environment
-- thinking about the cost of school lunches rather than being concerned with their nutritional content
-- spending billions on wars in countries that are not worth saving because it suits our military-industrial-complex mentality
-- having our citizen's interests systematically subverted to those of big oil, big drugs, big banks, big insurance, etc.

Does anyone think a $40 billion profit by Exxon is even remotely reasonable? That is more than $100 for every man, woman and child living in America, or over $400 per family, that is donated to just one of the big oil interests.

Changing Landscapes

When I was younger, the makeup of political parties ran along liberal and conservative fiscal lines. The questions were…
-- who paid for what (*federal or state*)
-- who had the authority (*federal or state*)
-- how much legislation should be directed toward or against business practices
-- how much welfare would be offered to the needy
-- how much social security should be given to the retired
-- how much power should unions hold
-- how big or small should government be
-- what industries should we subsidize, if any
-- do we bail out large companies that get in trouble
-- do we balance the federal budget

The Republican Party was generally known to be on the side of smaller government and bigger business, while rarely throwing a bone to the poor. The Democratic Party was in favor of tossing money at problems rather than coming up with real solutions. Since those happy days…
-- both parties have joined the race to see how much spending they can get away with because it suits their reelection efforts
-- Bill Clinton took as many issues away from the Republicans as he could – regardless of his actual political heritage or beliefs
-- Carl Rove did the same for Bush by accusing the Democrats of the same issues that were Republican's weak suits
-- political pork projects are even more out of control – like the multi-million dollar bridge to nowhere in Alaska just to make Senator Ted Stevens look good to his constituents – which was subsequently cancelled by then Governor Palin, who then kept the funds for Alaska anyway

In Recent years a change of political behavior became very clear. Republicans, having been hurt by their minority status, decided that just say no was more than an anti-drug philosophy. It became their marching song.

Another of their platforms has been the promotion of religious dogma by conservatives who can't seem to mind their own business. When Jack Kennedy, a Catholic, ran for President, he promised that religion would not influence his political judgments. When George Romney, a Mormon, ran for President he made essentially the same pledge. Their religious preferences were a private matter and were not up for consideration as public policy.

Today the advocates for religion have again come out of the closet, predominately filling the ranks of the Republican Party. They work to inflict their views on legislation at all levels of government. I suspect that resorting to a theocracy (*God based government*) would be the culmination of their dreams. Just look how well that has worked out for the Arabs.

The problem with merging church and state in government is the intolerance factor. Faith-based advocates are generally not the live-and-let-live types with a gentle agenda. They would happily put the force of law behind their rigid mindsets, and move the rest of us into lockstep with their obsessive need to promote religious dogma. Making abortions illegal would presumably be high on their targets of opportunity. Even if that particular issue is of no consequence to you, there could be other dictates to impinge on your rights and freedoms. And to what good end, if any? The world has never been well served when religion controlled the helm of a government.

To be fair and balanced, the Democrats have their share of radicals among their ranks as well. The main difference is that they seem to be more people-problems-to-excess oriented rather than the business-profits-to-excess oriented. Regardless, this does not excuse any extreme viewpoint. We need to reject extremism on all levels and instill tolerance, conciliation and compromise as the appropriate model for problem resolution and social advancement. The only alternative to this is a continuing, unnecessary state of contrived strife among politicians and little legislative progress. As for intolerance, perhaps minding one's own business would not be a bad starting point. No one has a lock on moral right and wrong and they should not be allowed to promote that focus through the force of law.

For and Against

As we know by know, politicians are continually against all proposals that are proffered by their opponents? The sport they play is to bash their adversaries, while at the same time offering little of worth in return. This is because if one is on record as being in favor of a specific idea they might have more difficulty selling their votes to the lobbyists. An even darker view of politics is that the public display of disagreement on issues is a game of <u>let's pretend</u> for the public's consumption. It is a manufactured derision that consists of posturing and obstruction. Votes are taken in the open, but the issues may be decided in smoke-filled, back rooms.   More often then not it is the most powerful members of Congress and their corporate backers that hold sway over the less powerful members.

Does anyone remember exactly when it was that compromise became a four-letter word in government?

The prevailing attitude in government is that politics is about confrontation and not about compromise. Perhaps new legislators do expect to use negotiation upon arrival in office, but very soon they learn that the boss system is alive and well in Washington. This is the protected environment where those who top the party ladder dictate voting policy to those members on the rungs below them. They can accomplish this because they control advancements, perks and appointments (*which lead to additional pay*).

The impetus of the senior politicians is to appease the lobbyists and to badmouth the opponents. Give nothing and propose nothing is becoming the political battle cry. As a result we have a smokescreen of exaggerated animosity accompanied by little productivity in Congress. This behavior is shameful beyond words, but few of us are willing to demand a change. The natural result of Congress's failure to consider other's point of view is that little is accomplished, and vital issues are sidelined or diluted.

In 2011 and 2012 Congress reached its zenith with the squabbling over a budget limit, spending, and taxes. This propensity to avoid these real matters is infamous in government, but somehow that behavior does not lead to embarrassment because so few of us are objecting to the sideshow.

When he was first elected to office, Governor Schwarzenegger of California failed miserably with initiatives that were aimed at changing the state's outdated policies. This occurred due to his going up against the entrenched powers, and he did little to consult with the opposition. It was simply the terminator in action. But Arnold was a person who could learn a lesson from failure. Eventually he set up a smoking tent where both parties could get together to work out their differences... with some success. What a novel idea to turn your enemy into your confederate.

Since politics is primarily the business of getting reelected to office, which means defeating one's opponents by any method at their disposal, using fair play or not. While a responsible voting record should be sufficient to produce these same results, the truth is that most voters have virtually no idea what their representatives actually stand for or vote for. A few may know what a politician's public pronouncements are, but this is a far cry from being privy to their actions and intentions.

When have you seen a politician's voting record in print? Rarely? Maybe never? Why isn't this information regularly offered to us by the press? On one occasion I read about a Governor's veto record which was presented as a measure of her mindset. I was impressed with the details that were presented in print. But this rare reporting was the exception that proves the rule.

Problems with Power

One of the problems with elected officials is that they have developed a system where the longer one is in office, the more power they garner for themselves over members with lesser stature. To put that into perspective, all Congresspersons are not equal when they come to their station. For junior legislators, the concept of one-person, one-vote is actually one-person, no-real-vote. They have long since been sold to the highest bidder or put under the thumb of those above them. This also means that the leadership is the major recipient of corporate funding in order to have them promote the corporate interest and policies down through the ranks. In a very public statement in 2011, the Senate Speaker told his conservative colleges to fall in line on a particular fiscal issue or risk their plum committee assignment. Enough said?

A possible solution to this corruption of values would be to set term limits for politicians into law. No congressperson could serve more than two consecutive terms. To be fair to those who are members of the House of Representative, their two year terms would be extended to six years, like the Senator's terms. If a congressperson were particularly well liked, they could run again after an absence from office. This would accomplish several things…
-- no congressperson would have more than one wasteful reelection campaign
-- politics would be more inclined toward public service rather than providing a job haven
-- lobbyists would have little incentive to give money to congresspersons for their loyalty because they could become independent, lame duck politicians if reelected
-- the need to cultivate lobbyists would be so abated that the congresspersons might actually vote on the citizens behalf
-- the powers of congressional leadership would be drastically diminished by virtue of shortened terms and diluted seniority
-- it is likely that the cast system, with committee heads holding most of the power, would come to an end

Jesse Ventura, ex-governor of Minnesota: *"Politics is the worst business in America."*

A friend of mine had a chance to travel with a Congressperson on a fact finding mission and was stunned to see what a thirst for power this person had…
-- kiss-up assistants were at his beck and call
-- no request for frivolous service would be turned down
-- he ate at the best restaurants, with food and drink prices meaning nothing because they were paid for by the public
-- special favors were expected and given wherever he went

So is it any wonder that these "representatives" sell their votes so easily to stay in office? Their attitude of entitlement also rubs off on the President and his wife. It has been reported that while First Ladies generally had two or three assistants, Michelle is said to retain in the neighborhood of twenty. Dare we say there are visions of royalty dancing through her head? And of course there are the pointless trips that the President takes at taxpayer expense.

Speaking of Speaking

It is interesting to note <u>when</u> it is that a politician is "outraged" enough to make an issue of something. It predominantly occurs when they are defending their misbehaviors or are seeking reelection to office in a tight race. The insiders in Washington are of course privy to why this pompous rhetoric takes place. So Congresspersons apply the appropriate grain of salt to what is being said, even when they are a target. They also know that their fellow politicians do not ordinarily go out on a limb because they have much to lose. They...
-- must first run their ideas past the powers that be, or risk censure if they step outside of the party line (*Just look at the Republican pinhead in 2010 that defended BP, and quickly offered the lame apology that he was misunderstood. He had been confronted by the leadership and told to retract his statement or step down from a prized committee post*)
-- can lose precious bargaining chips that can be bartered with other politicians or lobbyists
-- might risk alienating some of their voters by being candid
-- can not easily deny what they say in public

Remember the line from The Godfather or the advice that Jackie Kennedy-Onassis ostensibly received from her mother? It went something like: Never tell anyone what you are thinking *(so they can't use it to your disadvantage)*. For this and other reasons, our politicians rarely express their innermost thoughts unless they are desperately in need of publicity for their home campaigns or committee posts.

Sound Bite Politics

With the advent of campaign war chests and frequent access to TV broadcast time, politicians have long since discovered that the seconds-long ads work well for them. This politicking technique succeeds because a message can be delivered to the public without their having an opportunity for return information (*criticism*). As a result, these nearly valueless sound bites are not challenged as they might be in a debate or community forum. The consequence of this format is that…
-- there is a lack of pertinent information disseminated because image creation, not content, is the agenda
-- opponents are painted with false or negative ads that serve no educational reality, but they may stick in voters minds when they go to the polls
-- issues and platforms are typically ignored in an effort to avoid offending anyone, with platitudes ruling the day
-- the press contents itself with news about $400 haircuts, slip-of-the-tongue and other "issues" because they are in business of creating sensationalism for a scandal-thirsty public

The sound bite politics employed today have several implications in that they…
-- show a shameful disrespect for the voter by not delivering information
-- isolate politicians from experiencing or having to responding to contradictory points of view
-- permit politicians to imagine that they have an understanding of new bills - which they don't since they may not even read the laws that they vote on
-- turn politics into show business

No Where to Turn

Those of us who have an interest in in-depth information about our government's apparatus may be relegated to receiving their political analysis (*he says humorously*) from comedians like Bill Maher and

John Stewart. The problem with this venue is that their guests are predominantly liberal, and they may not have balanced presentations. Don't conservatives have something constructive to say, or even have a sense of humor? If you watch people like Hannity of Fox News, fairness can be as ethereal as a light breeze. He's a liberal basher in the extreme, which involves the repetitive voicing of innuendos and falsehoods.

The problem associated with many of the media's talking heads is that they anchor "news" programs which are populated with biased reporters and guest propagandist who…
-- have no solutions
-- show no insightfulness
-- espouse mostly anti-opponent-party lines

When they happen to book an opposing point-of-view spokespersons at the same time, the airwaves are filled with…
-- annoying childish banter
-- irrelevant arguments
-- frequently interrupted statements

All of this verbal nonsense may leave voters with the accurate feeling that there is no one listening to them, and that they might have no better choice than to give up on the system. Not so surprisingly this attitude works to the advantage of the incumbent politicians. They are then free to carry out their re-election efforts with minimal scrutiny from voters.

When there is the occasional criticism from the press, news editorials or public protest, it rolls off politicians like the proverbial water off a duck's back. They clearly have more important business to focus on, which does not often involve listening to their constituents. So much for representative democracy. While the Constitution framers wrote in fairly effective checks and balances on the three branches of government, someone forgot about addressing the (non)performance of elected officials.

Coffee or Tea Anyone

In 2009 and 2010 we saw the creation of the liberal Coffee party and emergence of the conservative Tea party. The latter came into being as a reaction to two situations… a lack of effective political leadership and the frenzy that was whipped up by the polarizing talking-heads. They gave people the impression that they were not being listened to (*nothing new here*) and that Congressional spending was heading the country toward bankruptcy (*we all know about the downgrading of the US's credit rating*). While there may be something positive to say for both parties' ideas, people have not gotten the idea that voting an incumbent out of office is more effective than blowing a lot of hot air at town meetings. What better method do we have to send a message to the ineffective Congresspersons than to remove them from office?

Vote for the opponent - the incumbent has already become corrupted

Holy Clinton-ism

On The Daily Show, Bill Clinton was a guest in 2008. He suggested that politicians have a really tough job, and that this is why they may be beholding to Political Action Committees (*PACs*). If you buy this self-serving drivel, politicians have to spend most of their time flying from Washington to their home states in order to raise campaign funds, to the point of exhaustion. Well, who developed that system anyway? You? Me? Hardly! It was the incumbent politicians who wanted to maintain an edge over their rivals so that they could remain in office without having to resort to merit, even though they know that the current system is corrupt and legislatively ineffective. Should we feel sorry for them?

If politicians wanted to correct the election process, they have the power to make if happen. After all they make the laws, don't they? They managed to pass the best health and retirement benefits in the world for themselves, right? The reality is that reelection to office is far more important to them then is their public duty. Bill's whimpering about their difficulties is nothing short of a pathetic vehicle used for creating a diversion, one which attempts to shield politicians from their irresponsibility. My guess is that he made these statements because he did not want to be tainted by the negative truth about campaigning, or its potential exposure to the sleeping public.

The Election Process

In spite of being repeatedly told that every vote counts, the reality is that every vote is worth (*ta da*) exactly one vote, or virtually nothing. The pundits and politicians love to point out the one or two small town elections that were decided by a single or handful of votes as proof of their thesis. The reason that we are constantly fed this propaganda is because it is a deliberate effort to prevent people from realizing of how powerless they actually are on their couches. It does not take a mathematician to recognize that one vote out of ten million equals exactly one ten-millionth of the total number, a really tiny fraction. If the people are told and therefore believed that they can be effective in controlling the political process, then those who are actually in control can reside comfortably, unrecognized in the ether.

From another perspective, your vote may actually turn out to be worth nothing, no matter who it is cast for. It's called Super Delegate. This is where the party faithful assign themselves delegate status without ever being voted in by the citizens. With the Democratic Party (*now isn't that a misnomer*), one fifth of the delegates to their conventions are these unelected good-ol' boys and girls. They can cast their vote for any candidate they choose, and they are responsible only to themselves. They are free to make backroom deals with whomever they choose, for their own benefit if they so desire. Short of the unlikely potential of a public opinion having some power over super-delegate voting, we have no controls levied upon them. Perhaps the most disturbing aspect is that when asked, these same people will defend this system in spite of its glaring injustice. This is why your one ten-millionth of the total vote may be worth zero. I assume you appreciate standing in a long line to vote, right?

When I (*especially*) watch the Presidential election process, there is an inescapable conclusion that comes to mind. The real power brokers must be amused at the pointless, non-issues-raising talk that constitute the debates, speeches, and sound bites that are made by the candidates and their surrogates. Don't those of us who watch these charades know the difference substance and pontificating? Don't they actually know that government doesn't work, and why that is? Is there a minutia of consciousness among the voters as to who is actually running the country, and just what they are up to behind the scenes? The answer to all of the above questions is a resounding No!

When we don't pay attention, we deserve the results. Good government is not an accident. Rather it is the result of people having knowledge and concern about its activity. The net is that big business runs America in the background, and they do not much care who happens to gets into office. They must be pleased that their control of politics is seldom revealed or is obscured by those doing their bidding.

In 2008 the Democrats took control of Congress and then what? Virtually nothing changed from when the Republicans had the power. There is just more bickering to cover up the fact that all of the politicians are beholden to the same business interests that throw money at both parties. And that they share the same obligations to provide these businesses with their service. Could it really be any other way with our morally and ethically corrupt two-party system? Why do you think there is so much inertia against...
-- third party candidates
-- universal healthcare
-- government negotiated drug prices
-- reasonable term limits
-- a simplified tax system

Why do you think there is so much legislation that is skewed in favor of...
-- investors and business – laughingly justified by the unproven "trickle-down" theory
-- tax incentives for big oil, while they make billions of dollars in excessive profits
-- hundreds of loopholes for the rich that most people will never know about, much less be able to use

-- subsidies that were originally designed to benefit mom and pop farms but now are mainly used to support corporate agribusiness …and the beat goes on.

Owning Your Mistakes

There is something dysfunctional in our nature that induces us to unnecessarily cover up failures, shortcomings and mistakes,. especially with politicians. Because the press can occasionally be ruthless in its quest for sensationalism (*as opposed to news*) this may be an almost understandable practice. No one wants to be put in the awkward position of having to defend a reasonable past behavior by responding to the slanted interrogations of the sensation seekers. It takes valuable time and detracts from more important issues. Even a lie will stick if it is given enough air time. But this fact of political life does nothing to justify the wide-spread deceit and corruption that is endemic in our elected officials.

John Kennedy took an unusual action for a politician some time ago by taking the blame for the militaries' Bay of Pigs fiasco in Cuba while President, even though it might rightfully have been attributed to a CIA intelligence failure. His mea culpa garnered him respect and contributed to a boost in his popularity. On the other hand, Richard Nixon denied his guilt in the Watergate cover-up for as long as he could manage, and was consequently induced to resign in disgrace. This personality defect caused him to preferred lying over revealing his flawed and felonious judgment.

John Fitzgerald Kennedy, President: *"An error doesn't become a mistake until you refuse to correct it."*

A press created issue a few years back involved an attack on the waterboarding of captured terrorists. In 2013 Rudi Giuliani, in a discussion about drone attacks, said the George Bush would not have gotten away with Obama's drone policy, as witnessed by the flack he took over water waterboarding. My take on this is that it only became an issue because of the administration's cover-up, not the appropriateness of the interrogation technique. Politicians just don't get that lying changes everything.

In 2011 when Congresswoman Giffords was shot in Tucson, the press was quick to blame vitriolic politicians and talking heads for their violence-inciting rhetoric. While I am inclined to support a degree of this logic, they went off the charts in singling out Sarah Palin (*no fan of mine*) for using gun-sight cross-hairs on her target map of the candidates that she wanted to be defeated in the 2010 elections. Then to compound matters, her staff claimed that these icons were surveyor crosshairs. Now Sarah is a woman who lives with guns and not surveying equipment. So rather than copping to a rather innocent use of this icon, she and her staff chose to fabricate a less than believable explanation.

People are generally forgiving of mistakes when the offender owns up to their gaffe and expresses contrition. When they don't, that's another matter. For politicians, the first line of defense is lying.

While I'm referring to guns, the right wing took the position (*once again*) that guns don't kill people, people do. This of course flies in the face of the correlation between too many guns and too many shootings. In the case of Giffords, a congressman suggested that there was no merit to limiting gun clips to ten rounds to prevent similar massacres. He said that he would be able change to a new clip in mere seconds. This lightweight thinker conveniently lost track of the fact that Gifford's shooter was tackled while trying to load another clip.

The Distraction Factor

Because Congress and the administration are all members of the same exclusive club, they will depart only so far from the norm to berate a fellow colleague. Yes, they rant on over petty issues about the other party to the ears of the voters, but they do not often engage in personal or meaningful attacks, except against their opponents during elections when their job survival is at stake. This stands as a bipartisan effort at political self-preservation.

In a 2008 hearing, the head of the Justice Department was exposed for giving false testimony to a Congressional committee, which is a felony. So did he lie? Apparently not! Did he go to jail? Not that either! Then when a politician was asked to comment on the situation, instead of offering an honest opinion he responded that the person had been "inaccurate", which amounts to a lie about a lie.

Political credo: *If I don't reveal your lie, you may not expose mine*

Dumb Government Tricks

The Secrecy Factor

When the politicians are not directly covering up their own corruption or obscuring their personal agendas, they may be actively engaged in promoting a veil of government secrecy which appears to be increasing in its rate of occurrence. This is in no small part due to a lackadaisical press (*which should come as no surprise*) that benefits from their relationships to those in power. Secrecy occurs when...
-- Presidents invoke Executive Privilege
-- self-serving document are classified
-- politicians exaggerate national security issues
-- the State Secrets Act is used to prevent information from being given to the courts (*since the courts can view evidence in chambers that is sensitive in nature, why should we prevent them from doing this when state-secret are involved?*)

Administrations engage in a policy of: no disclosure is better than some. The less that is revealed to the public, the less they can be criticized for, or perhaps jailed for. We suffer from government imposed secrecy in a myriad of ways. There are more than 1.000.000 people with the authority to classify information, or about one out of every four hundred men, women and children in this country. How many of these people do you think mark a document classified to save their own behinds?

Short of having the Freedom of Information Act (*FOI*) invoked, politicians are relatively free to operate in an environment which may be impenetrable to the public. And little is being done to prevent this according to a coalition of 67 organizations (*whose findings are rarely reported by the press*) that are dedicated to increasing government openness...
-- In 2007 the number of recorded decisions to classify documents was an astounding 242.000 (*how did they even find the time?*)

-- From 1953 to 1976 (*23 years*), the State Secrets privilege was used six times, but in the eight years since 2001 it had been used thirty nine times.

-- In 2000, 45 percent of government contract dollars were awarded under open competition. By 2006 only 34 percent of these contracts were awarded in this manner. Now you know why Cheney's old company Halliburton is still doing business in Iraq in spite of being accused of overcharging $billions.

Apparently this predilection towards secrecy has not been lost on state governments either. Since 2001 the state legislatures have passed more than 50 bills that expand their executive powers, impose confidentiality based on dubious federal regulations or programs, and close public meetings for alleged security reasons. Just what kind of security needs do the states have that the public does not have a right to know? Can you name even one thing, other than an occasional personal personnel consideration, that justifies a closed session?

There is even a veil of secrecy for those who donate big bucks to Presidential libraries. So why would these benefactors care about a President who is deceased? Well if you believe that these libraries do not act as propaganda organs for those companies and individuals who have benefited from close Presidential relationships, hmmm. These libraries should not be used to promote editorial content if their mission is the unbiased presentation of historical materials. They are, however, not so detached from outside influences. They are in the business of portraying a President's term in the best light possible. And that includes obfuscating dubious associations with others who may not want the true light of day cast on their activities.

Freedom of Information

The FOI act was design to open up the government to public scrutiny, but it is frequently thwarted by and effective tactic of administrative delays. Officials in want of privacy are becoming adept at throwing up procedural roadblocks that prevent divulging what they are up to.

If you would like to know more about this subject go to…
www.openthegovernment.com

An aspect of government secrecy that puzzles me is that we all have to live under this same system of rampant dishonesty. Our legislators are not exempt from the repercussions, just as we are not. They may initially achieve some short term personal gain while they are in office, but that ends at some point in time. So why do they feel the need to corrupt government for everyone including themselves and their children? Are they that myopic? The obvious answer is reelection.

Even when we expose governmental misdeeds there is little penalty for bending the rules or breaking the law. When agencies are asked to provide relevant data regarding a particular subject under investigation by Congress, some of that information may be left out. An investigation of the treatment of terrorist prisoners at our base in Cuba is a case in point. After the initial inquiry took place it was revealed that the CIA had destroyed videotapes of the persons who were tortured to extract information. Allegedly this was done to protect the identity of those agents involved in conducting the "questioning". Forget that their images could easily have been obscured to prevent identification. So the CIA broke the law by not retaining the tapes, and then they went on to fabricate a lie about their justification for doing so. Wouldn't you think that someone might be punished for this? Once again, apparently not!

Later there was another investigation of the original investigation whose only purpose was to embarrass the administration, and was not intended to right a wrong. Bringing the felon(s) to justice rarely occurs to in Congress, and rarely do any of these public servants lose their job for breaking the law.

Government Missteps

Government policies sometime have catastrophic repercussions. In the distant past, the denial of resources to the South prior to the US Civil War was a precursor of the prohibition that was used against the

Japanese which consequently brought them into WWII. We limited their access to the raw materials that could be used to further their expansion plans, and they vigorously objected to that restriction. This an example of how politician's propensities for using antagonism (*power*) can often trump using diplomacy.

While the appeasement policy toward Germany's aggression by Neville Chamberlain of Great Britain was a catastrophic failure, it should not have colored our national posture as much as it has. Since that ill-fated lesson of not relying on negotiations occurred we have participated in four major wars, with little to show for it in the last two… Vietnam and Iraq-Afghanistan-Pakistan. How long will it take for us to balance force with intellect.

When President Carter went on a fact finding trip in 2008 and talked to Hamas there was much criticism, especially from Israel and Israel promoters, for his engaging in that effort. How does communicating with an advisory get such a bad rap? Don't we have a State Department with this very mandate? To top off our imperfect Mid-East policy, we fail to negotiate in good faith with Iran, Hamas and Palestinians. We continue to set preconditions which are routinely rejected. Some countries enjoy poking the bully in the eye.

Jimmy Carter, President: *"Since Clinton left office there hasn't been a single day of good-faith peace talks between Israel and the Palestinians orchestrated by Washington. It is terrible and tragic and counterproductive to avoid communicating with people who disagree with us."*

Palestinian Oppression

First let me say that I am not a bigoted Jew basher. I have had many acquaintances and good friends over the years that were Jewish. My opinions reflect a lack of respect for some of the unfortunate attitudes that are manifested by government of Israel, and nothing more.

For years there has been an ongoing "Palestinian problem" that has not been properly addressed by this country, Israel or other nations around the world. The Palestinians quite rightly do not want to be oppressed by the Israelis that surround them on nearly all sides, and they will occasionally lash out violently against their landlords. Because their home land is being boycotted, they are at the mercy of Israel in nearly every direction. They have no…

-- trade route highways that are not subject to closure without notice or justification
-- ports that they are able to ship and receive goods from
-- real industry of their own (*who would order a product with an irregular delivery schedule?*)
-- permission to collect taxes to pay for fire, police, teachers, and infrastructure (*as if that is any of Israel business*)

In affect Palestine is a reluctant colony of Israel, and they have been subjected to harsh penalties when resisting their treatment. Because of these circumstances, 42% of the people who voted in their last election cast their ballots for Hamas, the armed resistance. This was surely because the Palestinians have seen their country routinely taken from them by…

-- Israeli settlements (*some 200 of them*)
-- roads within their country that they not permitted to cross even to get to their own fields
-- a forty foot high wall that separates them from sections of their own lands, and is manned by checkpoints

It does not take a genius to see that what is going on here is theft of land on a grand scale… not to mention a theft of dignity. How would you react if the states which surround yours …

-- decided to prevent the free exit and entry of goods and people between your state and its neighbors
-- forced some of your people off of their land in order to build new subdivisions for themselves
-- prevented you from having a tax-paid government to manage your affairs independently

You too would be furious I presume. In 2010 an advocate for Israel stated on a talk show that giving back territory to the Arabs was the worst thing they could do. Oh really? Maybe he should take a look at what giving up nothing for decades has accomplished. I guess that using someone else's land as a war buffer is deemed to be a valid excuse for domination.

The act of negotiating a lasting peace does not seem to garner much interest with Israelis. A possibility that may account for the conflicts that the Israelis have with their neighboring countries could be in the way that they live in the past. Their national psyche of insisting on remembering the Holocaust may act as a paranoia that prevents them from realistically dealing with the present. In addition, some Orthodox Jews use the Torah to justify their attacks on their neighbor. This is how a rigid, religious mindset works against peace while encouraging the wrath of other Middle Eastern countries.

In 2011 the Palestinians petitioned the United Nations to recognize them as a state. President Obama voiced strong objections regarding this matter. Apparently he feels that it is more important to placate the Israelis rather than to give colonized peoples their right to self-government. Haven't we been down this road for far too many years with only poor results?

Jordan's King Abdullah: *"Israel must choose between living with the mentality of Israel-the-fortress or living in peace and security with its neighbors."*

Why We Participate

A side effect of the "Palestinian Problem" is that the US has aligned itself with and financially supports the Israeli's repression. Unlike the more balanced European reporting, our press is shameless in their biased, limited information on this subject. As a result we are seldom privy to the inner happenings of the conflict, and we are then supplied with disinformation that is more sympathetic to the Israeli view then is it to the reality of the Middle East. As a consequence of this propaganda, the attitude of our nation is skewed in the direction where the Middle East countries barely tolerate us. The likely outcome of this situation is...
-- the world's continued dislike of Israel by moderate countries
-- intense hatred of Israel by Arab countries

-- more world terrorism

Is it worth that? Do we really think that some countries desire (*so they say*) to see Israel erased from the map is for no reason? And the world's generally-negative attitude toward them rightfully rubs off on the US for its complicity in this matter. It has been many years since we experienced the cold war and the degree of hatred toward the US that the Soviet Union was able to whip up until now. Being a balanced, responsible, and not overbearing member of the world community is an answer to the conflict, but we don't seem to get it.

My argument is not to castigate Israel as a whole but to identify the forces within its borders and ours that knowingly and through gross ignorance are preventing a Palestinian solution. From all its appearances this tragedy is being perpetuated by a powerful political coalition (*and their supporters in this country*) with land to gain. What is it about Israel that induces the US to support their colonialism to the tune of billions of dollars per year in military aid and handouts? We would surely not consider this level of funding for any other country.

We berate Russia, China and others for their repeated human rights violations, but remain strangely mute on the Palestine issue. Are we ignorant of what is happening, or is there something else at play that only the insiders know? How did having a discussion of this subject become so untouchable to questioning?

Once again we have positioned ourselves as the ugly Americans

The Viet-raq Wars

If we are to learn anything useful about politicians from our history, the war in Vietnam should have been a training ground. For those who remember the events of the '60s, they taught us that…
-- Americans like to trust their military leaders in spite of their often demonstrated lack of veracity
-- Presidents can not be trusted to tell us the truth when they have a hidden agenda, which is far too frequent

-- high level advisors in government survive their terms, often without integrity, because they are in the business of saying yes
-- the generals and the CIA will parrot whatever the White House demands until they are out of office, at which time a touch of integrity may strike
-- the regular troops in the field are never listened to because they might have honest, derogatory opinions
-- it is extremely difficult to control or oppress a people in their homeland because they have much more at stake than the invading foreigners ever will – look at how the Afghans (*with our hardware*) were able to force the Russians out
-- brute force is not a substitute for brains

In order to justify the war that we started in Vietnam we were told that...
-- a patrol boat attacked (*really?*) our ship, and that is what justified the "police action" for us
-- we needed to make the world safe for democracy
-- if South Vietnam fell to the North, the Russians and Chinese would spread Communism throughout the area and the neighboring countries would fall like dominos
-- people would be oppressed and millions would starve

What we were not told was that we wanted to develop Vietnam's coastline for oil. Well we lost the war, and oops, none of the above ever came true.

In the war for pacifying Iraq we were again implored to believe that...
-- they were building weapons of mass destruction, and that is what justified the invasion for us
-- we needed to make the world safe for democracy
-- if Iraq fell to the terrorists they would spread Islamic law and extremism through the area
-- countries will fall like dominos

We were not told was that our primary motivation was to secure the stability of Iraq's oilfields. Maybe we should have lost the war (*by going home*) and see what would have actually happened.

Since we are almost universally disliked by Middle Eastern countries and tolerated by some European countries, when we are gone they will only have Israel to focus on, which seems to be able to take care of itself. If we went home, the militant's stated reason for hostility (*our invading their land*) would be neutralized, and perhaps they might even want to get on with their lives. As it stands now, we are the Great Satin, which is an idea that their leaders utilize to rally millions of people to their cause. No great satin, no rally! Or is that too simple an idea for the pinheads in Washington to comprehend. Obviously it was for the Bush/Obama crowd.

Arab conquest of lands and people, which has been going on for centuries, has been replaced with a kind of religious multi-nationalism. It is not a single country that they represent, just one religiously-minded group. We are in their lands and they can be stirred up into hating us for it, just as they have always hated invading peoples. So why don't we get out of Arabia, mind our own business, and let them kill each other instead of us? Spending hundreds of billions of dollars in Iraq, Afghanistan and elsewhere has no obvious justification. The predictable results have been...
-- thousands of US soldiers dead
-- tens of thousands of US soldiers wounded
-- a near depression
-- a continued decline in our world stature

Denial of Culpability

For generations the US government has lived under the shadow of disrespect with many second and third world counties. Even when the Soviet Union was in its most repressive heyday, most of the world's non-European countries were leaning toward or actively supporting the USSR. Why? Since the end of WWII the US has shown a need to flex its muscles when dealing with others. And that penchant is not welcome in most of the world. Today Russia and China have very little to gain from any serious confrontation with the US, yet they continue to maintain a belligerent attitude towards us. They also engage in proxy wars by supplying terrorists that serve to diminish us. This occurs because...

-- they like the revenue from selling war toys
-- we have never learned the art of humility, conciliation and cooperation with other countries whenever we perceive that our interests are at stake
-- the need to win at any cost is what makes us lose

Our politicians foolishly support these bullying behaviors that are made inevitable by our unwavering support for big oil and the military-industrial-complex. Then we portray ourselves as the good guys, to the disbelief and distain of the remainder of the world. Instead of focusing on undermining corrupt dictators, we fight wars for oil, while all the time squandering that precious resource and other critical assets in the process So...
-- Could this act be any more counter-productive?
-- Could its narrow-minded promoters be any more ignorant?
-- Is there anyone left in Washington who has not been subverted by the lobbying process, to the detriment of this country?

Our difficulties around the world are largely self-inflicted bruises

Denial of Reality

When I worked at IBM I suggested to a co-worker that, to be fair, incomes should be taxed at 90-100% on all earnings above about $400.000, in today's dollars. My friend was vehemently opposed to this idea because he wanted his opportunity for wealth, the so-called promise of America. When I checked in with him after moving on to consulting work in California, he was still a clerk, presumably holding onto his unfulfilled dream. In the mean time he was paying a greater share of the tax burden then was equitable. Yet he was unable to get the message that his taxes were disproportionate (*from a progressive viewpoint*) to his inadequate income. The possibility (*or fantasy*) of greater financial success, not unlike thoughts of winning a jackpot in Las Vegas, are what keep people in their place and the wealthy in the place they would want to be. So some forty years later I sometimes wonder where my old friend is and how much of the apple he actually got a bite of. And did he ever think again about a fairer distribution of wealth.

Let me make one thing perfectly clear. Redistribution of wealth is not like playing Robin Hood of Locksley. Wealthy people are wealthy, to some degree, because the tax and business systems are skewed in their favor in countless ways and conversely against the poor and middle classes. Can you really believe that Bill Gate's business efforts are worth perhaps ten million times what his housekeeper may make? As an interesting aside about Bill, were you aware of the reports that his acumen involved halfheartedly developing a "windows" system for IBM while he worked on one of his own? And of course we know which one prevailed.

Anyway, promoting the redistribution of money, such as with a more progressive tax rate, can be an equitable method for adjusting take-home pay without resorting to the disincentive nature of socialism. Unfortunately the trend has been in the direction of a regressive tax structure since the Kennedy administration and JFK's mentor John Maynard Keynes became the authority on taxation. And both Bush administrations have seen that their already rich buddies got an even bigger slice of the pie, all with nary a peep from those who are most adversely affected by the steady stream of give-a-ways to the rich… the lower and middle classes. They seem to be satisfied with the small bone that they are occasionally thrown. More likely, this is what happens when people pay no attention to Washington, and continue to trust that their interests are being taken care of.

Thomas Jefferson, President: *A government big enough to give you everything you want, is strong enough to take everything you have.*

How often have you heard someone say that they would vote for a particular politician because they happened to advocate a tax cut or some other money give-away? These are the same folks who can not seem to understand just how tiny their portion of any tax cut is actually is…. nor do they pay any attention to the need to pay back the debt. It is incredible how easily duped the public is.

A nearly universal misconception (thanks to the disinformation provided by the wealthy) *is that the rich deserve their obscene wealth in spite of gross poverty and a shrinking middle class*

Then there is the problem of where the interest payments on our national debt end up. Of course it goes to the lenders. And that often means foreign governments that use it as a safe harbor for their oil or cheap-labor riches. Over time some of this money comes back to the US in the form of business purchases. What that implies is that the interest on the money we borrow to support our huge debt ends up with those countries that are buying up pieces of America. The money goes around and around while our assets diminish and our debt increases. Care to buy a Danish Budweiser or a Chinese nearly anything?

In 2012 the Chinese government had been given approval to purchase a US banking system. How much more proof do we need that our trillions of dollars of debt are coming back to haunt us. And the bone heads that got us into this situation are still in office. Can you spell: vote the @#$%-ers out of office?

Global Warming

For two terms the Bush administration ignored scientific facts and generated copious amounts of disinformation about the realities of global warming, which has the potential for devastating long-term effects on this planet. A part of that intellectually deficient effort involved exerting pressure on scientists to remove global warming terminology from their reports and findings. Talk about mind control. Then the administration refused to sign the international Kyoto accords that would set limits on CO_2 production, much to the ire of the countries who did sign. Instead of cooperating with this world wide effort, Bush installed a lobbyist from the oil industry to head up the group in charge of environmental policy and planning. Hmmm. Does anyone wonder what the results of that appointment were? Eventually when credible information about global warming was too far out of the barn for anyone to close the door, the above lobbyist went back to work as a consultant for big oil. And all of this was under the noses of Congress, who were either asleep or in bed (*more likely*) with the oil companies.

By the end of Bush's terms there had been evidence for this potential global disaster to the point of being overwhelming. Yet years later we are still without a dramatic plan to reduce the damage. Why? Because this would require...

-- a reduction in oil and coal usage (*oops, aren't those the same big businesses guys that spend vast sums to corrupt our public officials?*)
-- an expensive clean-up of our polluting utilities
-- the elimination of monster SUVs and trucks (*well, at least the other guy's SUV or truck*)
-- substantially higher mileage requirements for cars and trucks
-- pollution restrictions on industrial equipment, manufacturers and transport vehicles
-- mandatory, energy-efficient programs
-- converting to green construction

Say aren't most of those big business sectors? They are very powerful entities to offend, and there is a minimal effective effort at constructive policies on the part of our politicians who are beholding to them.

Touching on evolution... because the exercise of self-centered behavior was a necessary commodity in early tribal cultures we have retained this genetically inspired but sometimes unacceptable behavior trait. It is that nature which permits us to overlook the...

-- high cost of non-renewable fuel and materials
-- additional air pollution
-- depletion of finite oil stocks
-- support that our petro-dollars have for terrorism

On this last point we end up supporting both sides of the war on terrorism. Our dollars are in effect fighting against our own dollars. Where did you think the terrorists get their money if not from petro-dollars and therefore from us? Not from the sale of sandals and burkas would be my guess. Is it any wonder why the rest of the world has so little respect for the wasteful, military-industrial-complex oriented thinkers that permeate our government? And permeate is the right word choice here. It has the right smell.

In 2000 when the price of gasoline was $2.00, drivers rated fuel economy at 29th in importance when they were buying a new vehicle.

In 2007 with the price in the $3.50 range, the rating was only 22nd and SUV sales were up 25%. This lack of appreciation for our actions when buying gas guzzlers is unacceptable. We need to have more responsible behavior and less mindless arrogance. Is it really important to have a bigger gas hog then the neighbors?

If we and the rest of the industrialized countries could reduce consumption of oil by 50%, which is do-able by exercising green engineering, the economies of terrorist supporting countries that are supported by petro-dollars would likely collapse. We do have the technology at hand to…
-- build homes and offices that use minimal to virtually no cooling or heating energy
-- produce lighter weight, more energy efficient cars and trucks
-- extract most of the energy in the internal combustion engine that is wasted as heat (*some 70%*) and use it to charge batteries that would further reduce the need for gasoline.

The potential we have for reducing oil producer's income would undoubtedly lead to starving off much of the revenues that are used to support those fanatics who are intent on turning the world into two classes… robotic Muslims and their targets. We also need to stop pretending that electricity production is non-polluting. Natural gas fired plants and some of our dams may have only a minimal effect on the environment, but they are not the dominant methods used for electrical generation. Oil and coal burning plants deposit billions of tons of carbon dioxide into the air.

Global Pollution

When I was a kid I wondered where all of the smoke went from fireplaces, factory chimneys, and leaf burning (*my favorite chore*). It was carried up into the sky, and then what? I figured that the sky was so large that must be able to endlessly absorb the smoke. Today we should be aware that anything which is sent into the atmosphere will reappear down here. The world has a balance where nothing is lost or gained. The earth is a closed system where matter can only be…
-- reduced (*oxidized*)

-- converted (*combined or broken apart*)
-- absorbed (*taken in by plant life, oceans, etc.*)
-- sequestered (*buried*)
...but it can never be destroyed.

What is sent up into the air may fall back to earth as harmless ingredients due to interaction with the sun or with other molecules. At other times we end up with pollutants that return to harm us. Has anyone been to parts of California or China lately? Similarly, when we dispose of our waste into dumps it is only temporarily out of sight. The materials will eventually...
-- dissolved by contact with other garbage or molecules in the soil
-- form gasses that enter the atmosphere
-- be broken down by rainwater
-- leach into the earth
-- be transported about by ground water

While current waste storage technology slows these processes considerably, it does not entirely stop them. Whatever is used to restrain the spread of our waste is only temporary since everything eventually degrades. Why do you think the residents of Nevada are so opposed to accepting a nuclear waste depository?

Be careful what you throw <u>away</u> because there is no <u>away</u>

Because we have had so many quick and dirty methods for disposing of used materials, we have not stopped to consider the implications of those actions. When I was a child, my mom darned socks and my dad repaired household appliances as necessary, etc. But today is a different story...
-- we send our outdated electronics to the land fills rather than salvaging the materials
-- manufacturing companies dispose of their byproducts into rivers, lakes and streams
-- for years Los Angeles dumped untreated waste directly into the Pacific ocean
ocean going ships may disposed of their unwanted materials (*jetsum*) at sea when no one is looking

While this environmental misbehavior may have slowed in recent times, it should be clear that we still live on a planet that is gradually poisoning itself. And we may not be able to develop an antidote in time to reverse the process. But as usual we twiddle our thumbs and are unwilling to take those actions that are required to resolve our contributions to pollution. It is always easier to spend twice the money later then it is to correct something now.

We and the planet are one – the proof is coming ever more quickly

Defeating Solutions

At one time the Bay Bridge (Oakland to San Francisco) was scheduled to have mass transit occupy the proposed second deck. However, lobbying by automobile, tire, and oil corporations prevented this in order to sell more of their products. As a result of this mindset and corrupting of public officials, mass transportation for the bay area never blossomed in a way that would prevent the glut of pollution spewing vehicles during rush hours.

In the 1940's the city of Los Angeles had an electric trolley system named Pacific Railway. A consortium that partnered GM, Firestone Tires, Standard Oil and Mack Trucks purchased the railway in 1944. Shortly thereafter they dismantled the system to increase the market for their products, and this was the beginning of decades of traffic congestion in the LA basin.

In the 1950's a company named Alweg built a monorail system for the Seattle fair at no cost to the state. Their business plan was to have its rider-ship cover the cost of construction. The monorail was so successful that it paid for itself in eight months. Later this company offered the city of Los Angeles a similar arrangement to build forty miles of monorail over its freeways. But the offer was rejected because of pressure from auto and tire manufacturers. It would have dramatically reduced the need for busses, automobiles and tires that they run on.

In the late 70s, Texas oil companies were involved in buying up marginal rigs from small producers. Did they then use their newer techniques to enhance oil production, like water and steam injection or rock cracking by explosive charge? No. They capped the wells with cement to control an oversupply of crude. Then they bought up marginal refiners and stopped their production of crude oil to further reduce the supply. Have you noticed that the oil refineries tend to have their "previously scheduled" maintenance shut-downs at the times of increased demand in order to jack up prices? And all of these events occur under the noses of congresspersons who are elected to office to represent the public interest. The reality is, of course, that business interests and campaign financing come first.

Energy Solutions

The prevailing attitude has been to use as much fossil fuel as we may desired to power the world's economies because it is still relatively cheap and plentiful. Cheap, that is if we don't consider the environmental damage and the other indirect costs of that usage. Plentiful, if we don't look too far down the road. The downside to our current mentality which believes that we have unlimited supplies and an unlimited time to develop alternative solutions should be obvious. A few of them are…
-- substantial pollution
-- more greenhouse gasses
-- increasingly adverse weather
-- a dwindling energy supply
-- escalating prices
-- support for terrorism
-- unnecessary military adventures
-- reduced world security

Luckily there are several long term solutions available to us if we choose to implement them. While a few options may not be mature enough to put into production any time soon, a good number of them are. For example, this country is blessed with abundant wind at both coasts and in the Midwest. The electricity generating capacity of the heartland alone through the use of wind power would produce enough electricity to satisfy the entire country if we were to update the electrical transmission infrastructure (*erecting a major network of new lines and substations to transfer that energy*). While it would be a significant expense, what is this in comparison to the hundreds of billions of dollars that have been wasted in Iraq and Afghanistan?

Lately natural gas that is trapped below the surface in shale rock has been looking like an alternative to oil. The immediate problem is a lack of regulation and a cowboy mentality on retrieving it. Dangerous chemicals that are used in the extraction process have leaked into some water tables. But if that issue can be resolved we are in business with a viable fuel source.

There is also a virtually unlimited amount of heat that can be converted into electricity from within the earth's mantle. And the earth is not going to cool off any time soon. This is one hot rock we live on. We already tap this virtually pollution free resource where it is near the surface with geothermal generators in California and elsewhere. If we chose to move forward with this technology there is engineering that would allow is to recover this resource economically everywhere except perhaps under the mountains. But if we can drill for gas and oil miles under the sea, or have mines that are miles deep, we can do this as well. As a bonus we can now generate more power from less-warm ground water than was thought possible in the past. The bad news is…
-- the above tasks would confront the existing infrastructure of coal production, oil production, refining and delivery
-- some gas stations would have to be abandoned or turned into electric or hydrogen delivery stations
-- jobs disruption could be substantial as we convert from a petroleum based economy to a renewable energy economy

The good news, if you can call it that, is that we will have to make this change in the future anyway as oil supplies are depleted, terminated by hostile countries, or priced too high to tolerate. So rather than postponing the inevitable and putting ourselves at risk, we should start working to avoid the upcoming crisis with its even higher cost. With that effort comes the benefits of reducing pollution, global warming, and the military adventures involved in securing oil fields.

On a more local basis, new home builders can tap the heat source under most home sites. Since the temperature of the ground is nearly constant some feet down, looped water pipes can be buried to transfer that heat differential, compared to the above ground, to help cool a home in summer and help heat it in winter. Short of the initial expense and the minimal water circulation costs, this is a free energy source. When compared to the cost of normal heating and cooling over time, the savings are substantial.

We all know about compact fluorescent light bulbs (CFLs), but let me offer a relatively easy energy saving trick in some homes…
-- connect flexible tubing from the home's incoming water line
-- wrap the tubing around the drain pipe exiting from the shower, washer, and/or tub
-- run that line back to the inlet of the water heater, replacing the old connection
-- insulate the tubing and the water heater to mitigate heat loss

This will capture a good portion of the energy that is normally sent down the drain from bathing and clothes washing.

Or if you are building a new home, consider having your contractor build in an even more efficient waste water heat exchanger for this purpose. There are also contractors who can build homes which require minimum of heating and cooling. The greening of homes is relatively affordable technology, and it is here today. And there is no longer an excuse for not moving forward with it. We just have to insist on using this technology to…
-- get off the grid
-- realize long term savings
-- reduce pollution with all of its obvious and hidden costs

The CAFÉ Standards

Because the human mind is not generally well-steeped in logic it can be fooled by clever manipulators. We have a genetic tendency toward being believers rather than doubters. That wiring can and does work against us. Doubters and skeptics are generally frowned upon (*because they are different*) even though they represent important checks and balances against those who would deceive us. Apathy toward the critical examination of facts is part of the reason why scam artists continue to be successful in spite of the repeated exposures of their trade.

George Bernard Shaw, author: *"Accurate observation is commonly called cynicism by those who have not got it."*

Our willingness to be believers may not induce us to consider the implication of what we are told, and we may assign unwarranted credibility to the tellers. This would certainly be the case with the CAFÉ standards that were supposed to produce fuel efficient cars beginning more than 30 years ago. The government's initially stated objective was to create a progressively higher gas mileage average from each manufacturer over time. Who knew that <u>over time</u> would take the number of years that it has. In the mean time the public may have settled into the notion that we are actually doing something about fuel usage, but the facts indicate otherwise.

The best way to cut your car's fuel bill in half is to buy a vehicle that gets twice as many miles to the gallon... well duh

Prior to 2010 it was some ten years since the government installed a new mileage standard. There had been no changes in it during that time due to the lobbying by the auto industry. Even while automobile engines have become more efficient over the years (*thanks primarily to competition from Japan and pressure from California*), economical benefits have been cancelled out by the increasing bloat of the vehicles.

Auto companies know that they only have to meet the mileage requirements and not exceed them. As a result they have been busy catering to the shortsighted American appetite for size, which they helped to create through advertising. Big is where the greater profit margins have been. This is why in the first half of 2009 the Ford F150 truck outsold the Camry. Smaller cars with smaller margins are only built to keep the Japanese and Koreans from overrunning our market any more than they already have. Apparently winning the car sales wars with other countries is not a high priority in Detroit. So we buried our heads in the sand, presuming that all will be well if we just don't think about it now, to paraphrase Scarlet O'Hara's monologue in Gone With The Wind. And vehicle manufacturers lack the incentive to change that detrimental scenario. Now the Japanese are diving headlong into the large truck and SUV markets with their higher profit margins, which will leave Detroit where, exactly?.

While the manufacturers have been ignoring the future, we may have been telling ourselves that the CAFÉ Standards were accomplishing something. Could we be more wrong? The fleet mileage ratings from 1982 were virtually the same as those from 2006, according to the EPA... a statistic that is both unbelievable and unacceptable, and without a peep from the EPA. The years of window stickers, government bureaucracy, and false promises have amounted to virtually nothing... except of course for the wasted salaries of those who are employed to oversee this government/industry farce.

The clearest indictment of the auto industry is that after thirty years, the government is still "managing" fuel economy

It is surprising to me how often automobile magazines and auto newspaper articles glorify excessive horsepower while ignoring its obvious downside. For the US public, power sells because that is what we have been indoctrinated with for so many years. There has probably never been an issue of the leading motoring trends magazine that has not feature excessive horsepower on multiple pages. One issue involved super cars that can be purchased directly from a showroom floor that are reaching the 500 to 700 horsepower level, or nearly the same as race cars. With the top speed limit of 65 to 75mph on our highways, do we really need cars that can exceed that by 100mph or more?

Horsepower is essentially a measure of an engine's ability to burn its fuel quickly – Is this what we should be trying to achieve?

If engine technology hadn't improved dramatically over the last twenty five years, the mileage rating numbers would be far worse. So the expensive technology that we have created for the internal combustion engine has been wasted on the increasing weight that has been added to vehicles.

Oh yes, did I mention that the alleged mileage ratings that are posted by the auto industry were somewhat bogus? Prior to the 2009 models, virtually no car got the miles per gallon that were displayed on the window sticker unless it was driven down hill more often than uphill. Some, like the hybrid Prius, got dramatically less than their posted numbers in spite of a carefully fostered impression to the contrary through advertising. The people who run the mileage program have known of these discrepancies for years, and yet had done little to correct the testing algorithm. Neither have the auto industry or the politicians with oversight power. To the contrary, these are some of the same people that have prevented gasoline usage from decreasing.

When the mileage requirements first came out, ads were required to specify both the city and highway ratings because only the highway mileage was being advertised by the auto companies. Later a compromise was reached between the manufacturers and the government, the nearly meaningless combined city/highway rating that was used for a while. Now the Feds are letting manufacturers tout only the highway mileage again as if drivers didn't spend most of their time driving in the city.

In addition to the above regulations, the Feds elected to completely remove all truck-sized vehicles from the ratings game some years ago, except for a few light-duty trucks. This means that the poorest vehicle mileage ratings are never disclosed to the public or figured in the corporate mileage ratings. Those numbers are not even revealed to us in the automobile magazines, much to their discredit. No doubt this is due to the fact that so much of their advertising revenue comes from them. Information that the Hummer, for example, has a city mileage rating only marginally better than a thirty eight passenger diesel bus is not in the public domain. And the vehicle manufacturers will not volunteer this data without pressure from Congress, which does not stand up to big business, and prefers to cave in rather than perform a service.

In 2011 the government proposed doubling the mileage requirements for automobiles and light truck and vans. But these new standards are not due to go into full effect until 2016, with heavy vehicles being exempt until 2020 and then be phased in over five years. So the worst of the worst are given the biggest breaks. All the while, the industry has known that these targets were coming down the road, and have done virtually nothing to accommodate them ahead of the deadlines.

One last indictment against the auto industry is the decades of deceit involving the dealer sales system. No one who is paying even a modest amount of attention to this charade thinks that there is not something rotten in Denmark. Manufacturer suggested retail prices (*as with clothing*) are a fiction that is manipulated by the car makers, dealerships and their salespersons, against the interests of the consumers. Ads that tout prices below factory invoice are an example of this deceit. The dealer cost that may be presented to the public is higher then the actual cost to the dealer. This is because the manufacturers rebate a percentage of the retail price back on each sale. How long will we accept a system this corrupt before insisting on honesty? And the manufacturers do not object to this deceptive marketing because their primary interest is to sell cars.

Back to fuel. When the price of gasoline first rose to more than $3.00 per gallon after the Katrina hurricane, more people were driven toward economy cars than by any other effort that was enacted by Congress. That fact alone should make it clear that the bureaucracy has been thoroughly inept at lessening our reliance on imported oil or on reducing the greenhouse effect derived from that usage. People will only change their buying habits when they are pinched in the pocketbook. So rather that adopting a mileage standard that does nothing to curb demand, what we need to do is what the Europeans have done... double and tripled the price of gasoline as a way of punishing the biggest offenders and reducing the outflow of revenue. They still drive cars in Europe. But they also drive a wider variety of smaller, more fuel efficient cars, many with diesel engines. In fact, diesel cars have more than 50% of the market in Europe.

In 2011 Europe's mileage ratings averaged 35 miles per gallon vs. 22 miles per gallon here. Since modern diesel engines are a way of life in Europe, 40 miles per gallon is a reality, not a fantasy. So can we learn from their example, or must we be enamored of the massive, excessively-power vehicles that have been indelibly pressed into our consciousness through advertising.

In 2010 there was only one manufacturer selling a diesel car in this country, and that was a European company. US plans for building these engines are still years away if they even remain on schedule. About twenty-five years ago the automobile industry flirted with diesel engines. The problem then was that they elected to convert an existing gasoline engine to diesel rather that using a more sturdy, made-for-diesel engine block. As a result they were smoky, noisy, hard starting, and short lived. A typical Detroit non-effort.

While a steep rise in the price of gas would undoubtedly have a disproportional effect on the poor, there are adequate tax remedies to manage that negative side effect. Europe seems to have dealt with the problem over gas prices that in some places exceed $11 per gallon. Are they that much smarter? A more appropriate question might be: are we that much dumber? If we averaged 33 mpg vs. 22 mpg, the price of gasoline could go up by more than fifty percent without costing a penny more.

Then there is the true price of a gallon of gasoline which is far greater than the pump price. Just as with the tomato picking that is done by the illegals and is subsidized in a variety of ways, we do not charge the full measure directly to consumer for the costs that are incurred with gasoline consumption. Chief among them are military adventures that are employed to maintain our access to crude oil. Or are you under the impression that we had a benevolent interest in Iraq? If helpfulness were our true desire we would have employed diplomacy in the Middle East. Or perhaps we would have paid more attention to the life and death agonies that have been ongoing in Africa for years.

Rather than have the proposed mileage standards apply to each truck or automobile in a manufacturer's line, they apply to the corporations as a whole. The implication is that Detroit can go on producing gas guzzlers as long as it manages to sell a significant number of high mileage cars to offset that downside. The Big Three mentality has always been to have the large, high-profit vehicles subsidize small, low-profit vehicles, and the government does little to change this mindset. What do you think will happen to Detroit when the Chinese begin sending over small, well built, high mileage cars to the US? Detroit is so locked into the big car/big profit scenario that they have no concept of any other game plan, and may not be able to adapt this time around. The industry could all too soon learn a lesson at the expense of our nation when sales begin to drop like a rock… again. To make this point, the public is becoming progressively more interested in fuel economy as witnessed by the thousands of pre-orders that were make for the small, foreign, "Smart" car.

Travel with Excess

If you are not towing a yacht or camper, do you really need…
-- a 6.000+ pound truck to carry 100 pounds of tools (*maybe*) and a single occupant (*If you are not convinced that this happens with regularity, just check the HOV lanes for the conspicuous absence of these vehicles*)
-- the extra weight of a dozen surround sound speakers
-- the weight penalty of a rarely used seven or eight passenger seating arrangement

Maybe we should re-think the equation between indulgences and negative implications on the planet. My wife and I experienced an eye-opening example of vehicular gluttony on a trip to the Southern California coast. There were a torrent of massive, tricked-out SUVs barreling 60 to 70 mph down the Pacific Coast Highway's short, 50mph, intra-city highways with no concern that the signal light ahead had already turned red. What about…
-- teaching sane driving habits in driver's education?
-- saving some of the finite gasoline supply for someone else?
-- conserving the metals and plastic that cars are made from?
-- not acting like pampered morons?

Consumption Solution

After the $4-5 per gallon shock a while back, gasoline dropped below the $2.00 level and the automakers wondered what cars the public would be buying in the future. Perhaps they questioned…
-- Can we still build our beloved, monster SUV's and trucks?
-- Do we stop the R&D on electric cars?
-- Does the public really care about miles per gallon?

I think the manufacturer's questions about preferences could be responded to by expanding the gas guzzler tax dramatically, let's say with a $1000 tax for every mpg that a vehicle gets under 30 mpg. Then over time increase that number to 40 mpg and 50 mpg. In this scenario, those who choose to buy a vehicle that gets 10 mpg would have to cough up an additional twenty to forty grand more for their foolish pleasure.

Let's not pretend that 90% of the non-commercial, heavy truck and SUV drivers are satisfying anything more their egos. In those rare circumstances when a cargo bed is required or transportation for seven is a needed, they could phone up a rental company and get one for the day.

Getting back to the penalty side. If the manufacturers knew that their customers would be heavily taxed on excessive consumption, the angst about whether or not to build large vehicles would be moot. As an ancillary benefit, we would not have Congress's ineffective CAFÉ standards and the all of the people that are paid out of taxpayer funds to oversee that boondoggle.

The point I would make about the energy problems, such as the diminishing crude oil reserves and the terrorist sympathizers who control them, is this. There are generally simple solutions if we are willing to make practical, useful decisions. Perhaps it is a matter of punishing the biggest offenders into submission. This method of control is more cost-effective than pursuing solutions promoted by an ineffective, corrupted bureaucracy. But don't plan on getting their support any time soon. Oversight officials are far too busy receiving salaries to be even modestly concerned with efficiency or integrity.

Junk Cell Solution

In its infinite wisdom the government released everyone's cell phone numbers to telemarketers. Now we can not only be harassed by these leaches on society, but we can also pay for the privilege because these may be chargeable calls on your telephone bills. There is an opt-out capability though. Just call 888.382.1222 from the cell phone that you want to be ad-blocked. Oh, did I mention that this blocking does not apply to politician's when in vote gathering mode? So let me see if I have this right. We release the telephone numbers of all cell phones so that we can enable some government agency to exist in order to issue them and then enforce a blocked number list against the telemarketers. Is that a brilliant plan, or what? Well it does happen to employee more people in a government agency. Say, isn't the department director's GS pay grade is based on the number of employees working under him or her.

The War on Drugs

This has to be the ultimate in fruitless, counterproductive government intervention into people's lives since Prohibition was enacted. It produces immensely more harm than good. What could be more irrational than a grossly expensive and totally ineffective effort to prevent the distribution and use of illicit drugs? One definition of insanity is: repeating the same action and expecting different results.

This has been a long lasting experiment, yet it has failed to show any signs of success. People can still get drugs if they want to, and they do want to. Overcrowding the jails with non-violent offenders does absolutely nothing to change this equation. We have spent decades and billions of dollars on this thoughtless foolishness, and what tangible achievements can be shown for the effort? I don't believe it would be much of a stretch to say: nothing has. Actually less than nothing would be more accurate if we take into account the human damage this witless confrontation with pleasure has created.

I can only express anecdotal opinions about our war on drugs from what I read in the media since I am not out there in the trenches, nor am I part of the drug landscape. Apparently what we have is...
-- a great deal of holier-than-thou pontificating by the Feds

-- a succession of drug busts
-- immodest press releases shouting success
-- no tangible reduction in the amount of drugs consumed
-- vastly increased crime

Even more curiously, this unmitigated failure comes without any reduction in the DEA's massive budget. From the evidence that is there for all to see, it should not be difficult to conclude that nothing substantive has been accomplished, nor is it likely to be through drug prohibition. It should also be abundantly clear to anyone who cares to be objective that people will continue to obtain illegal drugs for exactly as long as they continue to desire them, not one second less, no matter what.

What appears to have been accomplished by drug interdiction, though, is an environment where the drug sellers (*as with the history of alcohol prohibition*) kill hundreds of accomplices to retain their slice of the market. Laws are thoroughly ineffective in dealing with drug demand, just as they were in the past. In fact it can be argued that these laws are counter-productive because people tend to crave what they are denied. Just look at the college and high school drinking binges that have become a right of passage for some.

If I am able to make this logical observation without difficulty, why can't those in our government do the same? Well one possible answer lies with the right wing's mentality of: pleasure repression trumps common sense. This does not imply that drugs are not harmful or that I believe that no actions should be taken to control their usage. What it does demonstrate is that the drug enforcement agencies use unworkable tactics, and they are not able or willing to make this simple determination on their own. Is it possible that they are so unproductive because their generous salaries are more important to them? Is it plausible that people in government could be this self-serving? Absolutely!

Much the same can be said about the past campaign against smoking. We raised the price dramatically (*like with drugs*), but this did not do nearly as much to discourage smoking as the out-of-the-closet, non-smokers have accomplished with their efforts at re-education and smoking restrictions in public places. What the drug

enforcement people do not understand, or more likely have chosen to ignore, is threefold...
-- making drug possession illegal encourages its misuse
-- drug use is a status thing, Jack, because it is imagined to be cool and alluring, and will continue unabated for as long as it is thought of as cool and alluring
-- drug use can be, and often is, a debilitating addiction that should be treated as a medical issue when appropriate

We would be much more effective at stopping the drug proliferation if we were able to convince the users that: it is only the dopes that use dope. An advertising campaign which showed simpletons and losers as the drug users might be quite effective in this regard. Advertising slogans like: "Your brain on drugs" may be cute, but are inherently meaningless (*disbelieved or ignored*) and ineffective because they do nothing to attack the basic fundamentals of drug use, which is experimentation, entertainment, and rebelling against the system. Getting high also reduces people's concerns about health issues.

We need to take the glamour out of drugs, but most assuredly not show our ignorance by jailing people for behaving naturally. We also should reconsider the belief that social problems can be solved by incarceration, more police, judges, and lawyers. The difficulty with trying to encourage this train of thought is that the current system is being promoted by government employees, police, judges and lawyers who either haven't enough common sense to find workable answers or have other agendas which prevent realistic solutions.

Less dogma and more intellect could go a long way, and might lead to...
-- fewer people in jail, and a subsequent reduction in the massive court and prison costs
-- fewer crimes that are committed to support the artificially high price of prohibited drugs
-- fewer dollars in the hands of thugs and terrorists

Rather than our politicians, police, judges and lawyers using common sense...
-- there is a massively expensive drug bureaucracy
-- the street price of drugs is artificially high

-- the cartels are fabulously wealthy and vicious, and they love us for it
-- the cartels can afford to corrupt governments
-- the cartels can afford weapons and their own troops
-- drug dealers commit crimes to protect their business
-- drug users commit crimes to support their habits
-- drug use goes on virtually unabated as new sellers and buyers step into every brief vacuum that is created by incarceration
-- more people are suffering from our pathetically ignorant drug policy then there would be if drugs were legalized, and far more than if it were also controlled

As for marijuana, its immediate decriminalization can be a viable initiative because it would...
-- offer cancer patients some relief from their pain
-- free up the jails housing the tens of thousands of non-violent inmates
-- take the profit out of the drug for the criminal elements that are the producers and dealers
-- allow states to tax the product

The downside could be increased usage, or maybe not. And we would almost certainly have to regulate this product in the same manner that we do with alcohol and cigarettes. Then the savings derived from not using our jail system could offset this marginal oversight expense a thousand times over. Of course there would be the many thousands of DEA, prison and related government worker bees that would have to find legitimate work. But is that worse than the current situation?

The drug problem is not so much a problem with drugs, which it is to a degree, but a substantially greater problem with the government employees who make a living off it. In 2011, in a reversal of policy, federal prosecutors, who apparently thought that they needed to do this, decided to launch a crackdown on the pot dispensaries in California. The owners were threatened with criminal charges and confiscation of property even though their businesses have been legal for 15 years in the state. They were given 45 days "to get out of Dodge". This change of attitude followed a two year period of intentionally relaxed enforcement by the feds. So how did we go from some compassion for the very ill, to none at all? What suddenly got into their heads? Obama who himself quit drugs? Time may tell.

Afghanistan Again-istan

The US had been encountering serious problems related to the reestablishment of the Taliban in Afghanistan. Their planting of poppies provides much of the revenue that is used to support the insurgencies in Iraq, Pakistan, Afghanistan and elsewhere. At one point, our government invited a cooperating War Lord to the US for an information exchange about the war. Then after pumping him for his firsthand details of the drug trade, the DEA (*Drug Enforcement Asses*) arrest him. This unbelievable action was directed toward a person who took a major risk to volunteer his assistance in our war effort. Yep, we jailed him! The unmistakable message to others who might wish to cooperate with the US is clear. We can't be trusted to act rationally as long as our policies are impaired by zealots that are masquerading as public servants. Could that somehow be what the intent of the incarceration was? Was there another train of thought?

We spend hundreds of millions of dollars in a failed effort to eradicate the poppy growing fields, only to alienate the poorest of farmers whose livelihood relies on this crop. Then our efforts drive them into the camps of the Taliban and raise the price of heroine, which in turn increases their wealth and power. Will we ever learn how counterproductive this war on drugs is? Isn't anyone willing to prevent this mindless waste of lives and resources? Can the access to drugs be any worse that the slaughter of thousands of people that is in some way due to our policies? The government could not have created a worse scenario for the US if they had put its minds to it, between the drug trade, the price of oil, our becoming the target of radicals, and the loss of world prestige.

Ruling by Religion

This brings me to an important, under-acknowledged point about politics. There is a contingent in America who would prefer to punish certain behaviors rather that understand and deal with them in a responsible manner. Among them are conservatives who are always on the loose-morals warpath, and are contemptuous of our natural excitement with various gratifications. They do their best to influence our government policies in the direction of their insensitive mindset.

If we could truly separate church and state in this country we would be far better off for it. But because of religion's pervasive influence in society we turn a blind eye to its negative and accommodating role in our problems. Perhaps this is because we believe that no harm can be done if the intention being promoted is deemed conscientious. But one man's responsible another man's oppression. So have you gotten the idea that some of America's problems, both internally and externally, are the result of these influences? If not, you may be a contributor to the difficulties.

True believers can't help trying to inflict their personal values on others, so I have to ask...
-- Is it really anyone's business, besides the mother's, whether an abortion is performed or not?
-- Is being gay or having sex outside of marriage really a sin that needs to be curbed by church or civil law?
-- Are the alleged family values actually important values or are they simply the crusader's values?
-- Does having legal, same-sex partnerships harm anyone?
-- Should any of the church's persuasions, whether noble or not, be encouraged by government?
-- Do we need to have "In God We Trust" and "Under God" promoted on our currency or in the Pledge of Allegiance?

On this last question...
-- What exactly is the benefit of repeating this pledge in schools or in public meetings in the first place?
-- Does repeating it mindlessly do anything to enhance our selves or the country?
-- Who are we trying to impress with this declaration of loyalty anyway?
-- As long as we are not working against America, is patriotism anyone else's business but our own?
-- If it makes a few people feel good, do we all need to follow in lock-step with them like sheep?

Prostitution's Bad Rap

Let's make on thing perfectly clear at the outset. Prostitution is only a crime against the repressive attitudes that have been promulgated by most churches in this country and have consequently been supported by our government. It is not a crime against people except in the eyes of those who have been indoctrinated with this repressive mentality since their youth.

The right wing thinkers in the US are continually on the war path against sexual freedom and gratification because they have been told forever that it is a sin to occur outside of marriage, and that sex is supposed to be utilized only for the procreation of children. So those who do not want to have children are supposed to do exactly what? Abstain? Because there are so many in this vocal, anti sex group, laws have arisen to punish those who step outside of their mindset.

Prostitution has been designated and vilified as the first occupation, and it has been a fact of life since long before recorded history. This status alone is quite an achievement for something so "evil". The religious right will contend that this profession is not victimless, but they rarely put up logical, factual arguments against it that are not a direct repercussion of it being illegal. That is not to say that they do not have thoughtful arguments. They do, however, tend to revolve obliquely around those antisocial behaviors that may occur due to repression and nonsense laws.

Sex is similar to an impenetrable balloon. If you press in somewhere, the result is an expansion somewhere else, but the volume remains essentially static. In this same light, prostitution, like prohibited drugs, is never going to go away, and we might as well deal with that fact in a reasonable, responsible manner. The current dogma about both of these subjects is clearly not working.

Societies through history have had more sensible attitudes toward sex than we have in this country. They indulge in a certain amount of pragmatism. If you can't eradicate a situation, work with it. And one problem is, of course, that there can be sexually transmitted diseases (*STDs*) derived from casual sex. But in this country, rather that have effective solutions, we prefer to listen to those who have been dominated by those preachers who have managed to get their collective ears. Sex is not inherently evil regardless of how many profess it to be so, or how vehemently the chorus of voices asserts that it is. It simply is natural.

Some other countries and areas within the US have taken steps to regulate this activity by relegating it to specific sex zones and mandating regular medical examinations. This is a far cry from the popular US stance of having sex police patrol known solicitation areas and make arrests for something that is none of their business. If I could make just one observation about the church-inspired mentality toward sex, it would be that these people just can't mind their own damn business. They need to get with the no harm - no foul perspective, rather than wasting the taxpayer's money.

In one way of thinking, dating can be thought of as a form of prostitution. It uses the money incentive (*dinner and a movie, perhaps*) with the exchange of sexual favors as reciprocity. But when this activity is completed with people who <u>may</u> be more than casually interested in each other, the arguments against their behavior fade into the background. So the real problem seems to be with the exchange of currency by those people who seldom know each other and may not meet again. I suggest that this is not too far distant from the more socially acceptable bar-pick-up scene.

As for prostitution not being victimless, victims are created by the very laws that are meant, I suppose, to protect us. No one denies that children and young adults can be harmed by imposed sex, and that they must be protected vigorously against this. On the other hand, only a fool would deny that aberrant sexual behaviors are frequently a function of state mandated repression. Take away the free expression of this activity and our innate programming can go a bit haywire. And it is not just the state that restricts our sexual freedom. Attitudes derived from religion are playing a big hand in that process of indoctrination.

Like the war on drugs, the war on sex has a similar result and influence on society, such as corruption and violence. Prostitution is pushed into the back alleys, and is controlled by those with a money incentive. Remove the money thing by legalizing this "service" and that nefarious incentive goes away. But this will take a serious rethinking of the subject, in association with a strong rebuke of the sanctimonious folks who manage to think that this is somehow some of their business. Sexual attitudes ebb and flow over long periods of time, so I don't see the majority coming to new conclusions anytime soon.

One study concluded that the laws we enforce against the sex trade cost everyone in the US $22 per year in police services. While that may not sound like a lot per individual, the total is spread across some $400 million of us from diapers to grave. And it does not take into consideration the toll on the people involved, which can not be measured in dollars. So by my math, sex police cost the US some $880 million per year.

Travel in Excess

There are rare times when Congresspersons need to travel in order to see dramatic national events first hand, like the devastation caused by hurricane Katrina… but not twenty or fifty at a time. Perhaps one or two could make the trip and report their findings back to their colleges. These "trippy" Congresspersons…
-- do speak English, don't they?
-- have phones, don't they?
-- know how to use email, don't they?

Then there are the politicians who accept travel perks from our largest corporations when it suits their fancy. Senate Majority Leader Harry Reid was one of the more egregious offenders in this crowd of easy takers. He had been given, as of a count in 2009, some 40 private (*non-government business*) jet trips since 2001 at who knows what real cost to the taxpayers. Have you ever been offered one?

Reid's response to the critics was "I am confident that I have never been influenced by anyone who provides me with the courtesy of a private plane". What we can learn from his statement is that...
-- confidence comes a bit too easily for Reid
-- he is not influenced by perks in the same way that ordinary people would be
-- courtesy is not another word for bribery
-- corporations are just nice folks
-- he is an out and out liar

Some might like to believe that Reid was doing his duty to our country while being lavished with perquisites, but how can we? The conflict of interest is obvious, although this does not seem to be part of his consciousness. Nor does it demonstrate anything resembling guilt or embarrassment found in his remarks about it. How can anyone not feel some measure of disquiet for unethically and aggressively taking advantage of a corrupt environment?

Representative Charles Rangel was another case in point. In spite of being admonished for taking corporate sponsored trips to Antigua and St. Martin, which is a violation of Congressional gift rules, he denied knowledge of their corporate backing. So let's see. He is either a liar or beyond dumb. Can you spell liar? And of course Reid and Rangel were not alone with their easy virtue. Nearly all members of Congress are known for taking a vast array of bribes from lobbyists and corporations. In fact it is so flagrant that many of us have simply tuned out this corrupt behavior. Amazingly, the graft is taken without anyone having done anything unethical or illegal, if you believe the Congressional fact-spinners. So how can the rest of us get in on this sweet game?

Bill Creation

No, this is not some guy that you might remember from High School. Rather it is the convoluted, inequitable process by which ideas are offered up in Congress in the hope of becoming law... usually. At other times these bills may become bargaining chips, such as with: if you support my pork, I'll support yours. It does not matter much if the other guy's bills are good, bad or ugly in this vote swapping scenario. Occasionally there is no expectation of a bill's passage because the motive behind it is a ploy that is designed to embarrass the opposition when they vote against it. Look to the "dead on arrival" bill to repeal the health care law by Republicans in 2012 as an example of this nonsense.

In an ideal world bills would be presented to benefit the country or right some wrong. Far too often, however, they are the creations of interest groups who were not elected to office, but have their Congressperson's ardent attention to further their own agendas. I refer of course to the PACs (*Political Action Committees*).

It would be helpful if we understood that a Congressperson's principal, unprincipled loyalty is not to their constituency but to the above mentioned groups who go about distributing their generous campaign funds, gifts, and perks. These lobbyists are also the same folks who are occasionally responsible for drafting our legislation (*no kidding*) when it suits their purposes.

More than once a bill has been crafted to "regulate" the very industry that writes it. In this situation the bill is more watered down than one might expect if it were proposed by an unbiased congressperson. Having bills that are written by others has become a convenience for our elected officials because they are far too busy dealing with fund raisers to think about the public good for more than a few minutes at a time. Because of this diversion of interest, it would not be unreasonable to wonder how much thought actually goes into evaluating the bills that are written by lobbyists. We should also ask how much of these bills are even understood by those who then offer them up for a Congressional vote.

Now you know how loopholes are created... intentionally

Bill Suppression

All bills that are written do not necessarily garner a vote in Congress just because they may have been drafted for that purpose. They must first be…
-- assigned to the appropriate committee - maybe
-- permitted by the committee chairperson to be debated – maybe
-- voted out of their committee – maybe
-- permitted to come to the floor for a vote - maybe

This means having a bill go through a succession of good-ol'-boy give and take actions. You give and they take. Or perhaps now you owe them one. Then if that labored process goes well, the bill's author needs to harvest support from his or her peers… more horse-trading. Finally the happy day arrives when a vote can be taken… maybe, unless there is a filibuster or some other procedure invoked that stops the bill dead in its tracks. Isn't politics grand?

Congress is what happens when an amoral, unprincipled body is in charge of making their own rules

Knowledge Suppression

Information that the public should become aware of is occasionally suppressed by the news media, politicians, corporations and government agencies because it is in their interest to do so. This distortion occurs because…
-- the news media is beholding to politicians and agencies who feed them propaganda
-- government agencies are obligated to politicians who fund their money-wasting bureaucracies
-- politicians are indebted to the large corporations who pull the strings with their campaign financing (*bribes*)
-- large corporations are obliged to… well to no one actually because they are truly the owners of government

These circumstances add up to the incestuous relationships that conspire to suppress meaningful information from being disclosed to the public and from beneficial laws from being passed. Perhaps the most infamous of these naked suppressions took place a few years

283

back when Ralph Nader was making a run for President. The press would only give disparaging lip service to his candidacy, and then just as often it would misrepresent his views. The press encouraged us to believe that a vote for Ralph was a wasted vote, and that it was tantamount to a vote for the Republicans because most of Nader's supporters would have been inclined to vote Democratic.

The information controllers went so far as to prevent Nader from joining the Presidential debates in the 2000 election. Third party candidates were alleged to be detrimental to democracy, and they were viewed as being a liability to a stable two-party system. Third party candidates may indeed be "injurious" to our political system because they foster the presentation of new ideas, and they may not permit politicians hide behind their Coke vs. Pepsi subterfuge (explained later).

Not too surprisingly the debates referred to above were run by officials from the Republican and Democratic national committees, not by the organization that stood in as their stalking horse, the Daughters of the American Revolution (*DAR*). That group were used to put an independent face on what was a patently bipartisan conspiracy. Shame on the DAR for getting its fifteen minutes of fame by being manipulated this manner!

When Ralph Nader arrived at one of these debates with a valid ticket for a seat in the audience, the thought police refused him entry into the auditorium, and threatened him with arrest if he insisted on taking a seat. His picture, and those of the others who were cast as enemies of the convention, had been placed in the so-called Book Of Faces (*persons who were to be denied admittance*).

The politicians and the interests that were behind this restriction of free assembly could not risk any breach in the wall of secrecy which prevents disclosure of who is truly running this country. Interfering with the controlled, two-party system might uncover that fact to the masses, they correctly reasoned. This control of process is only marginally less obnoxious than that which occurs in the banana republics that we have criticized for such activity.

Major corporations would like us to imagine that it is the politicians who are doing (*or preventing*) the public's bidding, but nothing could be further from the truth. A few of the real power brokers are the...
-- financial institutions
-- communications institutions
-- military industrial complex
-- automobile industries
-- health insurance industries
-- pharmaceutical industries
-- agricultural industries
-- oil, gas & coal industries
-- religious institutions

Voting for any candidate is an essentially a futile exercise, and it denies the truth of corporate manipulation of this country... regardless of which party is elected

Getting back to Nader, the Democrats to this day claim that his running for the Presidency in 2000 caused Al Gore to lose the election to George Bush, and they are still pissed at him. While I obviously am not a fan of GWB, I am less disposed to the arguments against Nader. It is disappointing that so few people had a clue as to his justifications for running. His platform was designed to put up an offence against the pervasive influence that big business has on our legislators due to legalized bribery. While that message does not seem difficult to grasp, it did none the less fail to capture much of an audience. If the Democrats could not distinguish themselves enough to overcome the less than one percent of the vote that was received by this third party, then perhaps they deserved to lose.

We should know by now that no matter whom the candidates may be, are our choices are always between twiddle dee dee and twiddle dee dum. Voting for candidates merely validates those who choose to corrupt themselves, this country, and deceive the voters.

One of the arguments that is perpetually put forward against voting for a third party candidate is that it represents a lost vote because that party has no chance of winning. Well what about the contention that that a "useless" vote sends an important message of discontent. Hasn't the formation of the TEA party managed to influence some

Republican candidates? Currently our populous is not disenchanted enough with the current state of politics to take the third-party step. This is no doubt because we have been indoctrinated since birth into believing that the current system works. Could we be more wrong? Wasn't the 2011 budget fiasco a wake-up call, even for those asleep on their couches?

The Balance of Power

The battle between the Democrats and the Republicans is not unlike the occasionally advertised competition between Pepsi and Coke for the pocketbooks of cola drinkers. This game is designed to eliminate as much outside competition as possible by ignoring or actively undermining the competing beverage companies. One could not be faulted for imagining that neither Pepsi nor Coke much cares who wins these cola wars because they are both winners as they divide up the spoils between themselves. According to press reports I have seen, they had gone so far as to prevent competing other cola companies from buying the prized, lighted-door vending machines.

In a similar way our corporations probably don't care who appears to be in control of government because in the end it is they who are in charge with their influence on both parties. They financially support both sides for a good reason. Their domination of process is very effective. As a result of corporate influences, politicians have made the term: populist candidate virtually disappear from our lexicon. It has been relegated to the political trash heap because it is no longer a viable campaign platform for generating contributions.

Years earlier the term: socialism went the same way. This was not so much because this form of economics was a dreadful idea, but because it might have reduced the corporate influence in politics. Power to the people was to be avoided at all costs. To my way of thinking there are two ways to look at the socialism… equality and justice. In days past, the Russians practiced a form of equality where the under-educated held an inordinate amount of power, and made destructive decisions through their centralized government. The preferred form of socialism is where justice and fair play are used as guidelines for making economic decisions. In this scenario no one holds power or wealth that is disproportionate to their contribution to the whole. Excessive wealth coexisting with gross poverty would be a target of this concept, and one that is regrettably ignored. Why? Can you guess who holds the power in America? A clue is that it's not the needy or under privileged.

Just like history being written by the victors, the distribution of wealth is dictated by the wealthy

When the lack of equitable tax payments by the super rich eventually became an embarrassment to the politicians who voted in their sweetheart loopholes and benefits, a Minimum Alternate Tax was inaugurated. It was deemed that the wealthy should pay some minimum tax to balance out their many benefits and tax loopholes. The result of this fix (*don't you just love that word here*) is that people with incomes in the millions of dollars can still end up paying a lower tax rate than those with modest incomes.

In 2011 the tax issue came up again when a billionaire stated that his rate was lower than that of a home employee of his. Obama took up the tax the rich fairly battle cry and was immediately met with the counter cry of class warfare by the Republican leadership. Hard as I try, the only warfare I can detect is the war by the rich who want to keep their wealth. And they offer no apology for their greed. Maybe we do need class warfare in order to correct the gross injustices that prevail in our tax system.

Minimum Wage

I would not care to be categorized as a liberal when it comes to politics in general, but what is it with minimum wage and healthcare in this country? We lost our top socio-economic ranking in the world many years ago, and we are now in the neighborhood of 14th place when compared to other developed countries. This has been an inexcusable downhill trend that can be attributed to declining public educational scores and the years of politicians listening to lobbyists and PACs instead of serving the people.

I remember when the minimum wage was $1.10 per hour. It was barely sufficient for a kid like me working as a stock clerk during summer vacation, and a far cry from being adequate for anyone trying to pay rent and raise a family. Yet not much has changed in the fifty-some years since then. Prior to the most recent increase in the minimum wage there had been more than ten years of fruitless discussions about it in Congress. Well actually it's been minimal talk and a lot of stonewalling by those who are financially beholding to, or are philosophically aligned with business. It is a shameful reflection on the federal government that there are many states with a higher minimum than the federal rate. Half a dozen states have a higher rate then even the latest, proposed increase, which required more than a year to phase in.

Following in lock-step with every proposed or incorporated minimum wage increase are the business lobbyists who predict that the economy could falter as a result of a boost in this pathetic pay scale. Their logic goes thusly...
-- because of the burden on small businesses, the lowest wage earners may be fired
-- product costs will increase
-- the poor will suffer doubly

So the corporate answer to the poorest on the wage scale spectrum is to let their pitiful pay be further eroded by inflation, as we had done for the last ten years. A case of: I've got mine, you're on your own.

During the last half century there has not been a noticeably adverse repercussion resulting from giving the lowest wage earners a decent break. A few store owners might have had to cut back slightly or temporarily on their business or lifestyles. A few low wage earners may actually lose their jobs at a handful of marginal businesses. But what is this downside in comparison to a benefit to the millions who scrape by on the pittance that we allow businesses to pay them?

In stark contrast to the above arguments, no one seems to complain about...
-- computer programmers, like myself, making $50 to $200 per hour and their adverse effect on the economy

-- the lawyers who have created a legal system that permits them to charge greatly more than that
-- dot.com whizzes that have drained hundreds of millions or billions of dollars from startup companies with their immense stock options
-- some doctors and dentists who can never make enough off of people's suffering

Even plumbers, electricians and other tradespersons may have billing rates that can be out of proportion to their skill levels. There is no detectable outrage from the public or a noticeable drag on the economy from these and other sectors. More importantly we do not rein in the drug companies or fix the broken, for-profit/not-people oriented healthcare system. But the poor, well that's another story. They are at our mercy, and we don't have much of that commodity to expend. We just don't give a damn. And by being poor they have no power or advocates to turn things around.

Why is it that we are so willing to penalize this undereducated, underprivileged class in this country? In stark contrast, if the corporations make millions of dollars off of the backs of its laborers, so be it? Would you have a problem paying an extra 25 cents for a burger in order to support a higher minimum wage?

This country is run by the wealthy, for the wealthy, with minimal regard for the welfare of the working class that make them rich

According to my education in business economics, increases in wages will...
-- increase demand for more products
-- which brings increased production
-- which brings increased productivity
-- which brings increased hiring
-- which quickly mitigates the aforementioned increase in wages

Sounds reasonable, doesn't it? Even if the above logic were not perfectly efficient, the net effect of increasing the minimum wage would be to slightly adjust the distribution of wealth... a little from the rich... a fair amount to the poor. But still, this minimal concession to the needy is anathema to the wealthy and their wealth promoters in government. They like their money, and they insist on hanging on to it.

Perhaps the best justification for a minimum wage increase comes from our neighbor to the South. Mexico Incorporated is run by a small handful of super-wealthy families (*one of whom became the richest in the world in 2010*) that feed off of the underclass. The result is that their…
-- wealthy remain obscenely rich
-- desperately poor run to America
-- underpaid police are corrupt
-- underpaid government employees are corrupt
-- drug cartels are out of control
-- bands of armed rebels run amuck because even the risk of death is a viable alternative to poverty

Meanwhile, back to all's fair in business at America. According to the Wall Street Journal in 2005, 1% of the wealthiest Americans earned 21% of the income while the bottom 50% of the people earned 13%. And there is good reason to believe that this situation has gotten incrementally worse in the subsequent years.

According to Forbes Magazine, the 400 wealthiest people, or about 0.00001% of the population, own 13% of the gross national product, or some $1.5 trillion worth. This is $1.5 million-million for 400 people! That is more money than they could spend in a lifetime if they went on a shopping spree 24 hours per day, seven days a week for the rest of their lives.

Even the middle class has come under financial pressure due to years of giveaways to the already rich by an out of touch Congress. Actually out of touch would be giving the President and those in Congress an I'm-stupid pass that they don't deserve. In reality they are well aware that their giveaways to the rich are primarily to themselves and their already well healed friends. Every tax cut is shamelessly designed with this elite class in mind, and has only a scrap or two to quell the unrest of the real taxpayers.

George Bernard Shaw, author: *A government which robs Peter to pay Paul can always depend on the support of Paul.*

One of the tragic side effects of disproportionate wages and other economic inequities is that it encourages the proliferation of crime. When people do not have adequate (*and we can all debate just what that might mean*) opportunities, a significant percentage of them will resort to anti-social behavior out of desperation or in the belief that crime will bring them a better opportunity. So rather than providing for a reasonable distribution of wealth in this country, we elect to build more and more jails in which to house the increasing number of miscreants that we have created, never recognizing how much the country is being penalized for its gross stupidity. Oops, I forgot that the rich are not impacted by this.

Let me point out that once again in 2007 the Congress did not ignore its own minimum wage. It raised its base pay to $170.000. And that is before taking into account their second-to-none health benefits plus their retirement plans which kick in after achieving office. Are your health and retirement policies anywhere near this delicious? Do you even have health and retirement plans?

It was reported in 2011 that the average wealth of all members of Congress (*based on their mandatory financial discloser forms*) increased 25 percent over the previous year… significantly better than the average American. While no one at this point has come forward to present evidence that their voting records have clearly contributed to this increase, it is hard to imagine that there are not copious bad apples in this barrel.

Minimum Health

First let me relay a statistic that was published in 2009 which appears to be credible. The average US cost (*not necessarily out of pocket*) for healthcare is over $8100 per person for far less than universal coverage. This results in millions of us who can not afford coverage, and millions more who must rely on high deductible plans to have any healthcare at all. Other industrialized nations spend half that amount

to cover everyone from birth to death. The reasons for this disparity are several…
-- the paranoia about socialized medicine that is whipped up by the doctors and insurance companies
-- high prescription costs to US citizens
-- inefficient hospitals and clinics with expensive, redundant equipment
-- specialists that are permitted to charge high fees for what sometimes amounts to minimal efforts… have you been to a dermatologist lately?
-- and worst of all are the nearly unregulated, for-profit, insurance companies that siphon off billions of dollars from the medical care system

On the last point above. Let me emphasize that American healthcare insurance is truly a for-profit system. This means that a significant percentage of your health cost goes to line the pockets of insurance stockholders and those executives whose salaries and bonuses are based on performance. Their pay, curiously enough, is not related to providing superior care. Rather it is based on how little healthcare they can get away with paying for.

Michael Moore, activist: *"We allow these (insurance) companies to profit off of the sick"*

Our Canadian neighbor to the north has a medical system which appears to work fairly well. Virtually everyone there has healthcare even though they may have to be on a waiting list for procedures. In that case they can fall back on paying for care out of their own pocket, if they choose. While my experience with this system is limited, I do acknowledge that are a number of people who have expressed negative attitudes toward Canada's socialized medicine. Perhaps it is a matter of not being able to please all of the people all of the time, perhaps not.

In contrast to the rest of the developed world, our country has the largest percent of personal bankruptcies resulting from people's inability to pay for their high medical costs. In fact until the housing crisis of 2007, it was estimated that one half of all of the bankruptcies in this country was generated by people who could not afford to pay for these bills. And we have yet to fix this situation.

In Canada and many European countries, virtually no one has had to initiate bankruptcy because of their medical bills. To the contrary, people do die in America only because they lack rudimentary healthcare. And what do we do about it? Mostly we believe the propaganda about the evils of socialized medicine. So instead of having the best healthcare system in the world, which we once had, we have the worst among the developed countries, and we allow it remain that way. The real death panels (*a phrase invention by Sarah Palin regarding Obamacare*) is to do nothing. A Harvard study found that 39.000 people die per year due to insufficient healthcare or to having none.

Regarding the details of the Canadian healthcare system as I understand it...
-- health procedures are rated (*weighted*) on two criteria... the *cost* of the procedure and its probability of its success
-- high risk/high cost procedures get the lowest priority
-- low risk/low cost procedures get the highest priority
-- healthcare is allocated based on a procedure with a higher priority before one that has a lower priority
-- if you have a poor prognosis and the cost is high, you may not receive benefits paid for by the state
-- if you have a good prognosis and the cost is not excessive, your procedure is assured
-- in between, the allocation of health services is based on balancing priorities
-- if you do not qualify for coverage you can arrange to pay your own medical bills

The bottom line is that more people are covered in Canada and the healthcare system is not drained of billions of dollars by the insurance companies. Perhaps one dollar in three goes to insurance – money that could be used to help people with their medical problems. Even if the Canadian system is not perfect, it is light years ahead of ours where vast numbers of people can't afford healthcare and may be forced to use the bankruptcy card or flood the emergency rooms (*which the rest of us end up paying for*).

An argument for some of those who are against socialized medicine is that it is a bureaucracy that decides who may live (*gets medical care*) and who may die for lack of care. If one ignores the actual mechanics of this system, it sounds scary. And this is what many Americans are led to believe.

So if not everyone can afford full healthcare due to its high costs, there must be some decision mechanism to manage that shortfall. Our current "strategy" is to have…
-- the highest costs in the world for less than full coverage
-- many who can not afford to make insurance payments
-- emergency rooms which are required to care for everyone, including the uninsured, and then pass that bill onto the insured
-- people that die because they can not afford doctors and medicine
-- bankruptcies that result from high health costs

When it comes to the various alternatives for healthcare, there are several different options…
-- let people die that have no insurance (*do you think this doesn't actually happen?*)
-- allocate healthcare only to those who can afford it
-- have an outrageously expensive, for-profit insurance system that converts billions of our premium dollars into their non-medical pockets
-- have those people with the better cost vs. prognosis receive the available treatment

My vote is for the last option. It is inherently un-American for a person's income to determine if they can receive treatment? Do we do this with school availability, police services, or fire protection? We might show caring for those who are injured in a natural disaster, but we care little about those in a healthcare disaster.

Medical coverage is good, quick or cheap... pick any two

Another feature of our imperfect healthcare system is that politicians are eager to protect the profits of the drug industry to the point where people have to travel to Mexico or Canada to be able to purchase lower priced drugs. Then our Congresspersons pass laws that permit the border guards to confiscate those drugs as a punishment of the desperate people who are trying to save money. So...

-- Why are American drugs cheaper in these two countries anyway?

-- Do we believe that adequate, affordable healthcare should only be available for the middle (*maybe*) and upper classes?

-- Since Congress's healthcare system is unequaled, why should they bother themselves with the rest of us?

Yet another inequitable side to medical care and medical billing is what I will call the two-tier system. This occurs when, if you have insurance, your insurance company pays the doctor a discounted amount of their purposely inflated invoice. The patient then covers the ever-increasing co-payment (*remember when it was $5?*), which goes to the doctor. (*This is the clever method of transferring more of the medical costs to the patient's back and off that of the insurance companies*). On the other hand, if you can not afford an insurance plan, you pay the full, inflated price. So those who least can afford health insurance end up paying the highest price, which subsidizes those who are insured. As a result, the poor go without coverage or use the emergency rooms.

Health insurance corporations are much like the casinos in Las Vegas. No matter which patients win or loose, they come out on top. There are few situations which might put their bottom line at risk. There is just the continuous inflow of money (*drained from your healthcare*) while the rest of us are trying to manage their escalating invoices.

For each dollar spent on healthcare, a third is siphoned off by insurance companies. Then they tout the virtues of the free market system, all while they are busy bribing elected officials to maintain the status quo. Meanwhile the naïve public pays their enormous medical bills and wonders what can be done... in silence. In 2010 Goldman Sachs reported that insurance companies are willing to lose an individual subscriber or an entire company (*due to high premiums*) from their roles because they make up for those losses with higher premiums. A smaller pool of clients does not mean lower profits. What is does mean is that they are willing to put their profits above healthcare for the country. For the insurance executives, it's all about their bonuses.

Never be confused about this - insurance companies are in the profit *business and <u>absolutely not</u> in the* healthcare *business*

Minimum Medicare

Another potential tragedy in the offing with healthcare is Medicare. Because the government is run by the members of the already-rich-and-got-great-coverage club, there is little concern for those who are not part of their good ol' boy system. Congress has made earning a living progressively less profitable for doctors who are willing to see Medicare patients. Unless you are in this elder category you probably didn't know there was a problem brewing. But your time to find out will be coming soon enough.

Now I am not here to defend the income of doctors. They are already sufficiently compensated for their efforts, perhaps not like it used to be... say down from an annual BMW 750i to an Infinity G. But a problem occurs when their billings, which are submitted to Medicare, might be paid at a rate of pennies on the (*inflated invoice*) dollars. As a result of this shortfall in revenue, there is a disincentive toward serving that type of patient. And some of doctors are beginning to deny Medicare-paid treatment to their patients. To put this situation another way, rather than having doctors satisfied with only a portion of their exaggerated bills from Medicare, they may disallow Medicare patient billing and start asking patients to pay their full invoice up front.

Let's say that a doctor might receive $20 from the government for a $100 procedure and $40 from your co-pay. The Medicare-denied scheme means that you could now pay $100 for a visit and then work to receive the $20 from Medicare, making to procedure cost $80, or twice as much as an insured individual would pay. This change in billing practice amounts to increased revenue to doctors and a major reduction in their government-required paperwork.

If one assumes the inflated medical fee are only used as a bargaining chip against the insurance companies and Medicare, then anyone who has to pay the full amount is being taken to the cleaners. With

the government-reduced fees that are paid to Medicare doctors we have the following...
-- medical societies allow the inflated bills to both Medicare and insurance companies because they know that they will be heavily discounted
-- people without insurance pay the inflated rate because some doctor's insurers will not permit (*as if it was any of their business*) their covered doctors to offer their non-insured patients a discount (*which occurred at what used to be my dentist's office*)
-- because the government wastes billions of dollars on pork projects, on too many bureaucrats, pointless drug interdiction, and a losing war, they have to cut back elsewhere, like with services to the public
-- Medicare patients who can not find willing doctors will have to foot their own bills or go without, which is an unacceptable scenario
-- in the worst case scenario, Medicare patients may have to cover 80 percent of their inflated bills if they can not locate a cooperating doctor who is willing to see them

Let me go back to the insurance companies' requirement that doctors not discount their services to the uninsured. The reasons behind this policy may be to...
-- obscure the discounted amount of doctor's invoices that they reimburse
-- prevent doctors from being in competition with the insurance companies for receiving dollars from patients
-- make sure that as much revenue flows through the insurance system as possible to increase their profits, and by forcing people to buy insurance

One doctor's office which stopped servicing Medicare covered patients and many other insurance companies, reduced their fees to correspond more closely to the income they would likely receive from third party billings. So instead of charging $100 for a procedure to get back perhaps $15 in insurance payments, plus a $35 co-pay, they began charging the patients $50 directly. And with that change they do away with the expensive submission of paperwork to either the insurance companies or government or both.

Many Americans are naively happy that there are health insurance companies to help them through medically tough times without

understanding how costly that really is. They might not be so pleased in knowing that the insurance companies are responsible for creating the artificially high medical costs while siphoning off billions of dollars from healthcare to support...
-- a huge insurance infrastructure
-- inflated executive salaries
-- extravagant bonuses
-- stockholder dividends, because they are public corporations

More and more doctors are being forced to either retire early from what is becoming an increasingly less economical practice, or to drop insurance coverage to maintain their income.

You might care to know that some CEO's of insurance companies are making bonuses in the <u>tens of millions</u> of dollars per year for their technical skills at reducing your healthcare reimbursements. Oh yes, they do make their multi-million dollar salaries on top of this as well. The bonuses are because these folks have become adept at squeezing the doctors and patients alike. To pin it down, the problem with healthcare in this country is that...
-- people pay obscenely high health insurance premiums for less than full coverage
-- doctors get pennies on the dollar for their inflated billings to insurance companies and the government
-- patient co-payments have steadily increased in order to pay off the doctors for their lower reimbursement
-- the government and insurance companies pretend that they are doing the consumers a favor
-- our corrupted leaders repeat the chant that socialized medicine is bad for America
-- advocates for socialized medicine have to defend their position against the lies emanating from the insurance industry. Guess who has the most money to spend on that debate?

The insurance companies have an incentive to reduce or deny medical coverage whenever possible because it directly affects their bottom line, which has nothing to do with providing superior health care. What seems totally arrogant and incomprehensible is that these companies occasionally will not disclose whether they will cover a particular procedure in advance of a person having that procedure. What? People are left to guess as to the affordability of going ahead with their medical care. Can you spell deterrent?

One solution for people without an insurance plan might be to purchase only catastrophic healthcare coverage. Then locate a doctor who will discount their rates for uninsured visits. This would result in an outlay that is more than the typical co-pay, but the cost of insurance coverage would be far less. Finding a cooperative doctor or dentist may be difficult though. I have been turned down several times with this request, but managed to find a cooperating dentist. Apparently some doctors like their higher revenue from the uninsured patients, and care little for these people's financial welfare.

Now it is not just lawyers that we have a good reason to dislike

Another option would be to find a company that acts like a brokerage by bargaining with doctors for uninsured rates that are comparable to co-pays plus receipts from insurance submissions. What does this say about a medical profession that forces people to think about using a broker?

Illegal Immigration

Conspiracy can be defined as a planned or executed illegal activity between two or more persons. It can also be engaged in between politicians and big business when they pretend to be doing something about aliens in order to placate US citizens. Depending on who you ask, we either do or don't have a problem. The do side seems to suggest that illegal immigrants…
-- are involved in a disproportional amount of criminal activity
-- raise the cost of emergency room fees for all because they do not have healthcare, and do not pay when utilizing this service
-- require us to spend millions of dollars on border control
-- use our schools, roads and other services without paying for the infrastructure
-- may not pay income taxes

The don't side seems to suggests that illegal immigrants…

-- will take many of the jobs that Americans won't
-- are a cheap, plentiful, and reliable source of manual labor
-- insure that the crops will be picked

The Heritage Foundation, a conservative think tank, has estimated that the lifetime cost of illegal immigration to the government at $22.000 per legal resident because of...
-- under payment of all taxes
-- additional school costs for their larger families
-- unearned income credits
-- driving without insurance
-- education in Spanish
-- expanded jail populations
-- social security benefits

So it turns out that our cheap tomatoes are not really so cheap after all. They are being subsidized by diverting their true costs into other sectors of the economy. Even if the need for cheap labor were a legitimate reason for permissive border control, the real cost of permitting a flood of aliens may be too high to justify.

Need evidence that the government is talking a good game rather that playing one? Consider our research facility at Area 51 in the Nevada desert. There are no fences at this top-secret location, just electronics that detects anything larger than a mosquito. Nothing gets past their electronic blockade undetected. This implies that we have the technology but not the interest to stop the influx of illegal aliens cold.

Perhaps we do not want to offend Mexico by reducing the US dollars that are sent back by undocumented workers. One theory about this is that the dollars sent to Mexico do not always chase American products and therefore act to keep a lid on inflation as our currency becomes their currency. In other words, if we can print and use US dollars that end up mainly as the currency in a foreign country, we have essentially gotten goods for nothing. It would be akin to our taking out a personal loan and then having to pay back only a portion of it.

Having a guest worker program may be an unenforceable plan that some are contemplating. If we permit aliens to enter with this type of visa, what would prevent them from staying permanently? We don't adequately monitor the foreign students or temporary visas holders (*potential terrorists*) now as it is. Why should we expect that this might turn out any differently with a work visa? The truth may be that government administrations have known how easily this program would fail. Perhaps they hope that people grow weary of the issue, and big business can retain its stoop labor pool.

Immigration Reform

In 2010 Arizona passed the landmark immigration bill 1070 that made headlines around the world. In response the Obama Justice Department sued the state in an attempt to overturn the law. In 2011 Arizona countersued the feds to...
-- enforce existing laws
-- build more border fences
-- provide more border agents
-- offer improved technology
-- reimburse Arizona for of the costs associated with the jailing of illegal immigrants who are convicted of state crimes

So what was the response from the Department of Homeland Security? Their spokesperson said...
-- "The countersuit had no merit." (*without offering any supporting reasons for that statement*)
-- "Border staffing is higher than ever." (*how much higher than what?*)
-- "Actions like this ignore all of the statistical evidence." (*which was also not provided*)
-- "[It] belittles the significant progress that our men and women in uniform (*a little flag waving here*) have made."(*no examples again*)

As I read the fed's argument I could not help but be impressed by the lack of any substantive information. Just blather designed to influence the easily influenced. And this is from the department that was headed by a former Governor of Arizona. It is another example of how easily government department heads obediently follow the prevailing political line.

Just Price Fixing

One out of many examples of how big business controls the government involved the Alcohol Control Board in California a number of years back. Because the state's liquor distributors wanted to maximize their profits, they lobbied the legislature to set minimum "fair trade" prices on beer, wine and alcohol. Let's see… lobbying, PAC money, new laws, yep they all go together. Then the state went on to claim that this legalized price fixing was designed to help the mom and pop stores compete with the big guys. Haven't we been fed these bogus story regarding mom and pop businesses before, like with farmers and crops? Are convenience stores really in danger of going under because of giant supermarkets? As a result of that beverage law there was no competition allowed by price among any businesses that sold alcohol in California. That is until a mom and pop (whoda thunk) liquor store owner decided to fight city hall. He began offering discount pricing, was threatened, fined, and sued by the state, but eventually prevailed in the courts. Chalk up one for the consumer, and for mom and pop who do not want government interference is their businesses.

Insider Trading Too

In recent years the Securities and Exchange Commission (*SEC*) has become more active in prosecuting insider trading on the various exchanges. But it has also had to ignore a gaping loophole in their process of jailing outrageous cheaters. Members of Congress have given themselves blanket immunity when it comes to (*among their other unethical behaviors*) using inside information derived from conversations with corporate executives and in other venues. As a result, some members have made millions of dollars from trades that would have landed you and I in jail. And they had shown no interest in cracking down on their own nefarious activities. Just one more example of why these self-serving public servants will spend massive sums of money (*sometimes their own*) and copious hours of campaign time to secure a seat in Congress in order to richly reward themselves down the road. Then in 2012 after an exposé segment on 60 minutes, Congress did agree to abolish the practice. 99 bottles of beer on the wall - when one of them falls, (*there are still*) 98 bottles of beer on the wall…

The Eric Holder Affair

In 2012 the NRA lobbied Congresspersons from both parties to hold Attorney General Eric Holder in Contempt of Congress. Their participation in this was prompted by their fear that <u>not</u> penalizing him for a failure to release documents about "gun-walking" to smugglers would result in future legislation restricting gun sales. I see it, but I just don't get the connection between guns and paranoia.

After months of procrastination, diversion, and finally refusing to turn the subpoenaed documents to Congress regarding the guns given to Mexican terrorists (*the so called Fast and Furious caper*), the House voted to issue a Contempt Of Congress citation to Attorney General Eric Holder. Holder was the first Executive Branch member to ever be sighted for criminal contempt. His refusal to provide the requested documentation was claimed to be justified owing to the support of Obama when he proclaimed Executive Privilege (*EP*) over the matter. Since Congress is not a judicial body, the contempt citation had to be forwarded to the Justice Department (*JD*) in Washington DC for prosecution.

Well any damn fool can guess what came next. Deputy Attorney General James Cole issued a statement that the JD would not pursue the indictment of Holder based on the President's claim of EP. They went on to affirm that therefore no criminal act had been committed. The Deputy then went so far as to articulate that their decision follows a long-standing practice across the administrations of both parties. The only option that was left up to Congress was to issue a civil contempt citation, which does not go through the JD. And since they did not expect any different action from the JD, case closed.

Corporate Coziness

If anyone is inclined to dispute the unhealthy relationships that take place between business and government they need look no further than the latest scandal at the Federal Aviation Agency (*FAA*) as prima facie evidence. According to the two whistleblowers who testified before Congress, the agency has routinely pressured its inspectors to ignore and soft pedal safety issues at the airlines. They testified that the FAA is cozy with airline executives, and that their managers have put those personal relationships above the welfare of the flying public. So we should ask the obvious question. Don't any of these dodos have to fly on scheduled airlines? Assuming that they do, why would they be inclined to put their own and their relative's lives in jeopardy for a friendship? Once again it is our genetic-emotional disposition to ignore potential problems and assume that all will take care of itself. Or in this case, it could be a darker picture of being well compensated for looking the other way.

Whistleblowers would not be needed in government or business if there were not corrupt practices that are ongoing

We all know that our government's regulating agencies are supposed to protect us from malpractices of industries and businesses. While this is very nice in theory, it is often short on execution. One example of the open door policy between business and government involved two executives at the National Highway Traffic Safety Administration (*NHTSA*). They joined Toyota after having been implicated in the agencies' grossly insufficient oversight of that same company. Does it come as a surprise to anyone that the problems Toyota had with unintended acceleration, inability to brake, and inability to stop the engine were downplayed by the agency? Toyota was so proud of negotiating their liability to minimal fixes that they triumphantly (*and don't you think a bit foolishly*) posted those results in a newsletter.

It appears that the two officials referred to above knew that they had an opportunity for a lucrative position with the company that they regulated, and they did not want to upset that applecart. One can only speculate at how often this breach of ethics takes place at our government oversight agencies.

More instances of how business runs our government revolves around safety issues with the toxin BPA that is found in plastics used by the food industry. There have been over 100 studies from government scientists and university laboratories raising health concerns about this compound. So what was the response of the Food and Drug Administration (*FDA*)? They pronounced that these plastics are not harmful in the quantities that people would likely encounter them. Then they said that in 2008 they relied on just two research studies which were funded by the plastics industry and backed by the American Plastics Council. This might not be as problematical if it were not for the ignored findings of independent researchers. BPA ingestion has been linked to breast and prostate cancer, behavioral disorders, and potential reproductive problems in lab animals.

Because they had such a good example set for them, the plastic's industry is using the same model that the tobacco industry used so successfully for years.... fight the science and postpone regulation and compensation. Ultimately the science against BPA may become overwhelming, but in the mean time the sales of these plastic products go on unabated. It's all about our genetic-emotional genes because we do not personally know the victims.

During an exposure of government graft, it came to light in 2008 that personnel at the Minerals Management Service (*MMS*) were enriching themselves by taking bribes from the industry that they are assigned to oversee. Not to give too much print to BP, but the infamous oil spill came about thanks in great part to the cozy factor between the regulators and regulated. BP allegedly had been permitted to violate numerous safety regulations which directly resulted in the loss of the drilling platform, eleven dead workers, and hundreds of millions of gallons of crude spewed into the Gulf of Mexico. Shortly thereafter, a senior member of the MMS retired, presumably to avoid testifying about his participation. So as it often turn out in government, white collar criminals frequently get off the hook. It's unlikely that anyone will be charged in the worker's deaths despite the need to hold BP and MMS people responsible for this horrific and preventable deed.

Should we require further proof of the incest has been rampant between the government and business, one has only to look at the statistics coming out about the oil industry regulators. In 2011 it was reported that one out of five employees involved in regulating this industry had been released from some duties because they may come in contact with family members there. Further, since mid 2008 ten people that were hired as regulators were bared for two years from working where they would come into contact with former employers. With the Bureau of Ocean Energy Management (*BOEM*), 35 percent of its inspectors have been disqualified because a friend or relative works for a company that they would interact with. Prior to a policy change that was enacted to identify potential conflicts of interest, coziness between the regulators and regulated went on virtually unchecked.

Rampant Leniency

Government agencies that have the power to fine companies and pursue court actions have frequently turned into mister nice guy with bankers. How often have your heard that the defendants neither admit nor deny wrongdoing when a case is settled? This is undoubtedly the feds way of speeding up the trial process. But is it right? Is this really punishment? Going hand and hand with this easygoingness are the pennies on the dollar that have been accepted in of court settlements. In the case of the Securities and Exchange Commission (*SEC*) v Citigroup Inc., losses of more than $700 million to investors had a proposed settlement of just $285 thousand. To his credit, the US District judge denounced and rejected the SEC's agreement as "pocket change" when compared to the losses that were incurred. Citicorp had been accused of selling slices of a Class V deal to investors in 2007 without disclosing that they were betting against half of the assets in the deal.

As mentioned earlier, in 2012 the Congress got around to passing an insider trading act specifically targeting trades based on the inside knowledge that Congresspersons pick up on the job. This was a bill that had languished for six years with virtually not support. When a TV expose' and a couple of WSJ articles brought this matter to the publics attention during Presidential campaigning, the attitude in Congress changed. The point I would demonstrate here is the public statements that two politicians made about it. They said that this law "will help restore public trust". I guess these deep thinkers are living in la la land, not recognizing or acknowledging the myriad of other areas where their bodies' integrity is sorely lacking. That particular band-aid is no fix for a gaping wound.

Ethics Free Zone

What we have in government is a runaway corruption train (*I do not use this term lightly*) with the engineer (*the public*) sound asleep. Politicians have learned that there will be virtually no downside to manipulating the system to suit their personal agenda, which is reelection, of course, and that they can do so with near abandon. Their actions are not the type of graft that one is usually imprisoned for. Rather it is the legalized solicitation of bribery from powerful, vested interests. Office holders know that the clandestine activities of government are largely conducted behind closed doors where the public can not exercise scrutiny, and that convenience makes them nearly invisible and invulnerable to inspection by their constituents. Their only fear might be that an opposition candidate may disclose…
-- dark secrets about their behaviors
-- what they voted for and against
-- who they are in bed with, both politically and personally

Of course this dearth of ethics does not just apply to elected officials, but to appointed officials and corporate executives as well. During the financial meltdown that was promulgated by the home mortgage derivatives scandal, the bailed-out bankers nicely gave themselves a total of $1.6 billion in bonus pay. After an uproar from the public (*while Congress did nothing*) a czar was appointed to look into this excessive pay scandal. In 2010 after months of "diligent" study, Kenneth Feinberg, a lawyer, came to the mind boggling conclusion that the corrupt thieves would get to keep all of their ill gotten pay

gains. His unacceptable logic was that their public shame was sufficient punishment for their misdeeds. Hmmm…
-- Do we even know the names of these allegedly shamed individuals?
-- Were they shamed enough to return any of the money?
-- Where did we get this moron Feinberg from anyway? Could it possibly have been from Wall Street?
-- How could this ludicrous decision have been made without some form of quid-pro-quo?

Curiously at the end of 2011 the major banks that were part of the melt-down scheme have yet to see even one of the chief executives indicted for fraud. While there is enough of that to go around, they appear to be off limits. And this is years after the bubble burst, so it can not be a lack of time to gather the incriminating evidence. One might ask: what should we glean from this about what the SEC's job might be? Is it to punish or to protect offenders?

Government Incorporated

Not too many years back the US government employed only one person for every 100 civilians employed by business. That number is now up to sixteen per, and climbing. Before long we will be in the same numerical boat as is Greece at eighteen, and you know how well they are doing, needing a huge bailout in 2012 to remain afloat.

Our national debt is being ignored by those very people who have the most control over it. And why, you should ask, is this happening? Well in a word it is reelection. They spend the taxpayer's money in massive amounts to placate business and line their government-pay-pockets. Unfortunately their constituents do not get the connection between US debt and political corruption. While we do not ordinarily identify Congresspersons as corrupt. I challenge you to come up with a better explanation for this behavior.

Fixing the Problem

Why is politics broken? There may be hundreds of reasons but here are a few that you may concur with...
-- people are innately self-centered
-- politicians, with minimal scrutiny of their activities, are at the apex of that behavior
-- we have been told forever that the two-party system is preferable to having third-party candidates and possible run-off elections, which conveniently limits the options of voters (*would you be ok with only 2 telephone companies, or 2 television networks, or 2 banks?*)
-- politicians apparently find some sadistic gratification in their artificial confrontations with the opposition party
-- campaign funding is more productive when the lobbyist are occasionally manipulated by politicians (*surprise*) who have discovered that stating their positions can be counter-productive to fund raising
-- incumbent politicians, with their established money sources and power bases, stand a far better chance of winning the next election because name recognition trumps performance
-- since getting reelected is the politician's prime directive, the majority of their time, directly or indirectly, is expended in that pursuit, and is not often used to produce productive legislation
-- getting along in the legislature means becoming subservient to the power brokers who dole out positions, perks and penalties
-- legislation is accomplished as much by who one will return a favor to, as by the merits of a bill
-- there appears to be a fear of Presidential power and, therefore, a reluctance to go up against it
-- there are no term limits to prevent the accumulation of power

When Nebraska joined the Union it sought to resolve a problem of wasted political energy by instituting a unicameral legislature. The members are selected in nonpartisan elections rather than in separate primaries. The top two vote-getters are then entitled to run in the general election. Because of no mandatory party alignments within the legislature, coalitions tend to form issue by issue, based on a member's philosophy of government, geographic background, and constituency. However, almost all the members of the legislature are affiliated with either the Democratic or Republican Party, and both parties explicitly endorse candidates for legislative seats. But because new candidates have to run on their positions rather than party connection, there is less influence peddling by those of longer tenure. While this system of government is not fool-proof, it could be a step in the right direction for the rest of the states. The problem is, of course, that there is an immense amount of inertia in the States and in Congress. Plus there is a heavy investment in the broken system that we are straddled with. No self-respecting politician wants to give up their advantage at reelection. And there are no practical measures available for the rest of us to redress the deficiencies.

Government straddles the line between self-serving the politician and serving the public... leaning heavily toward the politician side

On Being American

In 2009 my wife and I went to a Smothers Brothers concert. Because I liked them in the late 60's when they had a television show, I was very familiar with their ability to be irreverent toward government, war and religion. Their show was toned down a bit compared to their TV appearances, but it did have a skit about the Presidents that went something like...
-- Washington could not tell a lie
-- Nixon could not tell the truth
-- Clinton could not tell the difference
-- Bush could not tell anything

On leaving the theater I overheard an older couple who were annoyed that the Smothers Bothers would bring politics into their concert...
-- Did they think that their show was just about singing?
-- Where were these two pinheads when the brothers were doing these routines on TV and stage for a living?
-- Did they not understand what the show might be about?
-- Did they agree with the brother's previous censorship by CBS?
(*Nixon is reputed to have pressured CBS into firing them*)

The point for me was that these two questioned someone's right to present political humor as if it was unclean or un-American. I imagine that those two don't have a clue about the corruption that goes on in government, and that they blindly support the clowns who get elected to office. Being an American should mean that we do what is best for the country, and that does not mean being silent in the face of deceit and corruption. Short of working for an enemy, no one should be thought of as being un-American because of their standing up against incompetence and corruption in Congress or elsewhere.

Dumb Press Tricks

Pride and Prejudice

I'm going to lump the press into the same category as big business because they walk the walk and talk the talk. Ergo they are indeed big business. In stark contrast to my personal opinion, reporters might imagine themselves as being...
-- independent members of the fourth estate (*a coined phrase by Edmund Burke during a parliamentary debate in 1792 on the opening up of press reporting in the House of Commons in England*)
-- guardians against government evils
-- purveyors of the truth

In reality their reporting more often finds them in the categories of both government collaborators and show business outlets. By this I mean that their performance is often directed at facilitating political deceit and pandering to sensationalism, as much as it is toward probing for and providing pertinent news. During the 2008 Presidential campaign, one of the talking heads at a round table discussion conceded that he and his fellow reporters were responsible for creating a candidates momentum or loss of the same. This was acknowledged while displaying a look of pride. Interestingly there was no objection from the other journalists at this affair. So it is clear that they know the truth about their manipulation of the public, and they do not much care to correct it.

It is reasonable to assume that one of the presses' primary roles should be to ask probing questions to reveal the truth and expose dishonesty. Personal biases ought to be left at home and not be incorporated into the coloring of their reporting. Far too often this is wishful thinking. Let me demonstrate common press biases by first analyzing the appropriate technique for interrogating a witness in our courts...
-- unless the judge permits a lawyer to treat a defendant as hostile, statements that are accusatory may not be allowed

-- questions may not begin with a leading or assumption-directed phrases like: "Isn't it true that…"or "Didn't you…"
-- rather the phrasing must be: "Is it true that…" or "Did you…"

These rules of conduct should similarly be used by members of the press as a proper method for keeping their agendas out of the questioning. However it is not unusual to have reporters express their personal beliefs couched in their queries because there is no one to stop them… certainly not their bosses who must surely encourage that behavior. Attitude peddling puts the press in the position of making or tainting the news, rather than just reporting on it. One motivation behind the presses' methods of questioning can be explained as a tawdry effort to interject sensationalism into the reporting process because this is what viewers/readers want. As a result, we get what we ask for.

An unbiased press is a nice theory, but it is not the norm. To demonstrate this absence of straight forward reporting we might ask ourselves….
-- Do the media outlets have an obvious preponderance of liberal or conservative columnists on their staffs?
-- Are their news stories slanted in a particular direction without an accurate representation of both sides on each issue?
-- Do they voice expressed or implied support for one candidate or issue over another?
-- Do the reporters ask leading, rather than probing questions?
-- Are they inclined to be neutral?

Presses' Inclinations

One of the proclivities of the press is to report on an event or topic using the term: reportedly in order to attach a hint of veracity to a news story. What exactly does reportedly mean? It may mean that someone wishes to remain anonymous, and be able to pass along confidential information to a reporter. However this in no way implies that the disclosed "facts" have veracity. It may be that this is the quoted person's method of poisoning the waters of an opponent. Or it may be used to deflect attention from an issue. Far too often the press uses this ruse to get newsprint or air time. In point of fact, the press is less exacting with the truth than are most of us. After all they are paid by the word and not necessarily by a thought's merits or its authenticity. Why do you think the press drones on endlessly over stories that deserve little more than a passing glance? Did we really need...

-- six days of news about President Ford's funeral
-- the months of bylines regarding a college sex scandal
-- the endless rant about the death of a wife by her playboy husband
-- an obsession with the Congressperson who groped his staff members
-- focusing on Congressperson's who cheat on their mates (*which is immoral*) rather than their voting records (*which can also be immoral*).

And don't think that the anniversary of each traumatic event from recent history will escape there attention either. Nothing much has changed with Charles Manson in a quarter of a century, but he still hits the news on an annual basis. Where would the press be without a tickler file? The press can be so preoccupied with the specter of tasteless sensationalism because there is a ready audience for this kind of foolishness... sometimes called yellow journalism. No horrific story is allowed to go under reported. One of the channels in my area goes so far as to dedicate most of their evening news budget to as many police blotter stories (*murder, rape, pedophiles, hit and run*) as they can locate. Do we really learn anything valuable from this type of reporting? It certainly does not uncover what our politicians have failed to accomplish while they are in office due to their conflicted, money raising activities. But that disclosure would require real reporting which is not in most reporters' playbooks.

Mark Twain, author: *If you don't read the newspaper you are uninformed, if you do read the newspaper you are misinformed.*

News by Assassination

Now that cable television has become a major medium for the dissemination of news, we are inundated with the talking heads who both create and exploit controversy. They may express personal and occasionally vitriolic opinions, perhaps more than they present news. They drone on endlessly with tawdry attitudes that fill the airwaves and use tortured logic in an effort to make political hay for their favored issue, party or candidate. Because of this failure to be impartial, we should ask...

-- How dare reporters and networks align themselves into liberal and conservative camps anyway?

-- Is that the best way to present the news and inform the public?

-- Can't we find people with a balanced point of view and no political ax to grind?

-- Shouldn't we insist on honesty and integrity from the news corporations?

On both the ultra-conservative and ultra-liberal sides of the spectrum we have a string of commentators (*notice that I did not say reporters*) who seem to relish the limelight that they have created for themselves. Why else would they be invited to visit the late night variety shows if they weren't in show business? And this celebrity is accomplished at the expense of unbiased reporting. While a few may make an effort to present the news in a relatively impartial fashion, the majority are preoccupied with casting aspersions on their targets as often as they can manage. Forget that this contrived melodrama takes the format of...

-- innuendo

-- exaggeration

-- distortion

-- out of context quotes (*especially*)

-- deliberate misinterpretation

-- outright lies

I guess the current king of deliberate misrepresentation is Sean Hannity on the Fox channel, perhaps only because I do not listen to the radio talk shows. His biases can be so blatant and irrational that they have become annoying to listen to, which is a long way from being informative. Essentially he has cast himself as a rabble rouser with only a passing concern for the truth. Often that infrequent truth is couched among half-truths and lies. Corporations that employ these personalities do so, not for the straightforward presentation of news and the accuracy of their statements, but for the ratings that they seek. Audiences will believe almost anything if it is presented with enough conviction, emotion, authority and repetition. And this "news" may continue until well after an incidence has been debunked by legitimate authority.

In years gone by the three major network anchors appeared to disseminate a relatively dispassionate view of the daily news. In fact as a child I wished for presentations to be a bit more revealing or controversial, especially when it came to news about the politicians. But in a classic case of be careful what you wish for, that tide has turned. Much of cable programming that passes for news has an entertainment quality, and occasionally nasty quotient to it.

In 2013 Obama gave his State of the Union address. This was followed by the Republican reply, as has become usual. Marko Rubio was tapped as the up-and-comer in the ranks to deliver the opposition's message. During his speech he leaned awkwardly to retrieve a bottle of water and take a sip. No big deal, right? Wrong. The in-Obama's-pocket media turned it into a mini-indictment of Marko for the uncomfortable movement. So when the liberal press wants to degrade someone, they will not hesitate to pick on anything that they can get away with.

The social reporting on celebrities is even worst. Do we really need to care about the out-of-control lives of these pampered, self-centered brats? A case in point about slanted coverage would be the initial fifteen minute apology of Tiger Woods regarding his extra-marital affairs. While my wife and I thought that his contrition was reasonably on point, members of the blather media generally gave him poor marks for reading a prepared speech and for not taking any question. Like little children who wanted to play with someone else's toy, they felt that Tiger selfishly took control of the event. It did not matter that he responded to questions on the minds of most people. He was berated by these media for not giving them their fair share of time. Could that criticism be any more revealing of how they see themselves as being entitled? Talk about arrogance!

In the ninety days prior Tiger's TV appearance, the celebrity press was involved in hundreds, perhaps thousands of hours devoted to dissecting his personality, personal life, and illicit behavior. Their opinions were not labeled as such, but they were presented as insights by those in the know. The truth is that these commentators demonstrated virtually nothing beyond wild guesses, assumptions, and fabrications. In an interesting addendum to the above, the press saw fit to interview at least one of the women who were involved in affairs with Tiger. The person that I saw being given her fifteen minutes of shame lamented the fact that Tiger did not apologize to her since he had said that he loved her. Could this person possibly be even more self-absorbed than Tiger? He was married, you know. How does she figure that her rights were abridged? Did she ever think about the rights of Tiger's wife? Sounds like a sleazy bar-broad to me.

Creating the Issues

Rarely does the national TV press ignore an opportunity to criticize a candidate for changing their mind on a major issue… flip-flopping as they are inclined to call it. We should all appreciate that life and circumstances are constantly in a state of flux, and that only the most stubborn person would not be willing to learn a new lesson when the opportunity comes along. Yet the incident-creation types that wield the airwaves would have us believe that taking a new stance more often than once in a blue moon indicates a fatal lack of integrity. According to the press, if we can not believe what is said on some date forever, than how could we ever believe any other things that the candidate has said? This is either…
-- a fool's logic
-- a shallow effort to impugn someone's veracity without real justification
-- a shameless attitude that makes for good press

At a political rally in 2007 John McCain made a modest joke by paraphrasing the Beach Boys' song Barbara Ann. He devilishly changed a refrain to: bomb Iran. It was more interesting than funny, but the press invented a seamy side to the lyrics and tried to make an issue of it. McCain's appropriate and quick response was that they "lighten up and get a life". It was nice to see someone refuse to back down to the sensation seekers that have found a home in the press corps. That episode demonstrates how desperate some reporters are to get their fifteen seconds of air time to protect their job security.

I can imagine that the newspaper's daily editor/reporter meetings are not only filled with intellectual talk about which of the stories are more important than others, or which deserve the front page of the paper, or first position on the TV news broadcast. They must also discuss how to sensationalize them for the public appetite because that is what people want. If this were not true, there would not be dozens of pages and hours of television devoted to the latest campus shooting or a missing child. How does a campus shooting differ from the hundreds of other shootings that may occur daily? The answer is wealthy, white-collar offspring.

When we may want legitimate sensationalism, the press is mostly mute. For example, we know little beyond the daily body count of what is happening in Iraq and Afghanistan, which are government controlled news venues. There is seldom a mention of how much those countries' people may be suffering or (*especially*) why they blame Americans for much of that sorrow. After all, we need to be viewed by ourselves as the good guys. And the press corps has no incentive to upset that particular applecart because they feed off it. To get into the reasons why Arabs may blame us for their difficulties, we have to try to understand their mindset. They…
-- are religious in the extreme
-- do not co-exist well with other religions
-- can label non-Arabs as infidels
-- believe that their homeland is only their land
-- will not tolerate invaders (*everyone else*)
-- would rather live under religious tyranny than under democratic "oppression" because this is their culture
-- dismiss freedom as a political con that is played on the Europeans and Americans
-- might rather be blown up than submit to Western ideas
-- believe that an honorable death is to be revered and not feared
-- think we are too stupid to go home (*ok, on this last point they have my full agreement*)

Does any of the above make sense to you? These arguments against staying the Middle East do not seem to sway more than a handful of our politicians.

Press Promotions

The press is not with out guilt in manufacturing those false heroes which we may have come to admire. For example, when a President dies, the only people who are asked to bear witness about his presidency and persona to the media are the deceased's friends and well-wishers. Had I not been aware of Presidential behaviors that frequently have been dishonorable, I might be moved by this contrived adulation. It is not my intention to personally denigrate Gerald Ford and George Bush... just note that they were under-qualified office holders. Likable or not, the job of being President was substantially over their heads, as Gerry once conceded. And Ford performed a disservice to the country when he preemptively pardoned Richard "I am not a crook" Nixon, the de facto leader of the Watergate felons. Lately the wags are giving Ford high marks for this intervention in the justice process as responsible for putting that unfortunate event behind us. So with this logic, should we let all felons out of prison because it degrades our image? Even today President Nixon, the preeminent poster boy for *corrupt government starts at the top* is being forgiven by the press for his...
-- enemies list
-- paranoia
-- shady dealings
-- direct association with felons
-- being an un-indicted conspirator

Press Passivity

We apparently have short memories when it comes to recalling the negative aspects of our political history as they relate to our Presidents. Or perhaps we just can't stand to think of them as the felons that they occasionally are. Do you remember when President

Johnson had a juicy broadcast license for an Austin radio station delivered to his wife Lady Bird in spite of intense competition for the plum? Did the press have more than a passing reference or two to this event?

Prior to Nixon's journey into infamy, his aids were putting out feelers about having him nominated for a Nobel Peace Prize. This was ostensibly justified by his ending the Viet Nam war and ordering our troops home. So the act of stopping a previous, illegitimate policy of President Johnson was purported to make a world hero out of Nixon. Does anyone wonder just how Nixon's aids thought that they might be successful with their Peace Prize promotion? And aren't you just a little bit curious about what putting out feelers implies? Perhaps it means that they thought the Nobel committee could be manipulated in some way. Or a darker explanation might be that the mere mention of Nixon and Nobel in the same breath would enhance his image for the next election.

Does all of this slight of hand mean that we have not had a number of respect-worthy Presidents? No. But perhaps there were more in our early history rather than later years. While some of our recent Presidents may have performed well at their duties, that fact does not imply that there weren't a number of their peers who might have executed that job just as competently or better. It also does not necessarily follow that our most-revered Presidents had carried out their duties all that well in spite of positive press reporting. Americans just like to have our heroes regardless of whether or not it makes sense and is accurate. It is all part of the Indian and chief genetics that sanctions our respect for leaders even though it is out sync with their abilities or integrity.

Because of our gullibility, government officials can and do lie to us with impunity, and suffer little consequence from the charade

Who is in Charge?

Subsequent to the lawsuit that was filed by Dan Rather against CBS in 2007, it became evident that the press's practice of corrupt reporting goes well beyond its reporters. If one can put faith in Dan's contention about CBS management, the executives that own the news outlets are also responsible for misshaping the news. Their pressure to suppress or slant stories amounts to censorship, just as leaving out details or ignoring obvious conclusions would. Dan related that the documents which would have condemned Bush's unmilitary-like military record, and the opportune loss of same, had not been conclusively demonstrated to be either accurate or inaccurate. They were just conveniently missing. Yet CBS was alleged to have forced Dan into an on-air apology to maintain good relations with the White House. So one has to ask, do we really want news outlets cultivating cozy relations with the same government entities that they are supposed to be reporting on? Do we want the chickens hanging out in the foxes den and doing their bidding?

The Presses' Role

The epidemic-level of political malfeasance that is part and parcel of public office is made possible thanks to (*ta da*) the average folks who want to believe the best about their elected officials, and who seldom question what mischief they may be up to. This applies equally to the press because they can occasionally be up to no good as well. For example, they are less than critical of the…
-- political press handouts which may be accepted as gospel
-- politician's statements that are generally taken at face value
-- evasive answers that are allowed to go unchallenged
-- luxurious, taxpayer-paid, press-tag-along trips with Presidents that go lightly reported
-- shameful "debate" that goes on in Congress

Another aspect of the under-reported behavior that occurs while in office is the sense of entitlement demonstrated by elected officials. Take Barak Obama for example. Those who are fortunate enough to travel with the President on mind-numbingly-expensive jaunts around the globe are seldom critical of the cost, even though they should be fully aware of it. The perk is just too much to pass up in spite of the manipulation effect it has on reporters. Another White House directed exploitation is Washington's elite reporters being invited to party at cozy "press events" with the same officials they may be assigned to report on. And of course they want to be invited back for the next up-close-and-personal gala by limiting their aggressive reporting. This is not exactly the arm's length arrangement that the forth estate should have establish for themselves. Rarely has there been a President like Obama who pushed so many controversial issues that were against the will of the electorate. Being surrounded by yes-persons 24/7 and encountering minimal, in-depth press coverage may be the factors in developing this self-serving attitude.

The difference between reporters and automobile salespeople is that we all know that the later are deceitful

Yes, the press does provide a few stories that may expose some of the questionable behaviors of politicians, but this is usually done without crossing the line of press etiquette. When these disclosures do occur, reporters may be exposing just the tip of the iceberg with their limited follow-up. Or they may be mostly picking on those whose behaviors are over the top.

If the press corps were only marginally aggressive in their corruption reporting they could fill the news with political activity for which you and I might go to jail. In 2009 New Jersey sting operation, the feds netted dozens of high ranking officials, including some Mayors, who were indicted for corruption. Yet until the feds revealed these arrests, the dealings of this band of alleged felons were virtually unknown to the public. If you can have this many persons involved in an active conspiracy to subvert government, it should not have come as a complete surprise. After all how did the feds conclude that something was wrong if there was no smoke around this fire? So where was the press when the conspiracy was going down?

Another of the press's gifts that are bestowed on politicians is by allowing a lack of attribution by the government's rules-makers to their pronouncements and dictates. There is hardly a day that goes by without a press story assigning credit to some nameless, faceless, element, such as...
-- the Pentagon said this
-- the VA refused to do that
-- the State Department did this...

-- the Justice Department decided not to pursue...

Well who exactly are there anonymous people any way? I am fairly sure that the government buildings do not make our public policy. Because we rarely learn the names of the persons who are responsible for our government's actions, those who are making the decisions are conveniently protected by this veil of secrecy. Others in a position to know the inside story may have their own jobs to protect. Consequently they may be disinclined to risk any retribution with an ill-advised revelation. The result of this secrecy is that the bureaucrats are relatively free to set policies and practices that may be in conflict with the public good.

Do you remember when the press dutifully reported those trumped-up stories about the remains of Iraqi chemical factories being discovered in dilapidated tractor trailers for example? Right! Our countries' chemical factories occupy hundreds of acres, but those clever, sandal-footed Iraqis were so sophisticated that they could produce nerve gases in dirty, non-air-conditioned truck trailers in the middle of the desert. The shallow thinkers in our press initially bought this fabrication. Then there was VP Cheney's subsequent role in the manufactured WMD stories which his office blamed on other agencies for an information failure. Had the press corps and Congress been more diligent (*say at the sixth grade level*) we wouldn't be killing Americans in a country that wants no part of us and has so little regard for their own lives.

Our militaristic attitude may have been somewhat encouraged by the memberships of Bush, Cheney, Rice and Rhumsfeld in The Project for the New American Century, a non-profit, educational organization dedicated to a few fundamental propositions. Among their platforms are the beliefs that...
-- American leadership is good for both America and for the world
-- such leadership requires military strength, diplomatic energy and commitment to moral principle
-- we should rally support for a vigorous and principled policy of American international involvement

Now that the truth about the war had somewhat come to light, is it any wonder why Cheney chose not to test the political waters, much less run for President? Oh yes, and what became of the expose' of his previous company, Halliburton, and the allegations of their misappropriation of hundreds of billions of dollars from the war's reconstruction effort. And why were fees still being paid to them to help restore Iraq when that story was exposed? Where was there the press follow-up on this alleged theft of taxpayer money?

When there is no press accountability of officials, there is corruption

Press and Context

What may arguably be the worst case of the press's penchant for ruthlessly taking people's words and intent out of context is the controversy that erupted in 2008 regarding Reverend Wright and Barak Obama. Because Wright had expressed his frustration with the establishment in excessive terms, he was derided by the press in a most uncharitable manner. There is little doubt this was only because Barak was a parishioner in the Reverend's church, and would not have received any attention otherwise. While I do not understand Wright's rant about the government creating aids to control blacks and other odd statements, I judged his "God damn America" refrain to mean God damn the government for not making America color blind. You may not like the words he chose, but it would be hard to argue with the intent behind them, if I got it right.

Wright's later speech before the NAACP, however, could not have been more inspiring. Perhaps it was the speech of the decade regarding race relations, but one that will surely be ignored for years. His argument was that Blacks being different is not the same thing as Blacks being deficient, referring to the way in which African Americans are sometimes cast because of their local speech patterns. He went on to say that we are all different in a variety of ways and no one should be labeled as inferior because of that. I would challenge anyone to read his speech and come away without having that understanding reinforced. But the ever vigilant press jumped at the opportunity to repeatedly broadcast a few maliciously chosen, out of context phrases with which to condemn him. They apparently could not resist their prime directive to indulge in trivialization and sensationalism whenever possible. Wright's examples of discrimination against Blacks was to repeat two well known Presidential quotes in his poorly attempted accents of Kennedy and Johnson. He went on to point out that they had not been demeaned for communicating in their regional tongues. But when Blacks converse in their dialect they are put down as inferior. So how did the press present this to the public? Almost unbelievably they extracted the two phrases in such a way as to portray Wright as mocking Kennedy and Johnson, which by anyone's reading was not his intention. Then armed with their distorted reporting, they went on to disparage Wright as a vindictive person and someone who may have been out to damage Obama.

Talk about creating news from nonsense! I have no evidence to show that the press was attempting to do Obama a favor by allowing him to further distance himself from Wright, but they certainly maligned Wright for some reason. Maybe it was just another case of creating fodder for the sensationalism-hungry public.

More Good ol' Boys

Political appointments are a necessary evil of our system of government. There are so many positions to fill that someone has to do that job. The general public clearly has insufficient knowledge of who is qualified and who is not, as witnessed by the candidates that they elect to office. On the other hand, the President and his kiss-up-to-keep-my-job advisors are in only a slightly better position to make these judgments. As a result, those who offer up loyalty, money, or favors to advance an administration are likely to benefit (*no surprise*) from their "unselfish" service. Of course this behavior is not limited to the top levels of government. Rather it is endemic to government in general.

We have gotten so used to having politicians working for themselves that we may ignore their questionable campaign financing and overspending proclivities. Congress, in one example, has passed legislation funding the lavish funerals of our Presidents without asking

anyone's permission but themselves. Certainly they did not ask those of us who end up with the bill. Weren't these now deceased politicians paid more than enough to bury themselves? In addition to the generous funerals, there is the substantial cost of...
-- military bands
-- rifle corps
-- dozens of funeral cars
-- jets flying overhead
-- thousands of flowers
-- meals and lodging for the invited guests (*did you get your invitation*?)

Then we have to pay to fly the departed and their entourage to a final resting place on multiple Air Force 747s. Don't you wish you were part of this fraternity that treats itself so nicely on someone else's dime? No wonder Betty Ford was overheard to whisper "It's beautiful" at Jerry's funeral, as if she had some right to that extravaganza for which she did not offer to pay one red cent. Will you get a decommissioned Air Force One, as Regan did near his Presidential library? While President's Ford, Regan, and Kennedy funerals were grand productions, who are the benefactors of this showiness? You? I? Likely it is the politicians who may gain a degree of undeserved credibility from the: it rubs off on me effect of these extravaganzas. If we elevate our Presidents to this monarch-like status, then with innocent-by-association we tend to also elevate Congresspersons as a group. Perhaps there could be some small benefit to those who are obsessed with the rich and famous.

We should be aware that our leaders have not been, for the most part, particularly virtuous people since it is not even remotely possible in the world of politics. We should not behave as if they were saints after their deaths, because that demonstrates how little attention we pay to their performances during life. This adulation also tells politicians that what they are doing in office is ok, which is surely not the case. Part of keeping Presidential images from being as tarnished as their behavior often dictates resides with the incestuous association they enjoy with the press. The press is about as untainted as are the drug companies that offer perks to the doctors in exchange for their prescription business. Anyone attending a White House sponsored press events demonstrates their willingness to indulge in a conflict of interest and discounts their responsibility to the public. But then who do we have to complain to... the press?

My criticism of our Presidents is not meant to demean all of those who have held that position, whether they were bumbling, adequate or enlightened. It is only meant to put their performance into perspective. They and the millions of government workers run the largest company in the world and are certainly due some respect for that effort. What they are not entitled to is...
-- our mostly thoughtless support
-- their overly generous benefits
-- our tendency to treat Presidents like royalty
-- an average of $7.000/year more than we pay for similar work in the private sector

Unjustified respect for people imbues more power on the powerful, makes possible more wealth for the wealthy, and bestows more privilege on the privileged

I have mentioned the delinquency of the press many times and with good justification. They may fancy themselves as watchdogs of government, but it is not difficult to tell that reality and cultivated images are far different. During elections, voters are seldom given the kind of information that could help them make well-informed decisions. Instead they are bombarded with air time from and about candidates that spin the truth, rather then enlighten us. And the press is just as adept at spin as are the politicians. Their op-eds are filled with opinions, attitudes and disparagements that show little regard for facts. Even having their errors brought to light does not stop the prevarication as long as commentators think they can gain an additional mile out of a false statement.

Adding insult to injury, broadcasts are filled with commercials and teasers (*you know... stay tuned for whatever*). We are routinely bombarded with these "coming attractions" that are injected at the end of a news segment to peak our interest and keep us from changing stations. If we want the details about some issue that was mentioned we must endure the commercial delay. And we may have to wait for the second or third segment down the road before the

327

promised information is presented. Occasionally the teaser occupies more time then does that actual data.

Abuse Of Power

Pride and Prejudice

Years ago George Bush made what appeared to be a close friendship with Russia's Tsar-mentality President Putin. I guess his pride was telling him that he might be able to achieve what Regan had accomplished some earlier, which was nudging Russia into becoming a more democratic state. As events have turned out, Putin had been responsible for major backpedaling of democracy rather than on liberalizing it. Adverse political news in Russia is routinely suppressed, and dissidents are harassed and jailed. Apparently this lesson of runaway power is lost on some of us. Both of the Bush administrations presided over the gradual erosion of personal freedoms that have makes America what it is... free.

Just because politicians have been elected to office does not imply that they are knowledgeable, clever, don't have prejudices, or are even quick studies of difficult situations. This additionally holds true for the government agencies that are run by ex-politicians and political appointees. Just look to the reports of the blunders that were made by CIA and FBI over the years as proof of this thesis, such as with Iraq having weapons of mass destruction. Because we reside in a representative democracy most people remain detached from government workings, and simply choose to imagine that all is being managed well, without having a need for citizen intervention.

Assault on Freedom

Thanks to the some provisions of the Patriot Act, we have seen multiple assaults on our telephone conversations and emails without court warrants... laws that have been deemed to be unconstitutional by many. As a case in point, we have permitted the communication companies to bug American's phones, and then they have been given immunity from prosecution for those efforts.

GWB used another provision of this act, via his Attorney General (AG) Gonzales, to stack US Attorney's offices with his like-minded sympathizers without the traditionally required advice and consent of Congress. A number of attorneys were unceremoniously and unjustifiably sacked to make way for those conservatives who would follow a political line, as opposed to a legal line. The emails that demonstrated a conscious plan to dump the attorneys (*contrary to the AG's statements to the press and his sworn statements to Congress*) were "accidentally" deleted from Justice Department (*JD*) computers. Backup retention of these emails is required by law for the public record, but that did not stop the chief law enforcement officer of the US from being associated with both criminal deletions.

As is a familiar scenario in government, no one has been prosecuted for that loss of that data. A 2010 announcement by the Justice Department stated that the AG (their boss) would not be prosecuted for his participation in the firing and replacement of attorneys... another example of politicians taking care of their peer group. Just eighteen minutes of missing tape for those who remember the White House secretary's alleged lapse during Watergate.

A side story is the role of Monica Gooding, an aid to Gonzales. A US Attorney in Washington complained that she had tried to block the hiring of an attorney because of her prejudice against a person that was perceived to be a liberal Democrat. When incriminating emails surfaced and her complicity in the matter could no longer be denied, she broke down into tears saying "All I ever wanted to do was serve this President". So her version of serving America is to pervert the Justice Department into a just-us system for the benefit of a President. If the aids to Bush were so willing to circumvent the law, where does this dishonorable behavior come from? The answer is that it invariably flows down from the top.

We should recognize how important it is that the JD be fair and impartial without succumbing to political influence... all of us except for Bush and company, apparently. While these lawyers can be fired at will, the longstanding policy has been that they have their jobs for life. This goes a long way toward guaranteeing their impartiality and resistance to political persuasion. People from the JD have testified that its mission had been seriously perverted by hiring politically oriented lawyers and firing existing, career lawyers.

Rev. Martin Luther King Jr., social activist: *"Injustice anywhere is a threat to justice everywhere."*

American Monarchy

While presidential excesses are by no means limited to Obama, he has set a new benchmark for over the top travel spending. It is not just foreign royalties that fly with a fleet of luxurious jets to far off destinations for a few hours, rather than using the phone to conduct business. Are you aware that his frequent travels include…
-- a second jumbo jet for the press and other VIPs?
-- several planes for the President's many vehicles and staffers
-- airplanes bringing in tanker trucks for the President's planes to guarantee that the fuel is not tampered with
-- contingents of anti-terrorist military located along motorcade routes
-- copious supplies - ranging from lighting, to red carpets, and speaker stands, that are just the tip of equipment-iceberg
-- Michelle Obama taking her hairdresser (*can she no longer comb her own hair?*), along with a large contingent of superfluous staffers, aboard Air Force One trips, with nary a peep from the press
-- vacations to Hawaii that have been reported to cost taxpayers about $1.5 million per week
-- a trip made to Africa to underscore the President's commitment to malaria containment (*I guess the phones were down that day*)
-- in the first weeks of the nuclear problem in Japan, Obama played golf and took his family on a trip to Brazil (*Does that remind anyone of the Bush administration's lack of reaction to Katrina?*)

In the election year of 2012 Obama used the travel resources of the White House to make various trips to "swing" states at the taxpayer's expense. The House Speaker, Boehner, criticized these trips as merely political, which if true must, by federal law, be paid for by Obama's election campaign. One of the trips was said to be nothing more than a "fake fight" with Congress regarding federally funded student loan rates. This criticism, of course, misses the point since the President has the resources of regular press events at which he could easily voice his concerns, either directly or through the White House press office. So we end up paying millions of dollars for his lavish trips which are purely political in nature, and then the President lies (*implicitly*) about their need for the public benefit… obviously without remorse over their costs. The entitled can never spend too much to become embarrassed, apparently.

EPA & Spilled Milk

In the: it doesn't get sillier category, the Environment Protection Agency (*EPA*) has determined that since milk contains oil (*butterfat*) it falls under their purview of regulation. Then to top that gem of wisdom off, they ruled that the EPA has the authority to force farmers to comply with its rules to file "emergency plans" to illustrate how they will cope with spilled milk. This includes showing how they will train first responders as well as build containment facilities. Can our regulators get any more outrageous then this? Are the nut jobs in control, or what?

Unconstitutional Actions

A political threat to freedom involves an action that was ostensibly motivated by the threat of terrorism. It regards Bush's issuance of Executive Orders (*EOs*), which are written commands that carry the force of law behind them. Wait a minute. Isn't that supposed to be Congress's job? One of these overreaching EOs signed by Bush stated that all US regulatory commissions must have a Policy Advisor (*PA*) supplied by the White House. Does that remind anyone of Russia's need to have a political officer checking on its generals and bureaucrats? Apparently these PA's will be in place to make their own laws by reinterpreting existing laws. This might not be so dire if it weren't for the fact that these people were spineless yes people employed to further Bush's political and religious agendas. This packing method is not much different from the court stacking that has been criticized about Caesar Chavez of Venezuela, or was attempted by Franklin Roosevelt when he tried to grab power to promote his New Deal agenda. You may recall that he wanted to nominate one additional Supreme Court Justice for each sitting judge over seventy years old. This would have amounted to a dilution of the votes of those judges who had opposed his plans.

Most Americans probably feel that they had nothing much to fear from Bush's frame of mind, and wanted their government to take more effective actions against world terrorism. This sounds good on paper, but freedom is not a guarantee. There is always someone who is willing to take pieces of it away from us. I can just imagine hearing the weasel-brained advisors whispering into Bush's ear telling him how easy it would be to circumvent Congressional authority with EOs. They might even have pointed out that because the legislature is typically slow to react and is not up to speed on what's happening inside the Oval Office, EOs would be an expedient way to promote an agenda without concern for Congressional action overriding a veto. The Nixon administration demonstrated a similar disregard for legalities when they authorized the Watergate break-in.

Hiding behind Privilege

The Supreme Court has ruled that the Office of the President has legitimate reasons for keeping some conversations from becoming public. The purported logic is that Presidential confidants and foreign agents need the freedom to speak their minds without the threat that they will exposed to the world. So far so good if one buys into that self-serving argument about government secrecy, and then ignores its very real impact. Political decisions should not be kept from the public except when forming a strategy against an aggressor or with some personnel issues. However, we have lived with the unsafe principle of government secrecy for so long that it is unlikely to be supplanted any time soon.

There have been Presidents who found it expedient to take advantage of the courts ruling on secrecy in order to hide their dubious behaviors behind privilege. Bush used this subterfuge to cover up the events surrounding the firing of a number of US

Attorneys and his justification for going to war with Iraq. He also ordered people in his administration to disregard subpoenas authorized by Congress in their search for malfeasance at the Justice Department. There was no actual national security risk at stake in this last case, just the prevention of an open government where unlawful behaviors could be exposed. Secrecy is rarely appropriate in any setting, and it is even less so in government.

A populist backlash to state secrets has been the establishment of the website Wikileaks. Its apparent goal is to remove this veil from government and force it to operate in the light of day. But the bureaucrats are busy doing what they can to stop that information flow, including removing the website and prosecuting contributors.

Getting a Perspective

Bin-Ladin and company may have killed thousand of people in the World Trade Center, but the war in Iraq and Afghanistan has killed even more Americans... over 6000 through 2011. Sadam Hussein may have murdered tens of thousands in an effort to tame his real or imagined detractors and maintain control of the country's contentious religious factions, but his absence from power has resulted in the deaths of tens of thousands more. This information is not to justify these actions but to put them into perspective...
-- Have any of the deaths in Iraq been worth the price?
-- Has the Bush and Obama war accomplished much beyond the increased aggression by many of the world's Muslims?
-- Has it made the world a safer place in which to live?

Isn't it interesting that a Bush, who professed his adherence to God's law and to pro-life should be the same person that presided over a killing war that has lasted longer than WWII. Rather than conducting ourselves as one nation among equals, he preferred to act out his military fantasies at our countries' expense. One by one the Western countries that made up the original allied coalition became disenchanted as their leaders came to realize the futility and counter-productivity of the war that we began. It's too bad that they played follow the leader for as long as they did.

Infamous Quotes

Regarding the conflict in Iraq, Laura Bush had the arrogance to say on more than one occasion that "No one suffers more than George and I do over the war". This outrageous statement was even more disingenuous while they lived in their isolated, pampered, monarchy-like accommodations. I guess the deep sorrow of the relatives and friends of these dead soldiers didn't count for much in their minds. Is it that these two lightweight thinkers were completely out of touch? Or is it that they are simply unable to understand the difference between telling the truth and telling a lie?

Adlai E Stevenson, politician: *"Those who corrupt the public mind are just as evil as those who steal from the public purse."*

A comment that had been made many times by GWB while referring to the terrorists has been "They hate us for our freedom". Pardon me? Is there anything even remotely logical or sincere about that statement? Maybe they also hate us for playing tennis, not eating our pets, and using toilet paper. Surely it couldn't be that they hate us for invading their land and supporting their enemy Israel. Perhaps he also believed that they simply crave making war and we were a convenient target. He also showed a considerable lack of insight when he called the terrorists "cowards", ignoring that they...
-- have a deep religious faith
-- will not permit foreigners on their soil
-- will carefully plan an offence
-- will give up their life for a cause

Those sure are some cowards. Statements like those that GWB made boil down to a transparent attempt to deflect us from the truth about our aggressive military-industrial-complex and our appetite for foreign oil. Those are the real bad guys.

True believers are among the most dangerous of people because they will not listen to reason, much less understand it

Feedback from Iraq

A few years ago I "spoke" to a person from Iraq while I was playing online bridge and asked him how he felt about what the Americans were doing in his country. Without any hesitation his reply was "Sadam's hell was far better than Bush's paradise". This concept of living with the lesser of evils is apparently lost on the illogical minds of our leaders.

The Scott McClellan Affair

Talk about shooting the messenger. Before the ink was dry on his tell-all book "What Happened", the spin doctors in the Bush administration (*which I suppose was basically all of them*) were busy casting aspersions in the direction of McClellan. Their comments did not deny the facts of the book as much as they painted Scott as a person who...
-- was only interested in the money
-- hadn't complained to Bush's staff in the past
-- showed a lack of loyalty to the President
-- waited too long before coming forward

When the book was published, it revealed that the Administration had regularly fed talking points to sympathetic members of the press, and that the press did not reveal the sources of those stories. What this amounted to is dissemination of propaganda by the Administration in concert with the press to color the news in a way that was favorable to Bush. This would not be as disgraceful had it been accompanied by disclosure of where the news was coming from. However that was not the case.

Going back to the negative assaults on McClellan, let's say it was all about the money. So What! Can anyone reveal a politician who is not in it for the money, unless they are already wealthy? And then they are in it for the raw power. It is nothing less than hypocrisy for people to throw stones at others regarding a topic that they are guilty of themselves. Other criticisms leveled against McClellan were similarly weak and did nothing to enlighten the public. What these disingenuous arguments by Bush's staff were meant to do was to obfuscate the issues that McClellan had raised by creating a smokescreen of counter-charges. Then the press obliged these bullies in their cover-up by endlessly repeating the trumped up rebuttals, regardless of the fact that they were irrelevant. It is only important what Bush did or didn't do… not what McClellan did or didn't do. But the press never got that concept.

One of the interesting aspects of the "What Happened" book is the allegation that V.P. Cheney ordered McClellan to exonerate Libby for his role in the Valerie Plame affair (*the outed CIA agent whose husband had criticized the administration*). How many more behind-the-scenes adventures Cheney was a participant in may never be known. What stands out is the arrogance that he displays whenever he is questioned about his part in various controversies. One might think that Cheney's friends and associates would keep him at a distance after witnessing his lack of integrity in action. Since that appears not to be the case, we might properly assume that there is a society of business and government leaders who believe that they can act as they see fit, and that our normal rules of conduct and laws do not apply to them.

More Bush Brilliance

Among other thoughtless things, GWB apparently saw an opportunity to democratize the Middle East, and he showed little interest in what the repercussions of that mindset could be, such as…
-- raising the nation debt to astounding levels
-- being responsible for the deaths of tens of thousands
-- arming the terrorists with a cause to fight for
-- inflating the price of energy

In fact GWB did not even understand that the Muslims are not nearly as interested in democracy as they are in their belief in the Qu'ran. So much for his research staff.

Presidents Johnson and Bush were faced with the same quandary regarding ending wars that they inherited or initiated. How could we cut and run, then dishonor those who had already died was the lament. Did they imagine that the next soldier who might die would reflect on those who have already died in vain if he could save his own life? And even if he were so illogical as to think that his sacrifice was reasonable, would that be justification for even one more unnecessary death? History can be a weak validation for current behavior. The only question that matters is: does continued fighting help or hurt this country? No other argument need be taken into account. This question is analogous to the decision that should be made when deciding whether or not to sell a stock. Is the sale correct today? A rational thought process should be taken without any regard to the original purchase price or to those who have died. History is irrelevant in these cases.

How did we get ourselves into Iraq in the first place? The most likely answer is oil. Iraq has plenty of it and we wanted it, perhaps at a dirt cheap price. We didn't go there...
-- to rescue the people from a harsh dictator | they can be found throughout the third world
-- to prevent the proliferation of weapons of mass destruction | there were none
-- to bring democracy to a peoples who craved it | they are actually suspicious of democracy

The end result of our intervention is that the price of oil, which hovered around $30 per barrel, went incredibly higher, and not just for the US but for all of the oil purchasing nations. Don't you think they love us for that? And how do you imagine those extra dollars per barrel are being used? Possibly against us by the Arab nations that would like to see us taken down a peg?

An even more serious result of our starting this conflict was the awakening and emboldening of a religious subculture (*much like how the Japanese awakened America, the sleeping giant, in WWII*) whose goal is to dominate the Middle East. There are factions that want to spread their beliefs by any means possible. And because of this action we have provided them with the motivation and recruiting environment that they could barely dream of providing on their own.

In 2009 the Secretary of the Navy said at a ship commissioning "No matter how many times you attack us, we will always come back."

Do we really need to come back? Do we need to be the policemen of the world? Since there are some who understand the implications of this detrimental scenario that we have created for ourselves, isn't it curious that this logic not hit Washington in a big way? And why not? Just who is responsible for continuing this farce? The hundreds of billion dollars we spend go somewhere. Perhaps we should follow the money.

Pluses and Minuses

For a good many years this country had led the world in nearly every category that is important to us... scientific research, education, healthcare, retirement, automobiles, manufacturing, nuclear power, gas and oil production, electronics, etc. Today we are so far down the line on these lists that we are beginning to look like a second world county. About all we are really good at is building better war toys for the military-industrial-complex, and for selling ourselves goods that we buy from other countries. These activities do not generate the consumer products that can directly contribute to our economic welfare. They only encouraged the likes of the Johnsons, Bushes and Obamas in their foreign misadventures, quests for oil, and tolerating multi-national companies that outsource work to foreign countries. Then we use our toys to intimidate countries, and spend vastly more to insure the security that we have voluntarily put into jeopardy. I hold congress immensely accountable for our problems with their decades of...
-- insufficient spending on the replacement of our deteriorating infrastructure
-- excessive spending on pork and worthless projects
-- legislation for the privileged

So one has to ask...
-- Are there any fewer illegal drugs available because of the billions that have been spent by the dupes at the DEA?
-- Doesn't it cost billions to house the criminals that we have created with our drug policies?
-- Have our healthcare costs ever gone down?
-- Has the highway infrastructure or congestion improved?

-- Are there fewer immigrants crossing over from Mexico?
-- Have we made significant inroads into renewable resources?

Need I go on? This irrationality has helped take us to the point where our country is trillions of dollars in debt *vs.* $800 billion when Regan took office. And this debt has an astounding interest bill that can not easily be paid down for decades to come. Because politicians have treated themselves and their wealthy friends so well for so long, we can't guarantee that the Social Security program will be intact when the current crop of boomers wants to retire (*at the current rate of about 1000 per day*). Because we are living on credit, our huge tax burden will ultimately be passed along to our children and their children's children. How would you like it if your parents left you deeply in debt?

Supreme Principles

We would like to believe that the Supreme Court is composed of nine intelligent, impartial jurists who will make decisions that are equitable, reasonable and in accord with our Constitution. But if this were even half true, why would all Presidents be so anxious to make these appointments? The answer is that members of the court come with their own biases, and they will be selected for having attitudes that conform to the nominating President, regardless of faithfulness to Constitutional obligations. While it is impossible for anyone to be completely unbiased, some of us have a greater problem with this discipline than others. Judges and lawyers are typically appointed or elected for their beliefs rather than for their impartially. Presidents are known for trying to stack the court in their philosophical favor. When a like-minded candidate is installed, reinterpretation of the constitution is possible.

Fair and balanced... a fanciful flower that rarely blossoms

An example of agenda-peddling by the Supreme Court in favor of big business came up regarding the whistleblower legislation. The court ruled 6 to 2 that a particular tattler was not entitled to recover money for his fraud exposure because he lacked "direct and independent knowledge upon which his allegations were based". Sounds like double-talk that was designed to circumvent an important law enacted by Congress, and which serves a pressing need. The law was passed to penalize companies involved in illegal behavior, and to encourage those who will come forward with incriminating evidence. Do we really care how they came by their information, short of breaking and entering? The method of their discovery is hardly the point. But the Supreme Court saw fit to limit the whistleblower legislation based on a business-friendly, illogical, posture. Tattlers will now have less incentive to offer their service (*risking termination for no profit*), and the offending companies will be more immune from detection.

In another decision the court's 5 to 4 ruling overturned a long-standing ban on companies being able to set minimum prices for the vendors of their products. This price fixing scheme had previously been legislated to be illegally anti-competitive because companies could raise the price floor for their products in concert with other suppliers. In the court's ruling, price floor setting could be either competitive (*really?*) or non-competitive. So in their minds, a turn-about from the previous law was not necessarily anti-trust in nature. Apparently they would have us believe that price fixing schemes can occasionally be beneficial to the consumer, but don't count on it. This decision can be seen as support for reduced business competition because of a counterfeit rationale. So this court showed how easily it ends up in the pocket of big business and antagonistic to consumers.

Curiously, there is a pricing practice that has gone unchallenged for some time in the garment industry and probably elsewhere. Not only do major suppliers to large department stores dictate the décor of the selling areas that are dedicated to their products, but they may also tell those retailers what the selling prices will be, and how much and when the items can be marked down. Anti-trust? What else? Recently I used the Internet in an effort to find the best price on a hepa (*air purifier*) filter, and discovered that every seller of a particular brand had exactly the same price... that is every seller in the US. This universal price setting is not prima-facie anti-competitive if you believe the court.

In a 2010 Supreme Court decision "Citizens United v. Federal Election Commission" it struck down a provision of the McCain-Feingold election law. That law had prohibited corporations and unions from purchasing broadcast time for election matter that named a candidate within 30 days of a primary and 60 days of a general election. This decision freed up corporations and unions to spend unlimited amounts on "electioneering communications". In addition the donors were not required to be identified. The rationale behind this change was that most of this political spending occurs outside of contributions to a candidate's campaign, and that the campaigns were not accountable for the veracity, or lack of such, with the "communications". Really? What it did require is that there must be a "wall" between these Super PACs and the campaigns they favor. This is, of course, a flight of fantasy since their activity can not be controlled when it is done surreptitiously. And there is no firewall in place that would prevent those communications with candidates. In 2012 John McCain said "I predict to you that there will be scandals associated with this huge flood of money". The justification by the Supreme Court was that their decision was based on freedom of speech principles. Did they ever think about balancing probable corruption against the interests of the people? The classic analogy in opposition to this ruling is the prohibition against yelling "fire" in a theatre. And then there is the undeniable consideration that this money will be flowing from the super rich in concert with their interests, which are unlikely to be those of the rest of us. Could the court be any more wrong-headed?

In 2006 the Court ruled that is was not illegal for telecommunications companies to cooperate with National Security Agency's warrantless eavesdropping on internal telephone conversations and email. Some 30 suites had been filed since that information became public. To its discredit, the Court upheld the previous decision in 2012.

To its credit, the Court did rebuke the Bush administration for years of stonewalling on acknowledging global warming. The EPA had presented the Court with a list of irrelevant (*to the point of being ludicrous*) reasons why they declined to take action on automobile and truck emissions. One of the more specious arguments was that auto pollution is not deemed to be poisonous. That's news to me. How about you? Maybe these deep thinkers were standing behind someone's tailpipe for too long. More likely it is that the bureaucrats owed their allegiance to the administration instead of to the public. Then in its wisdom the EPA suggested that this matter should be resolved by a voluntary approach (*haven't we heard that nonsense before*), rather than by regulation. I believe we know how proactive and inclined to making changes for the better the auto industry has been throughout the years. Not! The ruling was 5 to 4 in favor of a critical environmental issue... one that should have been a 9-zip slam-dunk. This split should make us wonder what the agenda of the opposition judges was. Perhaps the Court's philosophy is all about not restraining big businesses on whatever they deem to be in its interest, as apposed to what is in the best interest of consumers.

Gettysburg Redress

In 2012 the Supreme Court affirmed the law that allows corporations to give unlimited contributions to political parties. While it was no unanimous, it was unfortunate. In upholding an oblique reference to the Constitution regarding free speech, the Court ignored the damage to free politics. Their ruling was like giving all of the hotels to one of the players in Monopoly and then expecting a fair game. What it did do is give those contributors with big bucks at their disposal another avenue to corrupt the already corrupted Congresspersons.

What we end up with this decision is an inclination to paraphrase Lincoln with: Government of the corporations, government by the corporations, and government for the corporations. I suppose that this is not all that bad for many Republicans.

Follow the Leader

What the previously mentioned abuses of power demonstrate is the ubiquitous dearth of ethics and integrity that pervades our society. This can happen for any number reasons. Because it takes a degree of cunning to achieve high office (*whether corporate or government*) the effort instills a pattern of slick behavior that may stay with those who succumb to the addiction of authority. Once a level of some achievement has been obtained, an executive can look around and see how often others have manipulated the system to get where they are. The message for many is clear. If others can do it with little retribution, why then why oh why can't I. Many of us may look at the leaders of business and government for examples on how to conduct ourselves in public and private. If we have not been privy to enlightened mentoring or strong principles in childhood, the perceived benefits of corruption can be influential on our formation. This is an outcome when we see that...

-- all Presidents lie to the public with impunity
-- great numbers of our political and business leaders become embroiled in corruption
-- far too many institutions are pleasuring their top officers with hundred of millions of dollars in salaries and bonuses

So whether society admits it or not, corruption trickles down from the top and pollutes those below. And we do so little to stem the tide.

Law Is For Lawyers

From My Perspective

One of the more interesting aspects of law and justice that I have observed on the legal landscape is that the fox is in charge of the chicken coop. The preponderance of lawyers in government results in laws that suit lawyers and the judges (*who are also lawyers*) who rule on laws. Curiously, while they occasionally may be involved with prosecuting conflict of interest cases, they don't seem to be aware of their own conflicted system. Or is it that they don't care?

Some try to justify the prevalence of lawyers in Congress as appropriate since these are people who are making laws. Using that logic, anyone in state and city councils or on homeowner association boards should be a lawyer, because only lawyers can properly have insights and make laws. Does that half-baked train of thought have your approval? A downside to a government full of lawyers is that they come from the privileged class. And what would you think their agenda might be when it involves wealthy vs. poor?

Who is at Fault?

It is obvious that there are numerous and frequent injustices in our legal system. This is not to say that I have any special insight into the legal process that others might not have discovered. It is that I have experienced the courts firsthand, and have looked at a few of the problems that are symptomatic of a less than perfect manner in which jurisprudence is exercised in this country. What we have is a system that usually works, but has glaring exceptions to the concept of justice. Well, usually doesn't get it. When power is pitted against principal, the civil rights of the weak are subverted in favor of those who have greater money, status, or connections. This concept is not just a pie-in-the-sky theory, and one I will reflect on.

In the mean time I will recall my 20-something experience with the South Daytona Police Department. After spending time in a dance hall, my friend and I went outside to await the return of the fellow who drove us there. In spite of being both sober and quiet, a clearly red-necked cop pulled up and demanded that we get in the back of his vehicle. "Vagrancy" was the mumbled excuse. He then proceeded to pick up a buddy and race recklessly through the town. We ended up at the police station, which turned out to be a small converted house with the dispatch in its kitchen. Through some miracle our buddy managed to see what had happened and followed us to the station. When I saw him at the door, my release of nervous tension resulted in near hysterical laughter. To get to the punch line, we were given 24 hours to leave town.

Lawyers Required

Have you tried to secure simple regulatory advice from some city or business office clerk and been told that you needed to contact a lawyer for the answer? Organizations are so afraid of litigation that they won't even discuss aspects of their own business without a warrant. Or what about doctors who are prevented from revealing information about a deceased patient to the police because lawyers have made sure that they are too intimidated to act on their own? Who says that lawyers make the best judges of fair and reasonable? Even the Attorney General's office in my state will not provide any counseling beyond disclosing the wording of a particular law. So if one wants to comprehend the implications of a law they must either be able to read gibberish and understand the statute, or (*and here's the good part*) hire a lawyer to do so.

In my case I was attempting to determine the statute of limitation on hidden constructions defects. This is hardly a matter to require a lawyer, or so one would think. Lawyers are in general at least as interested in protecting their sources of income as they are in serving the public good. the only relief from this overhead can sometimes be to file an action in Small Claims court where lawyers are not required. But these matters are restricted to petty cases that are (*duh*) not big revenue producers for lawyers.

Our legal system's lexicon reminds me of the many years when I was a Computer Systems Analyst. Initially I was educated to use obtuse jargon when dealing with programming issues. While many of the terms have become well-known today, words like megabytes, sectors, platters, software, downloading, hardwired, etc. were alien to most folks. My dad never quite understood what it was that I did for a living. Lawyers are also egregious in their use of the word game. Try reading and understanding virtually any contract some time. Over the years I have been able to decipher much of this terminology thanks to law courses, but the sheer quantity and nonsense relating to lawyer-speak is daunting. One of the excuses that you might have heard revolves around the need for precision, but I find this to be a specious argument. My programming education (*problem descriptions - facts determination - detailed instructions*) requires at least as much precision in communicating an analyst's findings to a programmer, and work-a-day English works just fine.

Occasionally a business entity will require that their contracts be written in conversational English, but this is a rare occurrence. And without pressure from Congress (*say, aren't most of them lawyers?*) nothing much changes. Because there are so few companies that require readable documents, I have to assume that their lawyers are arguing against that process. And there is no one in government who is willing to exert legalese oversight on businesses. As a landlord I come across rental documents that are designed more to obfuscate rather than inform. And these are the contracts that are being forced on lawyer-less renters.

Sir Francis Bacon: *"Information is power."*

While this quote's meaning may appear to be obvious, the full explanation is twofold...
-- by know something that others do not know, you have an advantage
-- obfuscate the information and you have an advantage

This gives a bit more insight into the power that information holds. Why do you think that the preponderance of our government's business is transacted (*unnecessarily*) behind closed doors, and is not reveled to the public? Information about their activities would certainly diminish our respect for them.

White vs. Blue Collar

It's a cliché to say that white collar criminals escape their fair share of punishment. Even if they do go to jail or are convicted in civil court, their sentence is not a guarantee that justice will prevail. The original O.J. Simpson trial was a case in point. Not only did the prosecution blunder unbelievably (*the bloody, shrunken glove did not fit so you must acquit*), but the Florida law allows retention of personal home equity making sure that Simpson paid minimal retribution for his subsequent conviction on wrongful death charges in civil court. This state's real estate law is a liability-escape route that has been used by numerous felons because it protects their home's entire value from being confiscated by the courts. This is a classic example of how easy it is to buy politicians if you represent a major business interest. In this case, it was made possible by the Florida Real Estate folks as a way of generating more interest in Florida property by criminals. Much of their ill gotten gains can be protected by purchasing a home.

Juries are generally more sympathetic to people of higher social standing than they are to others. Blacks far outnumber the Whites in their percentage of false convictions and severe penalties. The punishment for crack cocaine, for example, is greater than for powdered cocaine only because blacks are the major users of crack. Juries tend to vote with their genetic-emotional hearts rather than with their genetic-rational brains because they can not always be peers to the people who have been charged with a crime or are part of another ethnic group. Emotions frequently rule the day, even though a sober, thoughtful, judgment may have been required by the judge.

White collar crimes are viewed as being less serious then blue collar crimes which may involve violence. A person who assaults another will likely receive a harsher verdict than one who embezzles money from a company or raids a pension fund… which can causes untold anguish. Years ago a prominent West Coast mayor was involved in the purchase of a shipping company. Then he and his equally corrupt partners depleted the worker's pension fund before filing for bankruptcy, and they suffered no jail time for the raid. Those who were due retirement payments in their old age were the ones who suffered. Another example of a white color crime that lacked sufficient punishment was the slick wizard of junk bonds who got five years in jail for his felonious dealings. When he was released from prison (*early*), he was still a billionaire.

The Kenneth Lay Affair

We all know about the collapse of the Enron Corporation which was perpetrated by the actions of its executives. Because of personal greed and their manufacturing of false fiscal reports, investors and employees lost some $60 billion dollars in equity when news of the corruption hit the fan. While this may seem outrageous to most of us, it was eminently more tragic to those who saw their pensions or stock portfolios disappear in the blink of an eye. Can you imagine what it must be like to wake up one morning and learn that the income you have relied on for retirement had evaporated? After too many years of litigation, the Justice Department finally won their cases against Lay and his associates. Justice was served you say? Well not so, because Lay died before the government recovered any of the restitution money and the appeals court then saw fit to vacate his conviction. The logic behind this reversal was that because of Lay's death, his estate and its lawyers would not have an opportunity to appeal the conviction since they did not have the benefit of a living defendant. Maybe you <u>can</u> take it with you.

This court's reasoning does have a semblance of logic. But in an effort to protect the rights of a perpetrator, they ignored the tragedy of victims. It's <u>not</u> as if...
-- a jury of his peers did not convict Lay
-- there had been an appeal filed for flawed court proceedings
-- there were allegations of jury tampering
-- there were suggestions of prosecutorial misconduct

None of the above occurred. But because of our court system, the Lay estate was permitted to retain more than $40 million in ill-gotten gains. So his estate kept the money because they were said to be incapable of defending against the JD's conviction. Where is the logic in that?

The OJ Simpson Affair

What more can be said about this despicable organism? Well the good news is that his conviction on gun charges and kidnapping has put him behind bars for many years to come. What kind of sick SOB risks jail time for memorabilia? The answer is that the personal power he enjoyed for years had corrupted him ultimately.

The Scooter Libby Affair

First of all, what adult would call himself Scooter? Well no matter. The real issue is that there had been talk in Washington and in conservative camps suggesting that he should be pardoned for his crime. And I have no doubt the high moral values of President Bush were easily subverted to find justification for that action.

Those who make an issue of their Godliness are just as likely to be offenders of it... or maybe more so

The logic against issuing a pardon to Libby went like this…
-- no man is above the law
-- he was convicted by a jury of his peers
-- there was no injustice in his conviction
-- people in power should not receive special privilege from other people in power
-- we should not have a double standard for those with influence

However, these arguments apparently fell in deaf ears when it came to the ultra-conservative, right-wing elements. Integrity is not as great an issue with them when it comes to protecting a member of their peer group. While this type of behavior undoubtedly served us well in our long-past tribal days, it has no valid place in our current society. This episode should send a clear message that no politician can not be trusted to act on our behalf. So while Bush pardoned Libby in 2007 for his crimes against the American system of justice, none of the Justice Department evidentiary proceedings (*What are the details of the crime? Why should the sentence be set aside?*) were invoked prior to pardoning. It was pure politics in play. This action will stand as testimony that Bush, like Nixon before him, was one of the most corrupt Presidents in our history. When Bush left office in 2009, his rating was in the neighborhood of 25%... an all time low for any President. Something those in awe of him should remember.

What might learn from observing politics is that there will always be kiss-ups whose mission is to support a President's agenda and suppress evidence if asked. Like today's politics, British political history also had its Cromwells who saw it as their duty to protect the Sovereign at any cost. These behaviors can stem from both real and imagines threats. From another perspective, ingratiating one's self to a superior can be highly self-serving. Keeping your boss in power goes a long way toward keeping yourself in power.

Following Precedents

When it comes to judges and courts, precedents rule the day. What this means is that previous case law dictates how judges should rule or risk being overturned on appeal. Well, you may ask, how were the first cases ruled upon if there was no existing case law to refer to? The short answer is the Kings and Queens of England. They and their court made the initial judgments, and because of their power their decisions could be almost as arbitrary as they saw fit. After all who was there to object... except for the church on occasions?

To the contrary, some of our contemporary laws have been created by judge's rulings when allowed to pass unchallenged or were upheld on appeal. Occasionally new laws are made by the appeals courts when they strike down existing law. There are also times that laws garner new interpretations when there is a change at the bench. If a judge's legal thinking leans in a particular direction, then their judicial rulings may similarly tilt. The law is somewhat flexible since judges are attached to their own particular ideologies, just as you and I are. One positive factor that leads to judicial restraint is that judges may find it embarrassing to have a decision overturned by a higher court. Too many overturns, and sanctions or being voted out of office can be the result. These consequences may conspire to make judges reticent to create new law even when it involves a greater justice for the complainant or defendant. Oh yes, it is the legislators who are supposed to make new law, and it is the juries who are supposed to weigh the facts. A nice theory if it true. But the reality is that judges occasionally do make and reinterpret laws. At times they can even nullify a juries' decision.

Winning is Everything

Many of us may have come to the false conclusion as potential jurors that the mere fact that someone has been charged with a crime amounts to two strikes against their being innocent. Couple that attitude with a whatever-it-takes-to-win mentality of a prosecuting attorney, and you have a recipe for injustice. The case against the now-exonerated lacrosse players in North Carolina should come as a wakeup call for the judicial system (*which it won't*) and for the rest of us (*unlikely, as well*). Apparent a publicity-hungry prosecutor, who has since been disbarred, trampled on the rights of three students based solely on the dubious testimony of an alleged victim. There was no direct evidence of guilt (*DNA or otherwise*), and there were strong indications that the plaintiff may have fabricated her story. Had it not been for the financial resources of the three defendants, jail time would have been assured.

In another case, Michael Morton spent 25 years being innocent behind bars because he was wrongly imprisoned for the crime of killing his wife. The prosecution (*who has immunity from wrongdoing in office, even if it is intentional*) has been accused of hiding exculpatory evidence that would have exonerated the defendant. It has finally been revealed that Michael's son told the police it was a monster who killed his mother, and it was not his father. Years down the road, a repeat offender admitted to doing the killing. Yet this was buried and not used to release the father from jail. Eventually a coalition of lawyers and ombudsmen prevailed in this case, and Morton went free.

In 2008 the late Senator Ted Stevens was convicted in a Washington D.C. federal court on charges relating to his financial disclosers. He subsequently lost his bid for reelection. Several months later the Justice Department (*JD*) asked the judge to vacate the conviction when it surfaced that prosecutors had withheld evidence supporting Steven's not guilty plea. A released report then said that there had been "systematic concealment of exculpatory evidence that would have been corroborated his claim of innocence". In a bit of backtracking, this Schuelke report also said that while inadvertent evidence-disclosure failures shouldn't occur, the JD "meets its discovery obligations in nearly all cases". Well Mr Schuelke, nearly all doesn't really get it, does it? Perhaps his attitude would be different if he were the victim of overzealous prosecution.

The above cases and others like them raise several crucial points…
-- the judicial system can be manipulated by an unscrupulous prosecutor, leaving no easy way to control that abuse
-- access to money dictates how well or poorly one will be represented in court
-- there are hundreds of people being released from prison after DNA evidence has demonstrated their innocence
-- the system is far too expensive, complicated and time consuming to be fair and balanced
-- witnesses do die before protracted trials come to a conclusion
-- reasonable doubt is whatever the jurors thinks it is – or what they may be led to believe it is

In another case (*James Ray/ sweatlodge deaths*) the prosecution ordered the medical examiners office <u>not</u> to testify about their finding regarding conditions at the lodge. When this was learned through discovery by the defense and the presiding judge, the trial was in jeopardy of being declared a mistrial after months of testimony. Withholding of information is unconstitutional, but the prosecution wanted to win at any cost.

Winning is Nothing

In a three month period I received two settlement checks from class action suits in which I was (*simply by the circumstances of owning a product*) part of the class. The settlements ran well into the multi-millions of dollars for each of the cases. My shares came to 10 and 14 <u>cents</u>. In 2011 a major bank was confronted with a class action suit for not fully disclosing the downside of interest-only home loans. In the settlement, the plaintiff's lawyers were awarded $25.000.000 by a judge (*being of course a lawyer*) out of the $50.000.000 that was agreed to by the defendant. After this and other expenses are subtracted, the class may see only pennies here too. It's hard to be daunted at these outcomes knowing that our laws are made by and for lawyers. How bad does our legal system have to become before we insist that it be repaired?

In another "nothing" case, the twenty some companies who delivered their mobile home trailers to the displaced residents of Louisiana were sued because they contained dangerous amounts of formaldehyde in their products. So a settlement was reached whereby the companies would pay fifty million dollars in fines. Why do I mention this? Because the layers take was about 50%. So for those who have or may suffer health issues, they were paid about fifteen thousand dollars each. That's thousands vs. millions! What a grand legal system we have.

We all have probably noticed a number of ads on TV soliciting people to various class action causes, without disclosing as much. Most recently they have begun to add a disclaimer that the speaker is "a non-legal spokesperson". Why this change of dialog? Because there is nothing of a remotely legal nature about the ads in spite of fact that they prominently feature the names of legal firms. So what should we glean from these half truths? It is apparent that the firms are doing a bit of (*currently legal*) "ambulance chasing". That is, they are trying to gather as many victims (*usually of harmful prescription drugs*) as they can in order to qualify for a class action suits. When they say "you might be entitled to money" or some such inducement, they are merely speculating and hoping to line their own greedy pockets. By <u>own greedy</u> I mean that they have no serious empathy for their clients beyond the outrageous fees that they are given by the judges in this corrupt system. Class actions suits are often nothing more than a vehicle for lawyers to get rich while the plaintiffs get pennies.

So... In Conclusion

My Directive to You

There is seldom a day that goes by that the Wall Street Journal does not bring us multiple stories about the corruption of power due to our human nature. It is these behaviors that we must learn to curb if we want to reduce the injustices between people and control their felony activities. We need to be outraged at the harm that politicians and big business are inflicting on our country.

John James Drake

www.ingramcontent.com/pod-product-compliance
Lightning Source LLC
Chambersburg PA
CBHW050434290526
45786CB00006B/2026